The Age of War

The Age of War

The United States Confronts the World

Gabriel Kolko

LYNNE
RIENNER
PUBLISHERS

BOULDER
LONDON

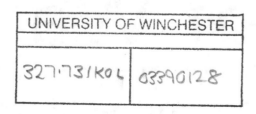
Published in the United States of America in 2006 by
Lynne Rienner Publishers, Inc.
1800 30th Street, Boulder, Colorado 80301
www.rienner.com

and in the United Kingdom by
Lynne Rienner Publishers, Inc.
3 Henrietta Street, Covent Garden, London WC2E 8LU

Library of Congress Cataloging-in-Publication Data
Kolko, Gabriel.
  The age of war : the United States confronts the world / Gabriel Kolko.
     p. cm.
  Includes bibliographical references and index.
  ISBN 1-58826-414-9 (hardcover : alk. paper) —
  ISBN 1-58826-439-4 (pbk. : alk. paper)
  1. United States—Foreign relations—1989– 2. United States—Foreign relations—
1945–1989. 3. United States—History, Military—20th century. 4. War on Terrorism,
2001– I. Title.
E840.K65   2006
327.73009'0511—dc22

                                                                    2005029743

British Cataloguing in Publication Data
A Cataloguing in Publication record for this book
is available from the British Library.

Printed and bound in the United States of America

       The paper used in this publication meets the requirements
  ∞   of the American National Standard for Permanence of
       Paper for Printed Library Materials Z39.48-1992.

     5   4   3   2   1

To Raymond Feddema,
with deep appreciation

This book owes much to his stimulation and insight.

Contents

Introduction

THE AGE OF WAR DEALS WITH THE CONTOURS, MOTIVES, AND GOALS of US foreign policy since 1950, but especially since the year 2000. Specific events make all books that treat current affairs somewhat precarious, but the larger patterns that concern us here have scarcely altered over the past half-century. It is understandable that intelligent people should be preoccupied with the events reported in the daily press, but they are most comprehensible in their historical context; that context is what this book is about. It is far more risky to focus on particulars as if they have no precedents or are not a part of an older, longer pattern. Indeed, a major fault of many assessments of US actions abroad is precisely such a disregard for the meaning of its conduct and the circumstances that led to them. US foreign policy is a whole cloth and can be understood adequately only in its historical framework.

Compared to the period before World War II, US priorities had altered fundamentally by 1950. In 1940, after the global war had begun, the United States spent only 18 percent of its federal budget on national defense,[1] and its overall concerns still reflected the Great Depression's traumatic impact. But after 1946 there was no consensus among members of Congress that permitted a restoration of massive social spending, and even many Democrats opposed it. The unanimity that bound the two parties together was the fear of communism and a belief in greater military expenditures, and the kind of social values that dictated budget commitments before 1941 never returned again—down to the present. By 1948, with the Cold War raging and enormous economic aid being sent to Western Europe, 46 percent of the federal budget was devoted to defense and international affairs. By 1952, with the Korean War, it was 72 percent, and domestic priorities were a thing of the past.

President Lyndon B. Johnson's "war on poverty" was intended to reverse this pattern, but the war in Vietnam kept that from occurring, and by 1968 nearly half of the federal budget still went to the military and international affairs.

Basically, domestic priorities were not so much expendable—there was too much pork for congressional districts for that to happen—as flexible, and if cuts had to be made, they usually came at the expense of nonmilitary programs. Numbers varied, and much more of the nominal budget went to domestic outlays once self-funding programs like Social Security automatically came into play by the late 1970s, but the military was now ascendant both psychologically and in monetary terms. The Pentagon's fascination with high technology meant its demands on the budget were essentially limitless. Futuristic weapons—many of which, like the anti–ballistic missile system, never worked—got immense funding, while many essential domestic needs were underfunded or ignored altogether. After Social Security and welfare were deducted, the military still got the lion's share of federal outlays—more than two-fifths of it in 2005.

But the United States was now much larger and more complicated—and more expensive—than it had been before 1941. The result was a basic neglect of human necessities and an increasingly decaying public infrastructure of roads, bridges, and much else that people require for their health and welfare. Some of the pumps around New Orleans essential to keep it from flooding, for example, were a century old—and there were no funds for new ones until catastrophe struck. The same is true of many vital public facilities elsewhere. The population has more than doubled since 1939, and its requirements and expectations have increased greatly. This transformation of the basic goals of the nation, to the neglect of domestic needs, is an ongoing process whose origins began after World War II. In this book I deal with these changes as an aspect of US foreign policy frustrations and failures since then—frustrations and failures that have occurred despite its monumental efforts and equally monumental social and economic costs.

1

Warfare at an Impasse: The Road to Vietnam

EVERY MAJOR POWER EMBARKING UPON AN OFFENSIVE WAR IN the twentieth century was convinced that it possessed a coherent military doctrine that would surmount often daunting political, economic, and technological challenges to attain victory. To have assumed that its strategy would accomplish any less would have been tantamount to acknowledging the inherent irrationality of its adventure. As the nation most engaged in making war in the latter half of the twentieth century, the United States attempted to produce a unified, effective, strategic vision that would guide its effort to master political and social developments throughout the world after 1949. But with the failure of conventional war in Korea and the Soviet explosion of a hydrogen bomb in August 1953, US leaders believed that it was more imperative than ever for them to formulate a realistic basis for future action.

The task they confronted was inherently insoluble because, like the major European powers before it, after 1945 the United States could not discern the relationship between innumerable specific foreign policy and military dilemmas—to which it responded instinctively in a usually incremental, ad hoc fashion—and its overall priorities. The men and women who defined US foreign and military policies developed justifications for them based on inherently activist and quite inflexible premises, thus frustrating the rational calculations and restrained behavior essential to balancing the real capabilities of the United States, which were very great but ultimately also finite, with its myriad interests. At the same time, the question of military spending obsessed President Dwight D. Eisenhower and most of his key economic advisers, who sincerely believed that a growing budget deficit and inflation were profoundly subversive to the fabric of US society and its values. But although its

New Look doctrine threatening massive retaliation with nuclear weapons promised more destruction for less money and initially allowed the administration to make substantial cuts in the military budget's share of the gross national product, it still did not resolve the decisive strategic contradictions in US policy.

It was immediately obvious that US dependence on sophisticated weapons aimed at industrial and urban targets in the Soviet Union and elsewhere, as well as its conventional weaponry, could not cheaply or quickly win wars in the Third World, if at all. Such local wars usually originated in conflicts that neither the Soviet Union nor China could control, and threatening them with nuclear cataclysms was simply irrelevant. And the fact that the Soviet Union after late 1949 was also engaged in a technologically advanced and expensive arms race meant that the United States could no longer impose a permanent ceiling on its military outlays. Moscow's ability to put an earth satellite in orbit by means of a long-range missile in October 1957, before the United States could do so, simply reinforced the reality, obvious since 1949, that the certainty of mutual destruction in a nuclear war made the Eisenhower administration's massive retaliation doctrine meaningless. A grave deterrent to the irresponsible use of US power now existed. The New Look was less a coherent military doctrine than a reflection of Washington's futile postwar efforts to define an effective grand strategy.

No less crucial to the growth of US defense spending was the fact that after 1950 the military budget became increasingly important to the health of the US economy, attaining the role of the principal counter-cyclical economic tool that NSC-68 (the secret guideline for rearmament) had planned, and although Republican conservatives strongly objected to the very notion of deficit spending, when forced to choose between fiscal prudence and the costly pretensions of being the world's policeman, they invariably chose the latter. Few members of Congress, regardless of their beliefs, could willingly accept the reduction of military expenditures in their own districts lest they be defeated in the next election. Since funding the military was the only expenditure on which a bipartisan consensus existed, economic policy to attain full employment and growth was based on arms outlays rather than on direct satisfaction of social needs.

But the very existence of the arms race and weapons generated its own imperatives. Above all, it required fear—what John Foster Dulles once described as "a feeling of need in the face of danger" lest "the Free World's efforts . . . rapidly decline."[1] Such permanent tension negated a serious role for diplomacy, which the Eisenhower administration discouraged repeatedly, especially relating to European issues after Joseph

Stalin died in March 1953 or to Indochina. For sustaining the image of an allegedly omniscient and omnipotent Soviet menace after 1946 kept both the US Congress and public mobilized behind the expensive, hazardous Cold War. This dependence on terror as a unifying catalyst caused the United States to employ—partly cynically but increasingly due also to its own paranoia—the most dubious statistics to create descriptions of Soviet power and intentions that bore scant relationship to reality. In the end both US leaders and experts were utterly unprepared for the schisms in the Soviet bloc and the subsequent stunning demise of the entire communist system. These cultivated anxieties also mobilized European nations to join the North Atlantic Treaty Organization (NATO) and other alliances, and Washington used them as well to deplore the menace of "neutralism" elsewhere. Fear thereby integrated diverse countries under the hegemonic direction of the United States, until the inherently divisive economic and political qualities of the industrial capitalist nations caused these alliances to unravel, if not disappear altogether.[2] But even as both truth and realism became the first victims of such a doctrinal offensive, the consensus it produced within its own ranks did not enable the US-led world order to overcome the profound limits of its military and political policies.

There were even more decisive reasons for NATO's creation than fear of the Soviet bloc. From its very inception, Washington also intended that NATO serve as its instrument for maintaining its political hegemony over Western Europe, forestalling the emergence of a bloc that could play an independent role in world affairs. Charles de Gaulle, Winston Churchill, and many influential Western European politicians envisioned such an alliance less as a means of confronting the Soviet army than as a way of containing a resurgent Germany and balancing US power.

Publicly, the argument for creating NATO in 1949 was the alleged Soviet military menace, but the United States always planned to employ strategic nuclear weapons to defeat the Soviet Union—for which it did not need an alliance. In any case, no one in Washington believed a war with the Soviet Union was imminent or even likely, a view that prevailed most of the time until the Soviet Union finally disintegrated. There was also the justification of preventing the Western Europeans from being obsessed with the fear of reconstructing Germany's economy, and US military planners were concerned with internal subversion. Most important, a framework for containing German power, once it had restored its economy and rebuilt its military, was crucial. When communism capsized at the end of the 1980s, NATO's nominal rationale for existence died with it, but the principal reasons for its creation—to forestall

European autonomy and create a framework for controlling Germany—remained. Therefore NATO had to be perpetuated.

Washington Searches for Options

Rather than accept the lesson of Korea that conventional war was no longer plausible or the obvious fact that nuclear "deterrence" was far too dangerous, Washington compounded its contradictions and confusions after 1953, neither augmenting its power at less cost nor discovering a definitive means for coping with events in the Third World without dire risks to itself. Although its official strategists wrote about the need to wage limited war to deter a present or future enemy, the United States found it exceedingly difficult to accept a conclusion to a conflict short of military victory, much less to accept negotiated compromises that allowed the enemies of those it supported to continue politically. Precisely because it had an instinctive addiction to triumph that was incompatible with the constraining premises of limited warfare, there always existed a risk that the United States would escalate what were intended to be finite interventions into protracted conflicts. Such impulses invariably overshadowed its other objectives and priorities, confusing and usually reversing them.

But if the United States ultimately could not articulate a comprehensive doctrine that offered an alternative to Armageddon, it did act, if only in wars that generated yet other grave dangers but in the short run seemed to solve some of its pressing immediate challenges. This path of least resistance succeeded temporarily in many places, even though its new techniques of intervention increasingly impinged upon the credibility of US power. Indeed, credibility, via the domino theory with which it was invariably associated, symbolically linked the fate of an entire region to events in virtually any one country within it—including those of only minor intrinsic significance to US interests. Credibility was inherently biased against diplomacy and nonintervention; it became a growing obsession that increasingly shaped US calculations and actions after 1950, entangling and ultimately subverting efforts to define a strategy for avoiding another Korean debacle. In Vietnam, credibility, more than any other single motive, eventually produced a calamity for two nations and stalemated US military power in wars that in fact made it appear less awesome than ever before. To create the fear that the United States would go to the brink of war to attain its goals, which included no further communist territorial gains, was permanently enshrined in US objectives under the Eisenhower administration. It produced an inherently belligerent posture and an open-ended commitment wholly inconsistent with a coherent, regulated, diplomatic, and military policy. Such a stance was preordained to generate monumental surprises.

After Korea, the United States believed that it might avoid another massive deployment of its troops in Third World contexts by relying upon friendly leaders and their armies to cope with local rebellions (many of them radical but not necessarily Leninist), aiding them with equipment, training, and funds and turning them into proxies of US power. Its concept of a "flexible response" to the communist menace after the Korean War assigned a crucial role to such local allies, ostensibly making Washington's willingness to use nuclear retaliation at the appropriate time and place more believable. But such a posture immediately created a need to view all governments ready to cooperate with the United States in this manner as both legitimate and worth preserving, thereby involving it in the politics of innumerable nations where political instability was a permanent fact of life.

Annual military aid in the form of equipment, advisers, and training to nations in Latin America and Asia quadrupled under Eisenhower, and the creation of integrative regional military alliances—Southeast Asia Treaty Organization (SEATO) and Central Treaty Organization (CENTO) to begin with—further tied Washington's destiny and credibility to that of its proxies. Reliance on the military as the single most promising power group in Third World nations became official policy, although that did not preclude support for other tyrants. Augmenting this dependence on officers were systematic US efforts to improve the ability of local police departments to perform political functions. "Public safety" missions and equipment were sent to thirty-eight countries throughout the world over a seven-year period (1955–1961), and many people were brought from those states to undergo training in the United States. Even more important was the great expansion of the covert activities of the Central Intelligence Agency (CIA), a supremely flexible mechanism that allowed the United States both to intervene in countless wars in innumerable countries and to deny responsibility in case of embarrassment or failure. Its "clandestine service" consisted of 2,800 people by 1952, not including a larger number of contract personnel, but under Eisenhower the service almost doubled again to become the CIA's largest budget item. The CIA could attempt virtually anything with impunity and often did with great success, as in Iran in 1953 and Guatemala in 1954, giving Washington "unconventional" means to become enmeshed, for better or worse, in many more nations.[3]

It was now much simpler for the United States to attempt to guide a country's political destiny covertly. Even though a great deal more could be undertaken at far less cost than in the days of conventional armies, this new reality also quickly entangled its definition of the credibility of

US power with the fate of innumerable dictators and corruptionists. This very ease caused the United States to intervene in various wars it might otherwise have avoided—ranging from larger military aid missions, as in the case of the Ngo Dinh Diem regime in South Vietnam after 1954, to sending the fleet armed with nuclear missiles to Lebanon in July 1958. What began as part of an effort to make military responses cheaper, as well as more flexible and measured, ended by implicating the United States in many more potentially dangerous situations, not least because the stability of its proxies depended on politics and conditions within nations that soldiers and guns could scarcely stabilize. The result was an even greater loss of control over its military and foreign policy because seemingly incremental, nominally small decisions pushed Washington in unintended directions that eventually determined its broad preoccupations and interests. For whatever its covert successes, which cannot be minimized even if we know much less than we would like regarding many of them, its deepening fixation with credibility and the sheer magnitude of the US global efforts predestined it to some obvious public failures. They, in turn, compelled it to escalate its involvement in various nations to avert the appearance of impotence.

It was in response to dilemmas such as these that Eisenhower at the end of 1958 authorized the creation of a single integrated operational plan (SIOP) for fighting a general nuclear war, which initially targeted 725 locations in the Soviet Union, China, and elsewhere. Whether it was retaliatory or preemptive depended on the judgment of a few men—and air force computers. The SIOP overkill strategy, with as many as three nuclear bombs allocated to some targets, "frighten[ed] the devil out of me," Eisenhower wrote, and the army and navy forced important modifications on what was, ultimately, the air force's pet strategy. The British feared the Americans were again contemplating a preventive war and during the Cuban missile crisis of 1962 gave full vent to these anxieties. But versions of the SIOP, only somewhat less cataclysmic, guided official US policy until the late 1970s. The world lived on the brink, far more dangerous than anyone dared imagine. But there was also a crucial element of irrelevancy in US thinking, a fascination with extreme danger that was a menace to itself and the world, if only because it gave the United States a dangerous self-confidence that the politics of most nations in no way justified.[4]

The Third World Conundrum

Overt US military activism in the Third World, defined only as the employment of force without engaging in actual war, also increased greatly after 1949. Public exhibits of Washington's might ranged from using small numbers of soldiers and aircraft in one-third of the cases to deploying strategic nuclear forces in at least fifteen of over 215 incidents in the period from 1946 to 1975. These intimidating displays of power occurred more and more in the Third World, with a direct Soviet or Chinese presence in less than half of them. But no one in Washington ever attempted to formulate a grand political-military strategy to justify the many hazards inherent in the often mindless actions that successive administrations embarked upon.

To some degree, real or purported crises involving the US military were useful in sustaining the tension crucial to the maintenance of a hegemonic Cold War consensus within the United States itself, as well as in nations of the alliances it dominated. In addition, the US leadership system was so internally cohesive and analytically monolithic that it simply did not have the capacity to operate other than in the way it did. Intelligence and political analysis became self-reinforcing, and the outpouring of books and articles after 1955 on military strategy were written by advisers—former secretary of state Henry Kissinger being only the best-known example—whose consuming ambitions alone made it inconceivable for them to challenge the illusions and false assumptions of conventional wisdom or the mounting risks the United States was taking in the Third World. To do so would peg them as nonconformists and destroy their career prospects. Those in power could not realistically define the obstacles to attaining US goals in the world, much less challenge those objectives, and in this regard US leaders merely behaved as politicians and bureaucrats do in virtually all modern political orders.

The US dilemma in the increasingly unstable Third World resulted largely from its refusal to accept the nationalist movements and doctrines sweeping the less-developed nations. Indeed, it was the very absence of a significant communist role in most of the Third World that revealed the growing importance of economic developments crucial to the United States and the conservative role it played to safeguard its principally economic interests. Privately and publicly, US leaders nonetheless attributed to the Soviets a transcendent ability to cause or exploit events in even the most remote countries. They condemned "extreme nationalism" as an objective communist tool, in spite of the fact that its leading proponents were often the conservative Latin American or Asian bourgeoisie who advocated it to advance industrialization behind protectionist walls, just as the United States had done after 1861. The United States positioned itself on the wrong side of the great post-1945 decolonization wave, and it was suspicious and usually opposed to the innumerable liberation movements, taking their anti-imperialist rhetoric at face value. In a fundamental sense, US leaders never comprehended the complexity of Soviet motives and behavior throughout the world or the autonomous genesis of revolutionary movements. On this basis, they generally aligned themselves against the main noncommunist political developments that were altering politics in the Third World. Thus the United States sustained colonialism in Africa, intervened covertly in Guatemala in 1954 and Brazil in 1964 to thwart nationalists, and encouraged conservative nationalism in the Middle East in order to replace British power with its own. If the only consistency that emerges from such diverse efforts is the pursuit of national interest, the very attempt to make its will and needs felt in so many places also engendered the growing risk of failure, a loss of credibility, and inevitably the escalation of its involvement. It required only one such case to profoundly test the strategic and political assumptions on which US power was based and to plunge it into war.

Power and US Interests

But the US fixation was not merely the product of its desire to maintain hegemony and credibility or of its bureaucratic sclerosis, for its vital interests also goaded it to attempt to control changes in the Third World. By the 1950s, the United States was importing 48 percent of its total supply of metals, compared to 5 percent in the 1920s, and the health of its economy depended on supplies from the Third World. The dependence on raw material was qualitative also. As a result of the Korean War, the world price of all metals increased 39 percent from 1950 to 1952, and Washington's consciousness of the vital importance of the Third World rose with it.[5] Manganese, nickel, and tin are the basis of a modern steel industry, and by 1960 the United States was wholly dependent on importing them. In 1950 the United States chose to aid the French in Indochina lest all of Southeast Asia fall like dominoes and the region's "major sources of certain raw materials" be cut off. "I do not believe this country can survive," W. Averell Harriman, one of the postwar era's most influential men, warned a Senate committee in early 1952, "if the sources of the raw materials are in the hands of unfriendly people who are determined to destroy us."[6] This need increasingly required the United States to employ its covert and overt resources to regulate the affairs of states spread out over vast distances—a process hazarding conflict and war once US troops and equipment moved onto the scene.

Many indices of growing misery throughout the Third World help us to comprehend other profound changes that became much more acute after the 1950s and affected the political environment the United States sought to manage. Only a few examples here reveal the complexity of the issues, to which we will return later. In the aggregate, by the 1950s, population in the Third World was growing faster than new land area devoted to agriculture, and much more of the latter was being allocated to export crops than to food for local consumption. By 1950, agricultural production in per capita terms had fallen sharply in Latin America and Asia compared to 1936, and in many nations the agricultural labor force was shifting from a relatively secure permanent status to temporary employment. Countless other indicators reveal that when US leaders began to apply their military power and strategy to the world's problems after Korea, they had virtually no notion of how these and similar trends would create social upheavals and challenges for them in the future. The New Look and the threat of massive retaliation were simply irrelevant to such changes, as events in many nations increasingly transcended both US weapons and traditional communist parties.[7]

The United States had often intervened in various ways in the affairs of the Western Hemisphere after it helped Panama secede from Venezuela in 1902. "Dollar diplomacy" over the following decades involved sending warships and troops countless times to Mexico, Nicaragua, Cuba, and elsewhere, often merely to prevent threats of unwelcome changes. The studiously vague, increasingly inclusive "preemptive" doctrine that President George W. Bush enunciated on September 19, 2002, with its commitment to "forestall or prevent . . . hostile acts," was scarcely new; it was one of the crucial bases of US foreign policy throughout much of the nineteenth and twentieth centuries—notwithstanding President Franklin D. Roosevelt's proclamation of the "Good Neighbor" policy after 1933. Washington had never allowed local hemispheric politics to run its normal course, often citing hostility toward the United States as justification, and intervention of every sort in the affairs of these nations was an established instrument of its foreign policy long before 1945 and the Cold War. But much of the Third World was traumatized by economic hardships, and in response, a variety of nationalist and radical doctrines took hold after 1945—of which communism was but one. Innumerable US efforts to overthrow existing governments, many democratically elected, began after 1948, when the CIA managed to overthrow the Syrian regime. The Iranian coup in August 1954 replaced an elected nationalist regime with a shah who ruled as a tyrant until 1979—by which time he had so traumatized the nation that Islamic fundamentalists could overthrow him and install the present anti-American rulers in his place.

When the US government wanted to overthrow another government, it usually turned to military officers, after 1960 articulating a theory of officers as harbingers of "modernization" to justify its actions. It supported officers in Guatemala in 1954, Egypt after 1954, Brazil in March 1964, the Dominican Republic in 1965, Chile in September 1973, Angola in 1975, Argentina in 1976—and innumerable other cases. It also assisted Islamic fundamentalists in the Middle East when there was no better option, and it enthusiastically embraced the feudalist and Islamic fundamentalist rulers of Saudi Arabia, a relationship that has continued to this day. But after 1967 the United States also tilted heavily toward Israel—pledging it vast quantities of military aid, which continues, and making it a proxy for US power in the region. At about the same time, Pakistan became a proxy for Washington in the South Asia region.

To describe all the literally hundreds of US interventions in every corner of the Third World after 1945, ranging from merely showing the flag or landing US troops to sending arms to coup plotters, would require a separate book, which I and many others have already written. Activism was the rule under both Democratic and Republican presidents, but in January 1980 President Jimmy Carter, without consulting the State Department or Congress, formulated a doctrine whose ultimate implications could scarcely be predicted. It was common practice for presidents—before and after—to issue ill-conceived statements and threats to cope with far deeper challenges that have frustrated the United States. Carter warned that any nation seeking to gain control of the Persian Gulf region would thereby attack the "vital interests" of the United States—its oil supply—and "the terrain or the tactic or the level of our response" was entirely open. The Carter Doctrine was vague, and it might have applied to the Soviets or militant Islam alike, but that too was left open. The doctrine was not a policy but a highly activist stance, much like Bush's "preemptive war" declaration over two decades later. It was not the beginning of Washington's deep involvement in the Middle East, but it made it plain that it would do whatever was necessary to secure US control over that immense region. Today we live with the violent outcome of such command decisions.[8]

Vietnam and the Testing of US Power

Vietnam was the paramount example of how infinitely complicated the social realities in many Third World nations had become and how they would inevitably test the many regimes and elites on which Washington was so fatally dependent and with them the political foundations on which US foreign policy and military power had come to rest.[9] US leaders always responded to the events and issues in Vietnam in the larger context of their ongoing search for a decisive global strategy relevant to the entire Third World, perceiving Vietnam as just one manifestation of the innumerable challenges they confronted everywhere: the efficacy of limited war, the credibility of US power, the risk of defeat in one nation spreading to those bordering it, and much else. Vietnam epitomized the postwar crisis of US expansionism and power at a crucial stage of its intensive, frustrating effort to articulate a viable, flexible, military, and political basis for establishing an international socioeconomic environment congenial to it. It was mainly chance that designated Vietnam as the primary arena of trial, but by 1960 it was virtually preordained that the United States would attempt somewhere to attain those vital military successes essential to confirming its credibility. Otherwise, the failures and dilemmas it had confronted in Korea, Cuba, and elsewhere in the Third World since 1949 would undermine the very foundations of the conservative orders it was seeking either to establish in some nations or to defend in others.

The structural origins of the crisis in Vietnam also existed in varying forms in much of the Third World and revealed how social institutions and the people in them made conventional assumptions regarding warfare so irrelevant. As a microcosm of the times, the Vietnam conflict again elucidated the limits of human endurance and the way in which internal strife and war's destructive effects transform the very character of the conflict itself, including its eventual political, human, and social consequences. Both within the United States and Vietnam, the war produced dramatically new parameters of social and political as well as physical struggle, thereby frustrating the ability of leaders on all sides to control it. Vietnam once more exposed how unpredictable and terrible war's processes and outcome are—and always will be.

The causes of conflict in Vietnam existed in many countries and still do. Although it is impossible to ignore other vital factors, the single most important issue of the war in the south after 1960, as well as in the entire history of the Vietnamese revolution, was land and land-related matters. Before World War II, land ownership in Cochin was highly inequitable, and the larger part was rented by tenants who paid landlords 40 to 60 percent of the output. The landlords also dominated usury, further oppressing the peasantry, with 50 to 70 percent interest annually being typical. This agrarian crisis provided the communists with a favorable national environment in which to mobilize countless new followers after 1945. The party had sought to introduce only minor reforms where it had the ability to do so, for it feared alienating most of the landlords and preferred broad patriotic appeals for a united front behind the anti-French struggle. But it still benefited about four-fifths of the peasants in some manner, ranging from lowering rents to 25 percent or even abolishing them in some places to eliminating the worst abuses of usury and annulling prewar debts.

After the United States installed Ngo Dinh Diem in power and created a wholly dependent, artificial new nation in the southern part of Vietnam in mid-1954, Diem instituted his own "reforms," and he imposed a new elite of politically reliable Catholic refugees from the north upon the rural administrative and land structure. As an intensely devout Catholic in an overwhelmingly Buddhist nation, Diem employed religion in wars preordained to polarize the society, in the process reintroducing exploitive land relations and high rents. Simultaneously, Diem persecuted not just communists but all of the dissident non-Catholic religious sects that flourished in Cochin.

The Communist Party in the north, which defined policy for its southern branch, hoped to have the political accord it had signed with the French at Geneva in June 1954 implemented and persisted with this line, notwithstanding both Diem's and Washington's immediate denunciation of the Geneva agreement. The northern party's grave crisis over land issues during 1955–1957, its own serious problems in consolidating its economic power, and aid-linked pressures from both China and the Soviet Union to avoid risking a confrontation with the United States caused Ho Chi Minh and his colleagues to insist that southern party members behave as if the Geneva terms would be fulfilled. Their public profiles made it easier for authorities to round them up. The result was that about two-thirds of the southern party members were killed or arrested over four years, culminating in 1959 with intensified suppression that endangered the lives of all who remained free. Irresistible southern demands to approve armed struggle created a profound tension between the party in the south and that in the north that threatened to produce, at the very least, yet another southern resistance movement that Hanoi could not control and possibly a schism. As had been and remained the case so often elsewhere, the war that began in the south after 1959 was far more the response of desperate people to repression than the decision of revolutionaries to embark on the seizure of power.

The creation of the National Liberation Front (NLF) in the south in 1960 was the outcome of pressure from southerners upon the ruling party in the north, which sought to constrain it for several more years. But after Diem's long muzzling of the southern peasantry, the NLF obtained far greater peasant backing than the Vietminh had earlier been able to mobilize, above all among younger, poorer peasants, so that it possessed a crucial class basis and pursued a "poor peasant" land-reform line for five decisive years, reducing rents, redistributing land,

and carrying out similar measures. Given the extent of landlessness and oppression, it is no surprise that the NLF's initial support and subsequent persistence was greatest where such conditions had predominated, and notwithstanding the decisive US role in making it possible, the war always possessed characteristics of both a civil and class conflict.[10]

Such a broad social foundation for the fight in the south meant that it would be, like all comparable struggles elsewhere, principally a people's war in terms of its supporters and logistics—resilient and highly decentralized, with a great deal of local autonomy. Indeed, both physically and politically it presented the United States with vastly more difficult problems than had the Korean War, not only for these reasons but also because the terrain made concealment so easy. Vietnam, therefore, was a fundamental challenge not only to the succession of political proxies the United States had sponsored for twenty years but also to the very premises of its high-technology warfare.

When the United States in 1964 embarked step-by-step to apply enormous quantities of modern arms and the strategic and political assumptions underpinning them, it resolved to transcend the Korean War's frustrating stalemate in order to vindicate the credibility of its military power and political determination. To do so, the Pentagon had to discover and apply strategies that could not merely overcome the limits of combat but also neutralize the socioeconomic pressures that made poor peasants ready to fight for their cause and produce an effective political-economic alternative to the revolutionary cause. Above all, it hoped to establish a proxy who would not only create a viable social order but also provide most of the manpower essential for the tough, bloody combat that the war entailed. And if Washington was to avert the financial costs and public alienation that the Korean War generated, a premise that was crucial to its post-Korean strategic doctrines, victory would have to be gained relatively rapidly and not require massive numbers of US troops. At least as crucial, the United States had to fight the war in such a way that it did not, as occurred so often throughout the twentieth century, produce unanticipated cataclysmic social and institutional consequences within Vietnam that might thereby snatch political success from the hands of the militarily more powerful nation. No advocate of escalation before 1966 grasped the magnitude or even the existence of some of these challenges or ever imagined what the war's eventual outcome would be. And in this they shared precisely all the illusions and false expectations that had preceded all major conflicts in this century. After over a half-century of surprises, the ignorance and myopia of the men and women who embarked upon wars was as great as ever.

The Organization and Intelligence Impasse

Thousands of books have probed every conceivable dimension of the Vietnam War, but all that need concern us here is the war's relationship to two crucial questions confronting the United States as the preeminent world military power in the second half of the twentieth century: First, did the war answer or compound the strategic and political dilemmas that the Korean War had revealed and that successive administrations sought to overcome with new weapons and doctrines? Second, to what extent would the traumatic political, social, and economic consequences of making war themselves define its final outcome and thereby confound the military assumptions of politicians and generals?

Certain aspects of the Vietnam War differed dramatically from earlier conflicts, but the organization of the various armed services and the kinds of justifications they concocted for their bureaucratic autonomy remained much as they have been since World War II (and continue to this day). Such bitter service conflicts over emoluments and budgets, which translated into careers for many, bore no relationship to reality and often made it impossible after 1964 to judge the true state of the conflict and whether the United States was losing or winning. They also greatly increased the war's costs.

As in Korea, the US Army, Air Force, Marines, and Navy could not agree on the integrated use of their airpower, notwithstanding the increasingly ambitious organizational schemes and doctrines that emerged after the Korean War and especially after President John F. Kennedy's immensely pretentious experts from universities and industry, of whom the Defense Department's Robert McNamara was the most imposing, arrived in Washington with their quasi-magical innovative budgeting conceptions. The tactical aviation components belonging to the various services were assigned separate territories, some overlapping, which resolved intraservice conflicts but proved inefficient at crucial moments and much more expensive. The air force, internally divided into strategic and tactical aviation, strenuously fought the army's control over helicopters and a whole variety of planes until April 1966, when it traded away its claims in return for the army's forgoing new fixed-wing aircraft. Even the air force's commands were divided into three distinct units, and nominally overseeing the entire war in Indochina was the US Navy's Pacific commander in chief in Hawaii, who had been assigned what initially was a small responsibility in February 1962 and subsequently refused to relinquish his central place in the command-and-control organizational chart. It was a fact that rivalry among the services was a pervasive reality around which much else would remain subsidiary, and that they could fight only in this context.

The Vietnam War is a typical example of the decisive limits of the role of expensive and large intelligence services when rationality and realism conflict with the policy and ideological preconceptions of the highest officials. It was merely a harbinger of future US adventures, down to Afghanistan and Iraq today, and of Washington's refusal to acknowledge the limits of reality. There have been many able and honest people in the US intelligence services, but their basic mission of making facts shape policy has been doomed to failure from the inception. The higher one goes in these services, the more one finds individuals ready to cater to the policymakers' preferences—who, in the final analysis, also decide who rises in the bureaucracy. The CIA, on balance, remained skeptical of the war; analysts in specialized think tanks, such as the RAND Corporation, were even more negative; and there were an ample number of people who described the US failures and challenges with candor and accuracy. The government sponsored accurate and widely circulated studies of land and class issues in South Vietnam but refused to believe that land was important. Part of the problem was the quantity of intelligence produced. Thirteen intelligence agencies overlapped each other in Vietnam at one time, and in early 1967 the army alone was producing well over a half-ton of reports daily. Beginning in January 1967, one Pentagon office produced a digest of reports every six weeks; the Joint Chiefs of Staff tried unsuccessfully several times to restrict its circulation because it was sometimes too candid, even pessimistic, about the administration's basic military operations and assumptions. There was, in short, plenty of information available that described US failures and challenges with candor and accuracy—for those who wanted to read, believe, and use it. It simply made no difference because the gap between reality and policy was irreconcilable. Secretary of Defense Robert McNamara's later complaint that there were no "Vietnam experts" to whom he could turn was simply false. They existed, but he refused to heed their advice whenever they warned against the series of disasters that the United States had embarked upon.

The mere fact that it took Washington nine years to conclude that its client, Ngo Dinh Diem, had been predestined to lose the war, requiring the United States finally to play a decisive role in his assassination in 1963, reveals how immune basic policies and biases were to what had become common knowledge. That there was vastly more information to choose from actually made it easier for those who had prejudged their decisions (or had strong career and personal motives) to use whatever suited their interests and ignore the remainder. Careerism and sheer hucksterism surely played a major, perhaps dominant role as generals and officials issued press releases, covering everything from grand strategy to weekly "body counts," that justified their actions and led to promotions. These falsehoods and cultivated illusions created a fantasy world that promised imminent success if only Washington would authorize a relatively small increase in effort, and escalation followed escalation as the fear of losing the nation's credibility rationalized each denial of what was the increasingly irrefutable truth—that the military and political policies of the United States were both false and failing.

There were many falsehoods consciously nurtured throughout the war, and the CIA often objected to them. But the most serious result of this protracted, convoluted system of deceptions was the so-called order-of-battle controversy before the Tet offensive in February 1968. The lower the numbers of enemy combatants, the more progress the US military could claim, and so they refused to count the various local forces—roughly 300,000 men disappeared because admitting their existence would produce a gloomy conclusion. The military intelligence and CIA were constantly struggling with each other for analytic domination, and the CIA lost most of these bureaucratic turf wars. The CIA objected to a point, but most knew that their careers depended on being optimists.

But the communists fighting the Tet offensive had far larger military forces than most US officials believed, and the stunning assault changed the politicians' and, even more ominous, public perceptions of reality. The US defeat during Tet was much greater because of the overblown predictions of imminent success in the fall of 1967, which was also essential for Lyndon Johnson's reelection ambitions. The falsified data, in the end, were believed by those seeking initially to manipulate public opinion, and the Tet debacle was the beginning of the end for the protracted US effort to win the Vietnam War. It was indelibly clear that the war was not only being lost but also had become the most divisive, traumatic, and costly error in the modern US experience. But despite much reflection and debate, it was not the turning point in the US role in the world that it should have been.[11]

The Premises and Problems of US Strategy

Vietnam presented US political leaders with the opportunity either to resolve the accumulated strategic and military problems that had emerged from the Korean War and the global arms race, which the New Look and subsequent limited war thinkers attempted to resolve theoretically, or to compound them gravely. The crisis of military technology that began with World War I was intrinsic in the fact that the inflated claims of strategic doctrines justifying modern arms had protracted every major war since 1914. In the process of doing so, their monumental nonmilitary consequences—ranging from economic dislocations to the massive destruction of civilian populations and the transformation of their political attitudes—had defined the political outcome of conflicts far more than had the positions of armies. Military power became both increasingly indiscriminate and its strategies irrelevant to gaining mastery over enemies in the purely physical sense of that term. Insofar as its pretensions made war seem plausible or, as in the case of the notion of credibility, occasionally essential, it had also become fatally counterproductive. The Vietnam War was but one major milestone in humankind's repeated, futile experience in the twentieth century of making wars that profoundly shaped global political and social development in ways ultimately much more dangerous for the war makers. The illusions US political and military leaders cherished were ones they shared with those elsewhere who had earlier embarked upon similar fatal courses. What was unique, however, was the fact that the United States had both the will and the resources to aspire to lead the world longer than any other nation, so that after 1945 it engaged in many more wars than any state in recent times. Whether it also had the capacity to succeed in such a role remained to be proved.

The compounded frustrations, experiences, and concerns of the 1950s strongly influenced the step-by-step US intervention in Vietnam that led to the longest war in its history. In the beginning, Washington attempted to create a viable client regime under Diem, but its failure to do so led to increasing direct US participation, until at one time about three-quarters of a million of its military personnel were either in Indochina or involved in the war from offshore locations. US leaders hoped to establish the credibility of their military might, prevent a succession of regional defeats that they believed the "loss" of South Vietnam would trigger, and articulate new counterinsurgency techniques that could win local conflicts elsewhere as well. But when dependence on its local proxies to achieve victory became an obvious cul-de-sac and massive numbers of its soldiers poured into Vietnam, the US way-of-war sought to triumph by relying on huge quantities of technology and firepower, either on the field of battle against enemy soldiers and their alleged civilian supporters or through punitive air strikes to destroy the will of the Democratic Republic of Vietnam (DRV) to support the war in the south.

After 1975, several US military analysts diagnosed the fatal assumptions of what one has called the "Army Concept," which allowed tactics and operational successes (employing lavish firepower and the unique mobility that helicopters afforded) to dominate and ultimately define grand strategy—an approach ignoring that there was, at best, only a scant relationship between technology and the outcome of ground combat.[12]

Military writers have even cogently criticized the hallowed official presumption that political success would follow from military victory. But however valid such censure, the war the United States fought in Vietnam remained essentially a predictable phase in the inexorable escalation in technology and firepower that has repeatedly defined the nature of warfare everywhere since World War I, irresistibly making civilians and their societies increasingly significant military objectives. Vietnam was the most extreme example of this pattern only because the United States had far greater resources to do what many other industrial nations had earlier also attempted.

The decline in the use of infantry and combat manpower as a proportion of armies is a universal pattern. The US military's problem in Vietnam was that enemy fighters could easily hide until the initiative favored them and they could exploit the element of surprise. The principal US strategy was to flush them out in "search and destroy" operations, using the infantry to make contact and then quickly pulling back so that devastating artillery and air-munitions barrages could saturate large areas where battle lines were often nonexistent and civilians lived. The combat infantryman was primarily a bait, barely a fifth of army manpower at the war's peak, whose role was subordinated to the conviction that the massive use of aviation and artillery would decisively influence the war's strategic balance. A reliable measure of this increasing reliance on technology and firepower is the tons of munitions per person-year of combat exposure, using World War II as the base of 1 ton per year of combat: by Korea it had reached 8 tons per year, and it was 26 tons per year in Southeast Asia during 1966–1971. The United States alone used 15 million tons of munitions in Indochina, over twice the quantity it consumed in all of World War II and five times the Korean War level. Aircraft dropped half of it; in the case of the B-52s, from as high as 30,000 feet. The air force's own estimate was that in half the instances, B-52s struck where there were no enemies; about 70 percent of all artillery shells were fired for "harassing and interdiction" purposes where there was little or no combat. The results were enormous civilian casualties and damage, the transformation of Vietnamese society, huge outlays for the US taxpayer, and US military failure to win the war.

The incredibly expensive futuristic dimensions of the US military effort are painfully familiar, ranging from computer-coordinated electronic battlefields to extraordinarily complex $15 million aircraft, but the helicopter was the single most important innovation. Although it had been developed for use in Europe, McNamara believed the helicopter to be a decisive weapon in counterinsurgency, allowing highly mobile manpower and firepower to overcome jungle terrain. The army did not share his enthusiasm but was swept along, eventually concluding that its initial skepticism had been correct. Helicopters were costly to run and maintain, they eliminated the element of surprise, and they were vulnerable to ground fire: 4,857 of them were lost during the entire war, considerably more than the 3,500 in use in Vietnam at the mid-1968 peak. Senior officers tended to use them to direct combat, and the army later concluded that had been a serious error since it removed them from battlefield conditions and gravely skewed their judgments. Expensive weaponry and munitions became an even more important component of the war after 1969 as US manpower declined.[13]

The strategically indecisive weapons and equipment used to fight the Vietnam War made it enormously costly and produced new dilemmas. Leaving aside the war's impact on the balance of political and social forces within Vietnam itself, US technology had to efficiently attain its military and political goals, lest a protracted conflict create economic problems as well as serious opposition among the public at home. Indeed, although a very few US leaders always feared such potential complications, none ever imagined that the ultimate price of the war would eventually include the breakdown of the US military establishment in Vietnam in ways that severely affected the nation's ability to continue the conflict. It was the conjunction of all of these challenges that eventually forced the Nixon administration to reduce its presence in Vietnam greatly and to depend once again on a venal and incompetent client regime to win the war. In this way the United States, like so many nations before it, came to confront the limits of its power.

Economically, the Vietnam War differed fundamentally from the four other wars the United States had engaged in since 1898, for all the earlier conflicts had begun when the economy was in recession or still emerging from a period of idle productive capacity. In addition to advancing the nation's political goals, they had created new prosperity, producing neither structural challenges globally nor alienating a major domestic social constituency. But the massive escalation after 1965 began well into the longest sustained period of expansion since 1945, causing the rate of inflation in the latter half of the decade to become three times greater than during the first half, expanding the demand for labor so that the productivity of manufacturing fell dramatically, and weakening the dollar internationally. The Johnson administration was already heavily committed to its Great Society reforms, which benefited the poor and black communities most of all, and the question of how to pay for both a war and domestic programs required it to confront basic political issues and priorities. To reconcile this tension, the president had, at the very least, to manage the budget astutely.

McNamara emerged as the decisive figure in this dilemma, for Johnson trusted him until his fatal mistakes could no longer be undone. But McNamara merely allowed the services to spend whatever they thought they needed, and on March 1, 1965, he issued a "blank check" making it clear "that there is an unlimited appropriation available" for Vietnam. Like all his peers at the time, he believed that the war would not last long.[14] As needs exceeded the amount of funds he had budgeted, he merely extracted supplemental appropriations from Congress, and since Johnson considered tax increases politically dangerous, for over two years the president cut spending for the popular Great Society program to help pay for the war. Only in July 1968 was a new tax bill enacted. But notwithstanding his supreme self-confidence, which initially disarmed potential critics, McNamara underestimated the costs of the war for fiscal 1967 by over 100 percent, running up an $11 billion deficit for which reductions in domestic spending hardly sufficed. In fiscal 1968, which began in July 1967, the deficit was well over twice that amount, by which time Johnson had lost all confidence in McNamara, who belatedly concluded about then that the United States could no longer expect yet more escalation to achieve victory.

These compounded economic factors emerged and interacted with domestic politics and international finance to constrain further escalation. Suffice it to say that the structural inhibitions on US war making had become decisive, setting the context for a subsequent partial reduction of its role not only in Vietnam but, in certain crucial ways, elsewhere as well. The gap between the nation's vast desires and finite resources was now an obvious constraint and a source of domestic conflict and opposition, including from economic elites that since 1914 had consistently supported a vigorous foreign and military policy. The United States now found itself having to choose among its global objectives in order to attain any of them.

US leaders had obviously miscalculated the nature of a war against resourceful, determined enemies in jungle terrain, but they also misunderstood the costs and complexities of their own way of warfare and the extravagant technological fetishism on which it was premised. Only surrealists can aspire to capture the daunting realities of a high-consumption war providing its soldiers with innumerable imported amenities and utilizing stupendous amounts of equipment and firepower in a highly decentralized, primitive economy. The buildup that occurred was unprecedented in the history of warfare, and the Pentagon purchased everything it desired on a crash basis, cynically charging a great deal not related to the war to the Vietnam account. As an official review later put it, "The zeal and energy and money that went into the effort to equip and supply US forces in Vietnam generated mountainous new procurements, choked supply pipelines, overburdened transportation systems, and for a time caused complete loss of control at depots in Vietnam."[15] Apart from pure waste in terms of useless luxuries and futuristic weapons, the standard solution for equipment lost in the logistics logjam was to order more, speed being more crucial than economy. By the end of 1967 the Pentagon managed to impose some constraints on such extravagant spending, and its logistics control began, in its own words, to be "slowly established."[16]

But the inherent counterproductivity of the entire system was clear: it was militarily inconclusive and so costly that it precipitated serious economic problems at home and internationally. Above all, it transformed the nation the United States was seeking to dominate. The problems that the Korean War had created seem relatively small by comparison.

Transforming US Public Opinion

The Johnson administration completely failed to anticipate the war's impact on public opinion. US activism in the international arena after 1898 had depended on the public's acquiescence to, if not enthusiasm for, the policies that successive presidencies defined. After 1946, however, the sustained, growing financial sacrifices these wars imposed upon taxpayers required popular endorsement. Opinion on the Korean War shifted at the end of 1950, but the majority of the people ultimately backed it, especially after Eisenhower was elected president. That politicians might pay a fatal political price for their military policies was a dramatic and unprecedented development and a potential inhibitor of vast significance. The length of the Vietnam War, the economic and intellectual dislocations it caused, and the repeated dashed hopes from the Johnson administration's persistently optimistic prognostications caused a "credibility gap" in its relationship with its citizens and began to erode support for the war, especially among blue-collar, low-income voters without whom the Democrats could not be reelected. By 1967 the proportion of Americans favoring the war began to decline, until by the end of that year opinion was evenly divided. The Tet offensive in February 1968 caused approval to drop sharply, and it continued to fall. By January 1973, two out of three Americans opposed the war.

Vietnam revealed that profound disunity in US society would accompany protracted war and that the historical political underdevelopment of the population and the absence of a significant leftist party had nonetheless not eliminated the public's capacity, however inchoate its expressions, to become alienated in ways that might seriously constrain the nation's foreign policy in the future. At this time, as well, a Congress that for two decades had docilely acquiesced to the definitions and demands of successive administrations developed a greatly expanded capacity to evaluate and affect foreign policy and budget issues and began to challenge executive supremacy—culminating in driving Nixon from the White House in August 1974. Like countless millions of Europeans and Asians since 1914, the American people also had a breaking point that patriotic calls to glory could not neutralize.[17]

The Breakdown of the US Military

At the inception of the war, the Kennedy administration failed to foresee the loss of popular support, still less the emergence of an articulate and often massive antiwar movement, but there were some precedents for such opposition that might have forewarned them. There were, however, no precedents whatsoever for the breakdown of US military services in Vietnam, which raised the issue of the very viability of the principal instruments of US military power and strategy, particularly the army. The US Army in Vietnam was highly stratified; the officers consisted mainly of career men from middle-class and small-town backgrounds who often used their subordinates in ways that aided their own advancement. But there were also poorly motivated temporary officers, far more interested in survival than heroism, who were either Reserve Officers' Training Corps (ROTC) graduates or had been selected from the lower ranks after ROTC volunteers declined by two-thirds during the war. Of the approximately 2 million men who served in Vietnam, those who were low-income, black, and Hispanic formed a disproportionate share of the combat rifle companies sent on the dangerous search-and-destroy missions intended to flush out the enemy so that the skilled air and artillery personnel could saturate them with explosives. It was this group, roughly a fifth of the entire army, that avoided engaging the enemy as much as possible and attempted, in 788 confirmed cases from 1969 to 1972 (succeeding in eighty-six instances), to kill their officers for pushing them too energetically to fight or for denying them access to hard drugs. Never before had the US military experienced so much insubordination or such profound racial tension and frequent riots, much less heroin addiction among 20 percent of its personnel and the widespread use of marijuana and alcohol.[18]

Withdrawing US military forces from Vietnam by 1973 gave Nixon's presidency a political respite, and it also reduced the cost of the war because of both domestic political and economic pressures and the insistence of the other industrial capitalist nations that Washington protect the dollar from further weakening. But rather than resolving the crisis in US strategy, doctrine, and weaponry, Vietnam intensified it, leaving the credibility of US military power far more in doubt than ever before. Not only had weapons failed militarily, but politically and economically they had created irreconcilable dilemmas.

All modern theories of military strategy have ignored the simple reality that the skills and motivation of those responsible for the dirty tasks of implementing that strategy are fundamental and that there is no possibility whatsoever of victory when soldiers refuse to perform as expected. No one in the US military or among its civilian strategists had ever imagined the possibility of such an outcome to an effort of this scope. In the end, as the well-groomed politicians and generals who articulated strategies and made grand claims for their weapons became irrelevant and pathetic in wartime, the constraints on those in power were greater than ever, and their conventional wisdom collapsed totally.

The Structural Causes of US Defeat

The United States failed in Vietnam not solely because of its strategy and the technology used to implement it, nor because the political and economic institutions on which they were based were fatally flawed. At least as significant was the fact that in the very process of fighting such a war, massive firepower transformed the basic structure of Vietnamese society in ways that aggravated the already profound organizational and economic weaknesses of the US-dependent regimes in Saigon. Even though the war seriously traumatized the communist side too, reducing its military capacities, the social and economic impact of the US way-of-war decisively altered the framework and forces that would determine victory and defeat. The astonishing manner in which the Vietnam War ended revealed how profoundly counterproductive Washington's military arm had become.

The escalation of warfare to destroy or affect civilians increasingly became the norm among all the major adversaries during World War II. Notwithstanding the qualitatively and therefore morally distinctive Nazi and Japanese intentions and roles, the Allies consistently transgressed traditional legal and ethical standards concerning civilians and war crimes (e.g., mass bombings of civilians in such German cities as Dresden and the dropping of atomic bombs on Japanese cities). The Korean War saw the United States take yet one more large step away from the

"rules of war" by hitting civilians with the massive use of firepower. Although the Vietnam experience reflected the sheer overwhelming quantity of technology that US wealth could purchase, both the weaponry itself and its uses were the ineluctable product of the military premises and institutions that have guided much of the "civilized" world since 1914.

Such caveats notwithstanding, the United States carried the war against civilians in Vietnam to an extent that only Germany and Japan have surpassed in modern history. Astonishingly superficial anticommunist justifications were concocted to rationalize US behavior, but an additional animus of outright cruelty, especially among airpower advocates, as well as a racist undercurrent, reinforced it. More important, however, was a kind of amoral pragmatic conviction among US leaders that the United States could win the war more quickly if, by using every form of warfare available to it short of nuclear weapons, it emptied vast regions of the people essential to sustaining the enemy. What they did not suspect was that exactly the reverse would occur due to a variety of complex and subtle social, economic, and organizational processes that were easily predictable and today appear starkly obvious.

US generals and political leaders consciously sanctioned the use of massive firepower in much of Vietnam because, as General William C. Westmoreland put it, "it does deprive the enemy of the population" from which it recruited soldiers and support.[19] In the vast "free-fire zones," every person was deemed an enemy in fact if not in intent, and the stupendous amounts of unobserved artillery ("H&I," or "harassment and interdiction," in military slang) and bombs accounted for much of the war's tonnage. Civilians in these zones were deliberately driven away.[20] Search-and-destroy operations applied the free-fire principle in yet another way. Chemical warfare, which the Pentagon privately acknowledged exposed it to war crimes charges (thereby causing it to attempt to keep the program secret), was one more means of displacing people.

The use of defoliating herbicides in Vietnam began on an experimental basis in August 1961, increasing from 6,000 acres in 1962 to 1.7 million in 1967. Diem initially urged the United States to employ it against rice in order to deprive the NLF and its supporters of food, and by 1965, 42 percent of the chemicals fell on food crops, affecting civilians and combatants alike. In 1963, US experts learned that the principal defoliant, Agent Orange, might cause cancer, birth defects, and much else (a fear that was confirmed), but this knowledge failed to affect policy in any way. The Americans used defoliants for nine years, spraying 20 percent of all the south's jungles and 36 percent of its mangrove forests—resulting in irrevocable human and environmental damage. Bulldozing vast areas also caused permanent devastation: some

3,000 square kilometers (1,900 square miles), including food crops and water-control systems, were plowed under during the war.

The predictable result of such destruction by these and so many other techniques was the uprooting of a rural society, exactly as the US policy intended. Although precise data will never be known, even the Pentagon has conceded that between 700,000 and 1,225,000 civilians were killed and wounded between 1965 and 1972 in South Vietnam, an area with 18 million people in 1970, but US Senate estimates are higher, with deaths comprising anywhere from 195,000 to 415,000 of these totals. Diem claimed to have moved 8.2 million people—about half of the south—into nominally controlled areas by 1962 alone, and successive pacification programs repeatedly forced or drove peasants from their homes. At least half of all peasants, but especially those in NLF-dominated territory, were pushed into refugee camps, where their standard of living dropped by about two-thirds, and they also suffered incalculable psychic losses. In 1960 only 20 percent of South Vietnam's population lived in urban regions, but by 1971, mainly for reasons of physical safety and dire economic necessity, this share had increased to 43 percent—a growth rate five times that for the Third World as a whole.[21]

To some critical extent, therefore, the communists were cut off from the peasantry in large parts of the nation, and in this sense the US military calculus succeeded brilliantly. But the responsibility for sustaining the distinctive social order that emerged fell entirely on the United States and its surrogate, and the resources necessary to do so depended on economic and political factors over which both had very little, if any, control. The marginalized urban population lived on the sidewalk economy or was unemployed; worked as prostitutes in the case of 200,000 women; and survived precariously in a transitional, artificial, cacophonous urban world completely different from their native villages; but the US had managed effectively to rupture their relationship to the NLF. The personalism and apathy that the imperative to survive instilled quickly produced a deeply alienated population, yet US officials believed that uprooting a traditional peasant society in wartime would create an alternative to the communists. But this assumption totally ignored the fact that alienation in the context of urbanization also brought its own dangers: the puppet regime would have no legitimacy or stability unless it had the money and force to placate those now in the cities. It was relatively easy to destroy a nation but infinitely more difficult to create a viable alternative that could transcend the war's terrible impact on the values and behavior of millions of people in vital locations and positions, much less evoke their loyalties in times of crisis. The Americans' problem was not whether they could transfer military power to their surrogates, as they had often sought to do elsewhere after 1945, but rather whether they could establish those political, economic, and ideological institutions that are the prerequisite for enduring military successes in the Third World.[22]

It was this vast structural, social, and cultural transformation of a nation that increasingly altered the war after the late 1960s from one that was principally military to a conflict whose outcome reflected largely autonomous factors inherent in a gravely flawed social and human organization. That the NLF's means for dealing with the new realities of the nation were altered profoundly was unquestionable. But was that now so decisive? The Americans believed it was, at least to the extent that a significant constriction of the communists' mass following could become the basis, along with other diplomatic and military measures, for defeating them permanently.

The Balance of Forces in a People's War

In terms of their original strategic assumptions and real power, both the United States and the communists were significantly weaker in 1969 than they had been before the Tet offensive. The United States inflicted massive casualties on the NLF and DRV armies, and it repeatedly escalated its firepower and manpower to compensate for communist successes until 1968. But its strategy still failed to alter the enemy's will and ability to persist, nor could Washington afford economically or politically to increase its military commitments. And although the NLF and many of its supporters had either been driven out of much of the countryside or killed, the Pentagon's highly unreliable data on hamlet security said nothing about the loyalties of the peasants that its side claimed to control. Its experts knew that many of them, including those ideologically non- or even anticommunist, were making accommodations with the remaining NLF structure and often selling it rice.[23]

In the most fundamental sense, the war's future was no longer in the hands of either the United States or its enemies, subject to their decisions, desires, and resources. It had lasted so long that it had significantly transformed the basic nature of the contest, greatly reducing the importance of battlefields and armies. The process and character of the war itself, with its multifaceted social, cultural, economic, and political dimensions, now shaped the orbit within which the forces that determined victory or defeat were increasingly likely to occur.

It is certain that the communists believed, for reasons that seemed persuasive and logical to them as well as to the Americans, that they were far weaker after the Tet offensive than before it, and residues of their defeatism persisted until the war ended. The NLF infrastructure and manpower losses after 1968 were enormous, and the communists' central Tet offensive objective to rebuild their power in the cities failed abysmally. The marginalized urban masses remained immune to their appeals, and although a substantial minority were *attentistes* (opportunists who support the side that is winning), most of them were of doubtful reliability. In many rural areas the party's stress on physical security did not allow it to operate freely among peasants, many of whom had become apathetic or too traumatized by repeated suffering and repression to dare to make a visible political commitment to anyone—whether the NLF or the Saigon regime. Before 1966, the majority of the peasantry had supported the NLF for a variety of reasons, ranging from genuine conviction to conformity to neighborhood and family opinion, but after 1969 most were concerned with their own survival, which meant adjusting to power realities. Because of US troop reductions after 1969 and disintegration and corruption in the Saigon army, the NLF regained access to at least 60 percent of the Mekong Delta by 1974, and many peasants adapted to the new power balance, including selling rice at premium rates to the NLF. Compared to their roles a decade earlier, however, most remained relatively passive. As for the communist-led army, it emerged from 1968 so bloodied that it avoided a major battle until the Saigon regime's invasion of Laos in February 1971 compelled it to fight—and to win. And although it attained major tactical successes when its conventional army crossed the 17th parallel in May 1972, its heavy losses and failure to coordinate its military components infused it with a defensive, cautious mentality for nearly three more years.

The communists appeared to have been weakened in vital ways; even more important, their leaders believed it to be the case. The crucial point is that of all those overwhelming military factors that both the Americans and the communists thought to be decisive measures of power, none possessed anything like the significance attached to them. Neither side, ultimately, comprehended the nature and structure of the war after its initial military impact translated over time into a test of social systems and social forces that, although they included combat, increasingly transcended it.

The Vietnam Debacle

The Korean War painfully revealed to the United States how armies that are materially very unequal can become stalemated on battlefields, and in Vietnam it unsuccessfully attempted to respond to that lesson by developing a grand strategy based on massive firepower and high mobility. That the war was too costly and too protracted merely reiterated the lesson of Korea. Although the United States believed after 1964 that its military power would transcend past frustrations, by 1969 it had to confront the relationship of its own credibility and sacrifices to the nature and viability of the client regime it was seeking to keep in power in Vietnam. Would its endorsement of Nguyen Van Thieu and reliance on his policies cause the United States to lose the war regardless of the balance of military power? And was Vietnam but one reflection of the unresolvable contradiction inherent in the US confrontation with much of the Third World, and was its fatal dependence on corrupt clients elsewhere a harbinger of future defeats?

In essence, the Army of the Republic of Vietnam (ARVN) evolved from a style of military organization much closer to Chiang Kai-shek's during World War II than to the idealized forces that US officers and court strategists considered in their plans and theories concerning Third World armies. Thieu's Byzantine military system was essentially a mechanism for controlling the political structure and, above all, for preventing the army from mounting a coup against him; the US-subsidized economic order was a vast fiefdom for guaranteeing the personal fortunes and political loyalties of Thieu and his supporters. With over a million men nominally within its ranks in 1972, and after 1967 with its senior officers selected only for their devotion to Thieu, the ARVN was incapable of fighting seriously, much less with the modern arms the Americans lavished on it that it could neither service nor operate properly. Between 1965 and 1972 almost 1 million men deserted, reducing the army's combat strength by 30 percent in an average year. Roughly one-quarter of the men ostensibly in its ranks were "ghost soldiers" who had deserted, were dead, or held outside jobs—a status that allowed their officers to pocket their pay and allowances. The social barriers between officers and soldiers were immense and ranged from education to religion, Catholics being especially overrepresented among officers. And since soldiers had to serve until age forty-five, the families of nearly half of them lived with or near them, which meant that the population of wives and children around ARVN bases far exceeded that of the army itself. The US proxy was a typical moribund Third World military regime.

In January 1975 the ARVN had what appeared to be a crushing numerical lead over the combined communist forces in the south: over three times the artillery, twice the tanks and armored personnel carriers, 1,400 aircraft against none, a two-to-one advantage in combat troops, and three times the manpower. ARVN fired nine times as many shells at the end of 1974 as the communists and had huge munitions stocks and comparatively simple logistical problems. It was not the strength of the miscellaneous communist forces that won the war but rather the weakness of Thieu's army in all domains that affected warfare. By 1974 it was disintegrating amid the ravages of inflation and demoralization, ready to capsize before the first significant challenge. Had Hanoi not attacked in March 1975, the war would still have ended in the very near future because of economic and political upheaval, from which the communists would have emerged victorious after a period of social chaos.

Only such profound social, economic, and ideological decay explains why the ARVN scarcely used the huge supply of arms and training the United States had lavished upon it. When the communist army attacked in the central highlands in mid-March 1975, it expected the war in the vast mountainous region to last through the year and perhaps longer, and it was utterly unprepared to win total victory in a conventional war. But the ARVN troops immediately mingled with their families, the army disintegrated after very brief combat, and the panic that spread throughout the northern half of South Vietnam was wholly unanticipated by anyone. Relative to earlier battles, there was very little fighting, and the ARVN deserted and fell apart in a process that was social, psychological, and organizational but scarcely military in the narrow, traditional definition of that term. The germ of such a defeat had always been there for anyone to see, but none of the principals in the war had understood the essential factors that caused Saigon's catastrophe, and so the communists entered a huge territorial void relatively peacefully and wholly unready for the monumental economic and administrative tasks that suddenly were theirs. For them it was the second time since August 1945 that great power and responsibility had fallen into their hands because of forces that had little to do with their own strategy and efforts.[24]

The Vietnam War was the quintessential conflict in the long history of warfare in the twentieth century, one in which the social, economic, and organizational dimensions of wars overshadowed the purely military in determining their outcomes. In such a context, aspects of which now existed in various forms and degrees in many other countries, war in the accepted military sense became obsolete, no longer capable of producing victory in the conventional meaning of that term. Wars could wreck traditional societies, producing new socioeconomic configurations and problems that were terribly daunting to those seeking to build socialist alternatives, and the people who undertook to do so often failed because of them. But it was clear, as well, that the United States after Korea and Vietnam was also incapable of defining a strategy or fighting a war that surmounted the decisive political, social, and economic challenges, both at home and in whatever nation it was fighting, that inevitably accompanied conflicts of this magnitude. It might fight to a stalemate, as in Korea, or lose, as in Vietnam, but the victories it coveted by force of arms were now far beyond its ability to attain.

2

Prelude to Permanent Crises: The Background

THE UTTER FAILURE OF THE UNITED STATES IN ITS LONGEST, COSTLIEST, and most divisive war since 1865 occurred at a point in the world's political and social development at which the United States needed more urgently than ever a military strategy capable of preventing radical institutional changes in the Third World. This growing disparity between the magnitude of the task and US military resources for accomplishing it has been a dominant theme since the 1970s, constantly coloring the news that has penetrated daily lives in the United States and defined the obsessions of political leaders. Precisely because the parameters within which wars now occur have altered so profoundly, it is vital that we comprehend the implications of the changing post-1945 Third World contexts for military conflicts. The collapse of the communist bloc after 1989 coincided with growing crises in much of the Third World, which increasingly present challenges to US leaders, greatly magnifying their difficulties in regulating international affairs. Potential and actual civil wars in the Balkans and Central Asia have again become dangerous and urgent, and the balance of power there has been destabilized in wars that challenge both the United States and world peace in a manner unimaginable after 1946, making our globe more complex and precarious than ever before.

The economic, social, and demographic dimensions of the Third World crisis and its relationship to the industrialized nations are all so well known that we need only refresh ourselves briefly regarding those structural factors eroding political and social stability in innumerable countries. Such problems were the product neither of leftists seeking to alter their society nor of wars; ironically, it was preeminently the United States that in the process of furthering its own interests contributed greatly to the economic, social, and demographic forces undermining peace. The fact that conservative orders began to weaken, or even capsize, when there were not always many radicals present to affect the process created uncontrollable and complex new situations for the United States and other industrial states. The 1959 Cuban Revolution was the harbinger of such changes, for both the venal ruling elite and the class that supported it proved unwilling to defend their system from the inherently fragile challenge that Castro's amorphous coalition posed. Only later was Castro's movement radicalized, but by then the United States, which never would have tolerated a Marxist revolution in the Western Hemisphere at a point when it could easily have destroyed it, could not find the means to prevent it from consolidating its power.

Descriptions of the Third World's structural conditions demand caveats regarding the meaning of statistics and averages. In addition to the uneven accuracy of existing data, great variations between nations and regions make generalizations subject to important contingencies. Certainly not all places fared equally badly, and a significant number actually prospered. But such structural challenges to the social classes to which US interests were linked, although troublesome enough immediately after World War II, increased qualitatively after the 1960s and by the late 1970s were transforming many places. From the viewpoint of the Americans, it was less important that these trends were far from universal than that in a number of countries—far more, indeed, than it could cope with—there existed destabilizing social and political developments that might test, at least in the eyes of its officials, US military resources for controlling them.

Land issues were one crucial index of the epic transformation that was unfolding. In parts of Asia the population grew faster than available land and thereby produced smaller average landholdings, greater numbers of displaced peasants working as hired laborers dependent on seasonal employment, and a vast movement toward Third World cities. Some of these trends were at least partially offset by higher productivity, but the one nation of the region that experienced the most acute land problems, the Philippines, also developed the only significant guerrilla movement. In Latin America the land problem was far more than a case of one sick nation in a region: there was an overall malaise that affected much of the entire continent, above all most of Central America (where 1 or 2 percent of the farms contained half or more of the land), and absolute poverty grew along with it. Average farm size declined along with the changing structure of agriculture, and marginalized small landowners and tenant peasants increasingly became seasonal workers, were pushed on to poorer land, or were driven out of agriculture entirely.

Throughout the Third World, the growth of agricultural products for export emerged as the single most important cause of the people's poverty and displacement: in the quarter-century after 1950 the physical volume of agriculture for export from Africa, Latin America, and Asia more than doubled. This pattern affected Nicaragua and El Salvador profoundly, and the land and human crises there became armed conflicts. Due to the burgeoning US market for its output and "development" loans from the United States, the World Bank, and the Inter-American Development Bank to build roads and processing facilities that made possible the exploitation of vast areas once devoted to food for local consumption, Central America became the quintessential example of the traumatization of agrarian economies. The transfer of much of the best corn land to cotton for export to multinational corporations operating through local elites began in the 1960s with the Alliance for Progress, quadrupling the value of cotton exports in less than two decades. Cotton alone would not have harmed the peasantry so seriously, but with the burgeoning fast food industry in the United States and its voracious demand for cheap beef, Central America succumbed to intensive US and international bank pressures, uprooting and impoverishing the peasantry more gravely than ever. Raising cattle requires far less labor than cotton farming, and it absorbed hitherto isolated areas for grazing. It also demands a local infrastructure too expensive for smaller farmers, and foreign public and private funding was channeled through local oligarchs, who profited greatly as beef growing displaced more peasants than any other export boom before it. The quantity of beef exported from Central America rose about two-hundred-fold between 1957 and 1980. The area devoted to food crops increased slowly, due mainly to the opening of marginal, hitherto neglected areas, while the generally superior land allocated to export agriculture more than doubled in the quarter century after 1950 and by the end of this period nearly equaled land devoted to local food needs. To this day Washington advocates such commercialization of the region's agriculture and its integration with the US economy as part of an eventual hemispheric free-trade zone.[1]

In Latin America such trends caused the share of the population living in urban areas to mount from 49 percent in 1960 to 70 percent in 1989.[2] With populations and poverty expanding faster than economies, important elements of the somewhat modernized and growing middle classes began to question the traditional oligarchies' abilities to rule over such complex transitional societies without triggering social explosions. In some countries the well-off divided into rival camps in wars that undermined the familiar military-oligarchy alliances that had stabilized many nations after 1945. But urbanization notwithstanding, the number of rural poor in developing nations increased by 40 percent in the two decades ending in 1992.[3] Some countries, of course, experienced sufficient economic growth to mitigate such trends, and among them the potential for instability declined significantly. Coping with those who gained little or nothing from this great transformation of the larger part of the world—the displaced inhabitants of shantytowns linked to the vast polluted urban conglomerations rapidly expanding in most of the world's poorest nations or the scavengers and prostitutes and the dust of the human condition—emerged as a central challenge to those social elites on whose power Washington's influence largely rested.

That such daunting economic problems would be resolved easily or always peaceably seemed unlikely. For one thing, the export economies that they sought to develop for their own class interests, and under pressure from international development banks and the United States, existed in a global context in which commodity prices historically have greatly favored the industrial nations. Commodity prices have fallen since the 1960s but especially since 1995, and the terms of trade that poorer exporting nations confront have declined dramatically, starting in the 1980s. Unsustainable external debts plague virtually all commodity-exporting nations and greatly limit their ability to spend on social services. In 1997–2001 alone the combined prices of all commodities in US dollars, in terms of the purchasing power for manufactured goods, declined 53 percent throughout the world. Africa was especially hard hit by this decline in the terms of trade, and the lost income it suffered from 1970 to 1997 (excluding oil exporters and South Africa) came to over two-thirds of the net resource transfers to it and more than offset, by far, foreign aid. Such basic trends are reflected in current account balances, debt-to-export ratios, onerous foreign debts—and poverty.[4]

But such external forces aside, most Third World leaders pursued self-serving policies and accepted inducements from the United States and many other industrial nations that eroded any hope for balanced development and stability. Third World arms expenditures after 1970 grew nearly threefold by 1987, even in regions such as Latin America and Africa that were generally not at war, and in some years exceeded the economic aid they received. The ruling elites of many nations revealed their true feelings about their own futures by transferring capital to safe havens, an amount of money that by the end of 1990 was equivalent to 55 percent of their countries' total external debt. The Third World's debt to the richer nations continued as a permanent and paralyzing burden, especially since the prices they received for many of their exports declined. Notwithstanding a temporary restructuring of nearly half of it during the 1980s, the external debt of the developing nations increased to an all-time high of $1.270 trillion in 1991, only to catapult to $1.970 trillion in 1999; debt service payments increased 120 percent.

As domestic debt piled on foreign debt, in many Third World nations economic problems grew enormously, and the ultimate political consequences of the countries' de facto insolvency became increasingly unpredictable. Latin America's average growth rate during 1981–1985 was one-tenth of the 1961–1970 rate, and economies contracted in thirteen of the region's twenty-five nations as they struggled to meet accumulated internal problems and to cope with external debt demands, capital flight, and foreign investors' repatriated profits. Latin America's net resources transfer to the world in the period 1980–1989 exceeded the inflow of income from all sources by $160 billion, but its external debt still nearly doubled. During 1961–1970, before the region's ruling classes both eagerly and under pressure leaped into the foreign debt trap, only four Latin nations suffered from high inflation, as opposed to ten the following decade and nineteen in 1991.[5]

When figures such as these are translated into human terms, the eventual political and military risks of such structural trends become very obvious. The gross domestic product per capita in constant dollars in all of Latin America increased sharply from 1960 to 1980, largely because of Mexico's and Brazil's rapid growth, yet by 1990 it had fallen to 11 percent below the 1980 level. But such an overall descent, for which there is no precedent, obscures Peru's 28 percent decline over the decade and much else. Such averages also hide the extremely skewed income distribution. The income share of the wealthiest fifth of Latin America is far greater than in the developed world, where distribution is already highly inequitable. There was no longer any doubt that a vast region's problems now defied the industrial capitalist world's repeated gestures to ameliorate them. Real wages dropped in most of Latin America after 1980, especially in Brazil, Mexico, Peru, and Argentina. In 1970, about 40 percent of the region's population lived in poverty, and although it declined over the decade the proportion probably increased during the 1980s because of economic stagnation and population growth. But beneath "poverty," and included in it for statistical purposes, is "destitution," so that although 73 percent of Guatemala's population was classed as suffering from poverty in 1986, of these, two-thirds were in fact destitute.[6] Such enduring, recurrent structural problems, ranging from the breakdown of export-oriented economies to the conditions of marginalized peasants eking out an existence, by the 1970s had begun to define the now-familiar human and physical geography in which future political upheavals and warfare could occur.

Perpetual Crises: Global Aspirations and Reality

The guarantee of mutual total destruction—deterrence—had kept the uneasy peace between the United States and the Soviet Union after 1949, but it failed to bring tranquility to the remainder of the world. The United States took measures, from arming and encouraging those it backed in various countries to sending its own warships and troops, that produced conflict elsewhere. Crucial also was the dissolution of European colonial regimes throughout the Third World after 1945, with their arbitrary borders and ethnic components, which often created artificial nations only because the British, French, or other empires' ambitions had to be satisfied. Wars were increasingly local and regional, civil and between small states, fought with conventional arms that were more lethal than ever as well as more readily available. Europe after 1947 was far more peaceful than it had been in generations, but divisions in the internal politics and social structures of various nations elsewhere led to a great growth in civil strife. Other factors were also at play. There was increasingly a much higher degree of complexity in world affairs and warfare after 1950, and the role of outside powers in fanning instability was crucial. Moreover, dissidents in various nations could exploit the Cold War rivalries to their own advantages, thereby internationalizing many local conflicts.

Especially after the Soviet Union disintegrated, US leaders erroneously regarded crises in specific nations as finite events without long-term consequences, and this myopia made it all the easier to become involved in an upheaval or crisis in some way—which they were increasingly ready to do in innumerable places. In many instances this perception was reasonably correct, but it took only a few cases—Iraq and Afghanistan are two of the best examples—to show how symbolism and simplifications in world affairs can lead to protracted commitments and disasters. As wars in Europe and Asia revealed, the ultimate consequences or duration of any conflict cannot be predicted accurately, and nations that intervene casually in the affairs of others have to anticipate surprises in the form of tragedies and protracted bloodletting. The United States had no monopoly on this blindness to how things go wrong, but its increasing importance in world affairs, especially after 1980, made the grave issues of war and peace a question of its specific mindset; its flaws; and the political, ideological, and economic processes that constitute the motivation and objectives of its policies toward the world. But it marched into the future armed with the assumptions and institutions it had formulated after 1945, with scant insight into how the world was changing profoundly or the dangers of its responses. As we shall see, problems that preoccupied it much earlier, particularly but not exclusively in Iraq and Afghanistan, continued to plague the United States decades later. Its readiness to intervene in the affairs of remote places produced catastrophes for it, as it had for other ambitious nations in the first half of the twentieth century. We shall return to this hubris and obsession for activism again—and again.

To the extent the United States was the most active power on the world scene after 1950, wars and conflict since then have increasingly resulted from policies it pursued. The communist nations and parties were more and more defensive, revealing communism as the aberrant but temporary response of outraged people to the two great wars rather than the inevitability Marx predicted. It was, in fact, increasingly disintegrating, and by 1991 the Soviet bloc fell apart without a war or revolution; today communism exists only in name in a few nations.

Increasingly after 1950, but especially after 1980, it was in Washington that the crucial decisions leading to international war and peace were made, but there was also profound discontent in the fields and villages of numerous countries that no movement or party controlled, the product of the hard conditions of life. Many people remained deeply unhappy with their social lot and ready to join movements of protest, some of them secular and radical but others religious, that promised basic changes. Communism had disappeared but the world had become increasingly violent and unstable. More challenging yet to the United States, in a decentralized world of discontent and upheaval, with people in remote villages armed only with small arms, the weapons and technology the Pentagon had developed at immense cost to destroy industrial, urbanized targets in the Soviet Union were largely irrelevant. The Americans had prepared for decades for one kind of war with one kind of enemy, essentially in Europe, and they now confronted very different conditions elsewhere in the world. Such a mismatch of its military resources with its political challenges occurred earlier in both Korea and Vietnam and was inherent in the unlimited global ambitions of the United States. But by the end of the twentieth century, the irrelevance and obsolescence of its way of making wars was far worse than it had been in Vietnam—a war the United States lost. This was particularly true in the Middle East.

The Stakes in the Middle East

Petroleum has always been the Middle East's great prize, and no advanced economy can exist without it. Since 1920, oil has been foremost in the calculations of all nations dealing with the region.

The United States produced 69 percent of the petroleum it consumed in 1970 but only 38 percent in 1996. After the early 1980s, its production began falling in absolute terms, and its crude oil imports became even more crucial as its demand rose. From 1960 until 1996, its imports increased at least four times. The Persian Gulf region supplied 8.8 percent of US imports in 1983 and 22.1 percent in 2000—most of it from Saudi Arabia. The area's importance was far higher for Western Europe and Japan. In 2000 the Persian Gulf contained approximately 65 percent of the world's petroleum and about 34 percent of its natural gas reserves.

Projections are only approximate, but domestic US petroleum production until 2020 is expected to remain stable. Its consumption over the period 1998–2020 is expected to rise from 18.9 to 25.8 million barrels daily, and this increase must be imported. But the world competition for imports is becoming far more intense, especially from Asia. That the nations of the Persian Gulf states control the single most crucial factor in modern industrial power—leverage likely to increase—is a fact those in power in Washington know very well.[7]

* * *

The events of September 11, 2001, were the direct consequence of over fifty years of US involvement in the Middle East, the result of actions and policies over many decades that have destabilized the arc of nations extending from the Mediterranean to South Asia. Today humanity in general lives with these consequences. The region is profoundly unstable—and so are international relations.

It was in the Middle East that the intrinsic ambiguities of the US relationship to Great Britain, its closest military and ideological ally, shaped all the US actions. It did not want to weaken Britain either economically or militarily—after all, it loaned England large sums after August 1945 because it wanted a barrier to Soviet influence—but it also wanted far greater control over the region's oil reserves. The Truman administration very much wanted the British to continue their military role in the Middle East; if they did not police it, then Washington would have to fill the vacuum. Genuine friendship and competition motivated US actions throughout the period ending about 1956, when the two nations irrevocably parted ways in the vast area. Moreover, domestic political pressures from ambitious oil companies and the powerful pro-Zionist lobby, as well as the formal US ideological commitment to the "Open Door" principle and the growing need for access to the region's oil, overcame its nominal desire not to weaken Britain's dominant role.

Ideologically, the British and Americans had much in common, but the two nations were rivals for control over the region's oil, and each favored its own clients. British obstinacy and arrogance made it much easier for the United States to gradually supplant Britain in the area. More important, Britain could no longer afford the price of being an imperial power, and it was at a decisive disadvantage in coping with US ambitions. But it was not only access to oil that motivated US actions. It also feared a vacuum of power wherever the weakened British Empire—ranging from the Middle East to South Asia—was capsizing. Into such places an amorphously defined communist influence could enter.

Control over oil provided the context in which the Americans worried about the decline of British power, and so they accelerated it, principally for the quite impersonal sake of geopolitics rather than the profit of US oil firms. The United States had been a net exporter of oil before 1939, but by 1946 it was obvious it would import an ever-greater share of its petroleum needs. In 1946 the known Middle Eastern reserves were almost equal to those of the entire Western Hemisphere, and its output soared. By 1950 its reserves were equal to the rest of the world's combined—and the British controlled most of it. Everyone knew that the Middle East held the key to the future of the world's oil industry, and it was far cheaper to extract than US oil.

The Korean War intensified the US undermining of British power in the Middle East. The United States concluded that "ultranationalists" in the Middle East were the greatest danger and that the British were magnifying their influence by refusing to pay higher royalties. The minor communist threat in these nations could be handled with stronger "police controls." Washington believed that the British should pay the Arab states a greater share of the vast oil revenues. Secretary of State Dean Acheson later recalled that "in an unplanned, undesired, and haphazard way," the United States replaced British power in the region. But there was nothing haphazard about the way the Central Intelligence Agency (CIA) helped General Naguib el-Hilali overthrow Egyptian king Farouk—a docile British puppet—in July 1952, which then brought Colonel Gamal Abdul Nasser to power.[8] CIA agents dealing with Nasser sympathized with his commitment to purge Egypt of its royalist dynasty and stifle the remaining communists. Egypt, the single most important British bastion, through which its canal to its Asian empire flowed, thereby fell under US influence.

In Iran, however, the United States openly undermined the British, who controlled the Anglo-Iranian Oil Company (AIOC), but they both opposed the nationalist Mohammed Mossadegh. Mossadegh, who headed the crucial committee of the Majlis (parliament) and was the most prominent exponent of nationalizing the AIOC, was European-educated and played to the urban middle classes. He was opportunistic and willing to make use of the communist Tudeh Party if necessary, but he was also an anticommunist who was eager to modernize Iran in a vague but essentially conventional bourgeois fashion. The United States favored the young Mohammed Reza Shah Pahlavi, who courted them to offset British and Russian influence and who shared Washington's fear of Mossadegh's nationalism. Since Iran was virtually bankrupt, and the British paid 10–12 percent royalties whereas US firms had agreed to a 50–50 split in neighboring Saudi Arabia in 1950, that the United States would soon dominate Iran was inevitable. The US ambassador in Tehran thought the British were "self-righteous and arrogant."[9] In early 1951 they reluctantly agreed to a 50–50 split, but the Majlis nationalized the AIOC in March, and Mossadegh became prime minister the following month.

The Pentagon feared Mossadegh might increase Soviet influence, but the State Department at first encouraged his intransigence, and the British concluded that the Americans were undercutting their interests. Throughout 1952, however, the Mossadegh government created mounting economic disorder, the communists became stronger, and the United States became increasingly hostile to him. In July and again in November 1952 Washington offered Iran a $100 million advance if it allowed US firms to handle its oil, but the British were able to block the agreement. Mossadegh, who also feared growing turmoil, was naively convinced he could play the British against the Americans. By this time the United States saw Iran mainly as a dangerous island of instability open to Soviet exploitation, whereas the British were worried principally about maintaining their empire and the oil that was so crucial to their balance of payments.

Dwight D. Eisenhower became president in January 1953, and he authorized the CIA to cooperate with the British to mount a coup against Mossadegh. London stressed the communist danger, but Washington also decided that it would replace British domination. The following August, the shah was installed as a virtual dictator. Five US firms owned 40 percent of the Iranian company that took over oil production, but even the shah disliked the new terms. The Americans, not the British, gained by far the most.

The most important problem that the United States confronted in the Middle East was not the Soviet Union but relations with England, for the region's complex social, ideological, and political dynamics ruled out communist parties becoming of more than minor consequence. The British were removed step-by-step, but the Muslim world's labyrinthine cultural and political factors far transcended the US ability to understand them, much less shape them decisively.

In Iran, which was of crucial importance both strategically and economically, the US opposed and overthrew a nationalist, largely middle-class movement that was neither authoritarian nor traditionalist. Iranian nationalists may have been inefficient, but they were more likely than the Islamic fundamentalists to modernize the nation. In Iran the United States depended entirely on the shah and thereby made a grievous error. Elsewhere in the Persian Gulf the United States supported feudal and authoritarian regimes, all strongly Islamic. US policy was unprincipled and entirely opportunist. The British leaders who later wrote memoirs portrayed the Americans as anti-British, but Washington simply advanced US interests at the expense of anybody in the way. What was crucial in the longer run was that the United States buttressed Islamic and royalist regimes against their secular challengers and that the political, social, and ideological changes these modernizers advocated were repressed, although in some cases they discredited themselves. The choices the United States made in the Middle East meant that rebellion and discontent there increasingly took fundamentalist Islamic forms. Some fundamentalists were syncretic and quite irrational, but their views had a broader mass appeal than modernist and middle-class ideologies, and most were very serious in their fanaticism. Eventually, terrorism and anti-Americanism were the outcomes.

The United States replaced Britain only insofar as it controlled the region's oil, but otherwise there was almost no improvement in the fate of the masses or the kinds of political regimes that controlled them. The large majority of people in the Middle East needed and often desired elementary social services and rights, but most that spoke for their cause risked going to prison. Only the mosque was an acceptable locale for dissent. Instead of developing gradually politically or ideologically, the region remained locked in ignorance and authoritarianism, and repression became the rule. Washington endorsed most of it. There were, of course, some exceptions, but the crisis wracking the United States and the Middle East today is to a crucial extent the outcome of policies the United States pursued in the region after 1945.

The United States Destabilizes the Middle East

The United States confronted the secular nationalism that spread throughout much of the Middle East after the late 1940s unevenly and often uncomfortably, and the persistence of Islamic fundamentalism is to a crucial extent the consequence of its policies. By 1962 officers ruled five countries. They were anti-British but scarcely communist, and syncretic ideologies, which in some cases included moderate socialist notions, were the rule. These politically astute men played on Cold War rivalries to optimize the military and economic aid they received from both the United States and the Soviet Union. They were opposed to Islamic traditionalism and monarchies, but many of them were also inefficient, unstable, and corrupt.

In Egypt the United States supported Nasser, who became head of the country in November 1954 and spent the next two years consolidating his domestic political position. Nasser exploited the divisions among US decisionmakers, but they all had no doubt he was strongly anti-Soviet. He took money from the Saudis and sought to get the West and the Russians, as British foreign secretary Harold Macmillan later put it, "to bid up each other's price."[10] But in May 1956 Nasser miscalculated and recognized communist China, and two months later Washington canceled an offer to loan Egypt money to build the Aswan dam. Nasser then seized and nationalized the Suez Canal at the end of July, Britain's lifeline to the Persian Gulf and its former empire. Britain's leaders were convinced then and later that the Eisenhower administration had encouraged their plans to invade Egypt together with the French and Israelis, but the United States was against war and strongly favored a negotiated resolution of the dispute. The attack on Egypt began at the end of October, and the United States immediately declared that its alliance with Britain and France covered European affairs only, not Middle Eastern ones; at the beginning of December, bowing to the United States working through the UN, Britain and France ignominiously withdrew from Egypt. The dominant British role in the vast region thereby came to an end.

Britain's eclipse produced a political vacuum and a vastly increased US role. In January 1957 the Eisenhower Doctrine proclaimed that the United States was ready to protect any country asking aid "against overt armed aggression from any nation controlled by international communism," a vague formulation that created altogether new problems for the United States.[11] The entire region—especially Lebanon, Syria, and Jordan—was destabilized. US military forces intervened in the region a total of thirty-nine times from 1946 through 1975. Some interventions were huge in scale, but others were merely symbolic showings of the flag. What President George W. Bush on June 1, 2002, vaguely termed "preemption" had been in the arsenal of possible US responses for about a century. In the case of Lebanon in July 1958, 14,000 troops equipped with atomic artillery landed without clearly defined attainable goals. Now US credibility was at stake in an increasingly unstable political environment.

The problem was that Arab political complexities exceeded the US ability to master them. After 1949 the Middle Eastern states were indifferent to the Palestinian Arab cause, allowing Washington to pursue a relatively independent policy. It also banned arms deliveries to Israel and Jordan; the United States managed not to run aground on the shoals of the Arab-Israeli conflict for well over a decade. That situation changed, however. Over Eisenhower and Secretary of State John Foster Dulles's objections, Congress gave Israel modest sums of economic aid in the form of grants and loans, largely because of the Zionist bloc's skill in the 1950s in mobilizing Congress's ethnic voting coalition and the Democrats. For the United States, it was the beginning of far deeper troubles.

In the spring of 1967 Israel embarked on the Six-Day War, culminating in June, and conquered the remainder of pre-1948 Palestine as well as Syria's Golan Heights. Israel's actions were in large part a response to demagogic rivalries among the Arab states, but guerrilla activity during the preceding years had been only a nuisance to the Israelis. It gave them a convenient excuse to expand their territorial control over pre-1948 Palestine—plus the Golan. The war ended because of Moscow's threats and a tense, potentially very dangerous US-Soviet naval standoff. But it also initiated a regional arms race that allowed the Soviets to begin playing a crucial role in the area. In January 1968 the US ended its embargo and began providing massive arms aid to Israel, which reached $600 million in 1971 (seven times the amount under the entire Johnson administration) and over $2 billion in 1973—making Israel the leading recipient of its arms aid from that time onward. The difficulties the United States has experienced in the Middle East began with this decision. Today Israel still receives $2 billion in free US arms aid. Most of the Arab world, quite understandably, now considers Israel to be a proxy for US power. Virtually unconditional US support for Israel became the most important single factor in alienating the 1.2 billion Muslims in the world, laying the basis for increasing anti-Americanism and ultimately terrorism against the US presence abroad and even on its very shores.

The British decision in December 1967 to withdraw all its forces from the Persian Gulf region by the end of 1971 left the United States alone in the region, with potentially immense military and political obligations, when it was deeply involved in the Vietnam War and unable to fill the vacuum. US relations with Israel had been friendly but discreet until then, but Washington began to look for surrogates or proxies that could help it create barriers to the Soviet Union, which was unwilling to employ its own troops but ready to heavily arm states such as Egypt, Syria, and Iraq. The State Department argued that Arab nationalism was a greater threat than the Soviet Union, but successive administrations ignored its opinion and intensified the close association with Israel that would increasingly alienate the Arab world.

Israel, Iran, and later Saudi Arabia became Washington's closest allies in the region, and five major US firms controlled half the region's oil output at a time that both the demand and price for it was rising. The United States believed its reliance on surrogates was a solution to its regional challenges, when in reality it now had to defend and stabilize its proxies, expanding its definition of credibility to include their security. Doing so further enflamed Arab nationalism. From this point onward, the United States defined all regional issues as merely aspects of what it conceived as the overriding Soviet-US rivalry. Israel increasingly held a de facto veto over US policy on the Palestinian Arab question. When on October 6, 1973, the Egyptians struck the surprised Israeli army in the Sinai, which then pushed them back, the United States joined with the Russians in the United Nations to end the fighting. But the United States still regarded the Soviet Union as its main enemy in the region, rather than as another victim of the Arab world's cynical willingness to exploit any nation for arms. Not a single communist state was established in the region; Arab nationalism—which united the virtually medieval Saudis and secular Arabs—was far more of a potential threat to US interests. Of far greater importance was a massive Saudi and Gulf oil boycott that increased oil prices by 1979 to almost twenty times the 1970 level and had untold repercussions on the world economy. The Arab states were ready to use oil as a political weapon.

After 1967, the Arab-Israeli conflict ensured that anti-Americanism would only intensify and that the Arab world was increasingly alienated. The cycle of change and crisis, combined with its crucial importance as supplier of the world's oil, meant that the Middle East would increasingly frustrate the United States. Given its choice to assume immense responsibilities in the area and its need to depend upon proxy regimes, only crises lay before it.

The Dilemma of US Power in a World Adrift

Crises in the Middle East were but an aspect of a much deeper US endemic inability to understand the world it was seeking to regulate and control, a myopia that defined its actions everywhere. That blindness to reality only became deeper after 1950, and even the collapse of the communist world did not affect it. What is superficially described as uniquely destructive in the Bush administration's policies after 2001, including its references to the "axis of evil" or doctrine of preemption, all existed in various forms in earlier decades. It is this continuity in US foreign policy that warrants emphasis.

The result of these rigidities was the growing US inability to anticipate trends affecting innumerable nations' social and economic organization, along with their political and strategic implications for US interests and power. Washington's responses were increasingly ill-considered and often incompetent, offsetting whatever advantages the collapse of Soviet power might have given the United States. To take but one of many examples, in the case of the Angolan crisis of 1975, the head of the CIA's operation there subsequently complained that "frustrated by our humiliation in Vietnam, Kissinger was seeking to challenge the Soviets," and so he "overruled his advisers and refused to seek diplomatic solutions in Angola." "We were mounting a major covert action to support two Angolan liberation movements about which we had little reliable intelligence," the agent continued, thereby committing US arms and prestige to what became a terrible, destructive conflict that lasted for decades.[12]

After 1975, Washington remained uninhibited. It was still ready to send its military to threaten force, whether in the Middle East or Southeast and East Asia, but it learned little from its Vietnam experience, with its loss of control over national priorities. Its vast reservoir of arms and economic power allowed it to make the same mistakes over and over again. Nixon's support of Pakistan in its confrontation with India in 1971, notwithstanding his private acknowledgment that the rebels had good reason for their actions or the grave risks of escalation that might have involved the United States, was due to the fact that Pakistan was an ally fighting with US arms, whereas India, although friendly, had Soviet equipment and was neutral. In the White House's eyes, maintaining the credibility of US power as a deterrent demanded that it remain prepared to intervene virtually anywhere, which required it to give those Third World tyrants and corruptionists acting as faithful proxies its unquestioning loyalty and support. Its fixation with credibility, a virtually religious concept, as well as the domino theory, wholly negated the role that accurate intelligence and rational insight could play. For reasons such as these, Nixon supported Ferdinand Marcos's imposition of martial law in the Philippines in the fall of 1972. Similar thinking and action since then has made it impossible to predict when and where the United States would again get mired down. Such behavior made the formal foreign policy priorities the United States had on paper meaningless; its real priorities were capricious, and its addiction to interventionism made them arbitrary and often determined by where there was shooting. The US fixation on credibility, a function both of ideology and the very existence of military power, has existed for at least forty years and was crucial in bogging it down in Vietnam. Today it is extremely important in explaining US persistence in Iraq.

The Iran Crisis: US Failure

The US experience in Iran confirmed the fact that the United States was no stronger than its proxies. Assuming Britain's lucrative rights but also its responsibility to support the shah was one of the most crucial actions that the United States could have taken in the region, and its calamitous consequences persist to this day. By eliminating secular, middle-class nationalism, the United States overthrew those who favored modernizing options and left a resurgent Muslim fundamentalism as the status quo's principal opponent. The poor and the dispossessed, the majority of the people, provided fundamentalism with countless recruits. No other nation in the Middle East better illustrated the risks to the United States when it depended on proxies to defend its interests.

The shah was anti-British, but he was fully aware of US geopolitical goals in the region and how he might exploit them to reinforce his power. He relied on the military to sustain his regime, and after 1962, when he assumed virtually total power, his police also became crucial. He bypassed the nationalist middle classes and intelligentsia. By introducing a corruptly managed land reform designed to end virtual feudalism in many areas, he instead added to the problems of rural society and drove many peasants into the cities. By 1963 his main opposition came from the traditionalist, fundamentalist Shiite religious leaders, the mullahs, of whom Ayatollah Ruhollah Khomeini was the most important; the shah was not a Shia. Social upheavals and riots in the major cities in the summer of 1963 resulted in over 1,000 deaths. In response, the shah increased repression, and after 1971 the CIA and Israeli Mossad helped train Savak, his dreaded security organization. Iranian prisons were filled with many thousands, and the media, universities, and the like were tightly controlled. Washington increasingly depended on the shah, who became more tyrannical and alienated most of Iranian society.

The shah courted the Americans successfully, but he also wanted greater oil revenues and more sophisticated arms, and he even threatened to turn to the Soviet Union if the United States would not sell them. He encouraged US geopolitical visions and fears for the region, but he also increased his oil revenues. In early 1973 he announced that he would not renew the 1954 oil agreement when it expired in 1979—in effect, nationalizing oil and following in Mossadegh's footsteps. Nixon explicitly regarded him as an extension of US power in the region. The shah also spent $20 billion on overpriced US arms from 1970 to 1978, providing a market for one-quarter of its arms exports. Corruption and repression suffused his regime, and the shah and his family accumulated a huge fortune. By 1977 some 7,200 US military personnel and contract employees helped maintain his modern army, but the living standards for the large majority of the people fell. The visible class differences increasingly alienated the masses.

There was no class basis for the shah's regime, only the army and its satraps—and their ultramodern equipment. In September 1978 the CIA predicted the shah would remain in office over the next decade, even though bloody confrontations between Muslims and the police had begun earlier that year. The US embassy for years had relied principally on the shah's intelligence for its information, oblivious to Iran's political and economic problems until they were beyond control. Solely because he was close to the US government and purchased huge quantities of its most advanced arms, US officials assumed the shah was immune to challenges. In the fall of 1978 the opposition to the shah took to the streets, and the army learned it could not depend on poorly paid conscripts from the villages. The army disintegrated in several months, and the rest was inevitable. The shah went into exile in January 1979, Khomeini took power, and Iran became an Islamic republic—which it remains to this day. Washington was utterly surprised.

The Iranian Revolution of 1979 was a major defeat for US policy in the Middle East. Given Iran's size, oil resources, and strategic position, it was exceedingly important, an event whose consequences have profoundly altered the geopolitical makeup of the entire region. The Carter administration's deep unhappiness turned to fury when Iran's new leaders seized fifty-two Americans working in the embassy the following November. Never had the United States suffered such humiliation, and it was mainly in this context—with the impending crisis in Afghanistan also a factor—that the following January the Carter Doctrine was proclaimed. Any "outside force" seeking "to gain control of the Persian Gulf region" was threatened with an unspecified but possibly nuclear response anywhere in the world should US "vital interests" be attacked. The Carter Doctrine was not a policy but an impotent and pathetic gesture; the challenge was not the Soviet Union but a militant Islamic movement. Communism was irrelevant, and a botched US effort in April 1980 to free the hostages only added to its dismay. Washington had pushed the British out of the region, and it was now alone in confronting its immense complexities.

The Reagan administration picked up the challenge that the Iranian fundamentalists had created, and its chosen instrument was the secular Saddam Hussein, who became the dictator of Iraq in July 1979. At the beginning of his career, his party had vaguely socialist pretensions, which were then in vogue among officers, but power, not ideology, was Hussein's sole concern. He not only detested Islamic fundamentalism but also had ample reasons, going back to the 1960s when Iran began to supply Kurdish dissidents with arms and seized strategic Iraqi islands in 1971, to consider Iran an enemy. The United States, beginning under the Carter administration, encouraged Saddam to confront the Iranians, who were overarmed with US weapons; US officials secretly gave Iraq false intelligence on alleged Iranian weaknesses. In the protracted, incredibly bloody war that followed, successive US administrations even provided Iran some assistance, and the CIA helped to fund US aid to the contras in Nicaragua by secretly selling arms to Iran via Israel. But the large bulk of US efforts went to Iraq—and Saddam Hussein. The United States encouraged Iraq to fight a war it could not win, one that ended by benefiting only the United States, Iraq's reactionary neighbors, and arms merchants.[13]

Washington, together with Sunni Muslim Kuwait and Saudi Arabia, strongly encouraged Saddam to invade Iran in late 1980 in the expectation that Iraq would annex part of Iran and help prevent the charismatic Shiites from extending their influence in the region. As then President George H. W. Bush put it in early 1992, "As you may remember in history, there was a lot of support for Iraq at the time as a balance to a much more aggressive Iran under Khomeini."[14] But Iran had far more manpower than Iraq, and the war took much longer than expected. Iraq borrowed $95 billion, mainly from Saudi Arabia and Kuwait, and imported $42 billion in arms. The United States supplied Iraq with intelligence during the war and provided it over $5 billion in food credits, technology, and industrial products, most of it after Iraq began to use mustard, cyanide, and nerve gases both against the Iranians and dissident Iraqi Kurds. Each side wrecked the other's refineries, and at the beginning of 1987, with Iran desperate and angry at Kuwait for funding the war, the United States put its own flag on Kuwait's tankers and provided navy protection for them, increasing US warships in the Gulf from six to at least forty by September 1987. Had it not done so, the Kuwaitis and Saudis threatened, they would dump their vast holdings of US Treasury bonds. A cease-fire was signed in August 1987.

At least 370,000 people died, 262,000 of them Iranian, but Iran claimed 800,000 dead. No one really knows how to measure such horrors. The war cost Iran over $600 billion directly in lost oil and export income; Iraq spent almost as much and owed its neighbors vast sums. Their war devastated both nations.

The United States was Iraq's ally, in fact if not officially, and it urged Saddam Hussein to build a large army with modern armor, aviation, artillery, and chemical and biological weapons. It did not foresee what was obvious: he could also use his military power in yet other ways. Modern arms were far more than commerce for arms manufacturers. They also transformed the entire power equation in the Middle East and made both the region and the world far more dangerous. Given all the destabilizing elements in the area, most of which Washington had helped to create, it was almost inevitable that the Middle East would become the leading US preoccupation once the Soviet Union disintegrated. What was certain, wherever it might occur, was its consummately ambitious goals in the world and its confident reliance on its awesome military power.

The Trap: Afghanistan

Afghanistan revealed how unpredictable and complex the US interventions could become, thereby shaping future conflict in the world in crucial ways. The United States first laid a trap in Afghanistan for the Soviets, but it eventually fell into it also—the consequence of both adventurism and the unlimited hubris of its foreign policy. Events in Afghanistan were merely one more confirmation of the fact that once wars begin, no one can predict their consequences or how they will end. It is a consummate irony that the very same fighters who used US funds and arms to defeat the Soviets during the 1980s led the most important opposition to the United States after the mid-1990s and that many of the Afghan warlords whom the Pentagon supported with air cover, money, and supplies in the fall of 2001 not only fought on the Soviet side but today encourage cultivation of immense quantities of opium and prevent unity or peace from ever returning to that war-torn land.

Zahir Shah had ruled Afghanistan for forty years until July 1973, when he was overthrown by his cousin, Mohammed Daoud. Although the Pashtuns constitute about 40 percent of the population and the royal family was Pashtun, the country outside Kabul remained highly divided, with warlords, tribal chiefs, and the like ruling most of it. The majority of the population consists of Islamic fundamentalists. Diplomatically the country was essentially neutral and therefore of slight interest to the great powers. Daoud was an opportunist and interested principally in power, and he banned all opposition parties. Like his dispossessed cousin, he did not recognize the border with Pakistan. He also claimed to be a modernizer, and fundamentalists called his reforms atheistic. He talked of annexing the very large Pashtun region of Pakistan—containing about 15 percent of its population—and creating a vaguely defined new state, Pashtunistan, modeled after Bangladesh. Pakistan aided an Islamic insurgency to keep him preoccupied. Daoud was killed in April 1978, and a seriously divided communist party took over an area no greater than Daoud himself had ruled.

Left alone, the communists would have lost power very quickly; they began purging their own ranks ruthlessly. They almost immediately sought to give women equal rights and introduce land reform, resulting in diverse bloody rebellions, which Iran and Pakistan aided. When Islamic fundamentalists took power in Iran in January 1979, Afghanistan's geopolitical importance increased. Both the Soviet Union and United States began to pay attention to Afghanistan's acute internal divisions in what had been a relatively unimportant country, internationalizing an already highly volatile situation.

At the end of March 1979, senior US officials discussed whether "there was value in keeping the Afghan insurgency going, 'sucking the Soviets into a Vietnamese quagmire.'" On July 3 President Carter signed a directive authorizing secret aid to the opponents of the pro-Soviet regime, and as National Security Adviser Zbigniew Brzezinski recalled in 1998, the objective was "to induce a Soviet military intervention. . . . I wrote to President Carter: We now have the opportunity of giving to the USSR its Vietnam war."[15]

The Reagan administration believed ardently that confronting communism aggressively was essential, but that was hardly a substantive innovation. Although the Reagan Doctrine several years later proclaimed US readiness to give arms, money, and training to both opponents of existing alleged communist governments or to regimes allied with the United States and the proclamation seemed bellicose, there was scarcely anything original in the notion. For decades Washington had done so; the Afghan war was initiated well before Reagan came to office. As a senior CIA analyst later wrote, "Yet for the most part, the new administration continued the armament programs and doctrines of the Carter years."[16] Reagan was a complex and seemingly contradictory personality: he gave the Pentagon much more money for new weapons, and his rhetorical attacks on communism escalated sharply. These words were more than offset, however, when Secretary of Defense Casper Weinberger enunciated another doctrine in November 1984 that the National Security Council subsequently endorsed. Weinberger declared that US forces should be used only where vital national interests were at stake and never for casual symbolic reasons, implicitly downgrading the importance of "credibility." The United States should make no commitments unless there were "some reasonable assurance we will have the support of the American people and their elected representatives in Congress . . . for as long as it takes to win."[17]

If such a mandate exists, he insisted, US forces should be sent into combat with sufficient numbers and power to achieve victory and with clear and attainable military and political goals enunciated beforehand. The likelihood of such preconditions ever existing was very low, and the Weinberger Doctrine was intended to prevent some small, ill-thought out interventions from once again escalating into a major war involving US troops. And while the Reagan administration aided rebels in regimes it sought to overthrow, Nicaragua being the best known, the Pentagon opposed sending troops to Central America, very reluctantly agreed to send Marines to Lebanon in September 1982, resisted meddling in the Panama crisis, and in general became—mainly as a result of the Vietnam experience—the most cautious sector of the executive branch.

It was Weinberger's emphasis on using proxies rather than US forces to accomplish the basic goals of defeating its enemies and protecting its friends that was the administration's most important hallmark. In practice, none of its applications of US power were new, including its much greater reliance on covert operations. Virtually all US strategists before and since then have urged relying on local allies, hopefully "pretty good guys," as one described them, because perfect ones did not exist. No one advocated relying on outright villains, but in Vietnam, Angola, Namibia, and elsewhere the United States had worked only with villains as the most effective way of attaining its goals. Few had illusions that indigenous "good guys" would cooperate, and choosing the "bad guys" again and again exposed the weakness of covert action that supported anticommunist insurgencies.[18] Indeed, as the Americans learned repeatedly before and after, their local friends could become an insurmountable burden and even their enemies. It was precisely this scenario, termed "blowback" by the CIA, that occurred in Afghanistan and Iraq.

But dependence on proxies was in large part the consequence of the American public's unwillingness to repeat the Vietnam experience over again. Its pugnacious aspirations and massive military spending notwithstanding, the Reagan administration was fully aware of its need to acknowledge and then overcome the limits of US military power. It was not until the rise of the neo-conservatives and such hawks as Vice President Dick Cheney and Defense Secretary Donald Rumsfeld under the second Bush administration in 2001 that an uninhibited, muscular vision of the desirability of using military power again defined official strategy. Even then, however, military officers remained much more cautious than the academics and intellectuals in power.

In Afghanistan, the US objective was to see the Soviet Union mauled, not to help the Afghans, to bait the Soviets and create a bloody war for them on Afghan soil. There was also the added attraction that Soviet intervention would "inflame Moslem opinion against them in many countries."[19] Peace, on the contrary, was never a goal until the Soviets were hurt badly. That fact was crucial. That the Afghans had to pay an immense human price in the process never mattered.

The Soviets fell into the trap, encouraged by their erstwhile comrades in Kabul, whom they regarded as irresponsible adventurers who were unlikely to last much longer. At first they were determined not to send troops, but they also feared that the United States would replace the electronic intelligence listening posts it had just lost in Iran with installations in Afghanistan, for the CIA had begun to survey sites there—and the Soviets knew it. Moreover, the fall of the shah to fundamentalists in January 1979 and the political destabilization of the entire region made what happened in Afghanistan more important to them. In December 1979 the Soviets began to send the first of about 100,000 soldiers. Ostensibly, the Carter Doctrine was proclaimed the following month with this invasion as an excuse, but the Soviets only did what the United States desired.

The mujahidin received modest covert aid until 1984, when the Pakistanis and Saudis convinced the United States that the Soviets could not just be bled but driven out of Afghanistan altogether. In all, the CIA supplied the Afghan rebels with $3 billion in military aid over the decade, and the Saudis also contributed at least $2 billion. Pakistan's intelligence was in charge of distributing this equipment, which was the largest US covert operation in its history. It was equal to the combined cost of all other US covert operations during the 1980s—of which there were many that, like those in Central America, were far better known. Pakistan made certain that Islamic fundamentalists and Pashtuns received most of this aid—it wanted not just anticommunists to win but those who accepted both the existing borders and its primary influence over internal political affairs in a nation sharing a 1,500-mile frontier with it. The Saudis were just as ruthless in their political and theological partiality. Iran supported tribes hostile to both the Soviets and Pashtuns. But non-Pashtun tribes, especially the Tajiks, became far stronger than the Pakistanis desired.

Osama bin Laden, many of his chief aides, and most of the senior Taliban leaders gained their military experience in the anti-Soviet campaign that the United States and Saudi Arabia funded. At least 15,000 and as many as 30,000 foreign fighters joined the mujahidin, and the chief of Saudi intelligence selected bin Laden as the key leader of the important "Arab brigade." Bin Laden established recruiting offices in thirty-five countries—there were thirty offices in US cities alone—and this large network later became crucial when he created Al-Qaida in 1989. He had training camps in Afghanistan, the Philippines, Sudan, and Somalia over a period of time. Religion was the principal reason foreigners volunteered. Initially, they were fighting a jihad against communism, but they evolved into an international brigade espousing a distinctive synthesis of extreme Islam and violence that pitted them after 1989 against the existing Muslim states—and the United States. The Afghanistan war was the key incubator of Muslim fundamentalism and was crucial in establishing extremist Islamic movements in a number of nations. Without it, the world today might be quite different. Many thousands—about 2,000 in Bosnia alone—subsequently fought in Chechnya, Algeria, Somalia, Kosovo, the Philippines, and elsewhere. Some remained in Afghanistan, joined later by many others, and were crucial in the formation of the Taliban regime. Al-Qaida may have trained up to 70,000 potential fighters—and terrorists—and created cells in at least fifty countries. At first, Washington considered them anti-Soviet freedom fighters, financed with US money and instructed in destructive technology by US-funded agencies.

Around 15,000 Soviet troops were killed and many more were wounded in Afghanistan. A total of 620,000 served there, and in May 1988 they admitted defeat and withdrew. It had been their Vietnam, as well as a crucial factor in ending communism in Russia. It seemed to conclude exactly as the United States had planned a decade earlier. There were other crucial reasons for the disintegration of the Soviet Union, but its futile war in Afghanistan was certainly one of them.

About 1 million Afghans died because of this war—some because of Soviet bombs and artillery, others caught in battles, many from hunger—and the nation was left in chaos. Tribes and factions still fought each other. Millions were refugees, mainly in Pakistan, but as many as 2 million had fled to Iran. After a few years, Pakistan decided to end this anarchy, and it was instrumental in creating and funding the Taliban movement, many of whom had been trained in religious schools in Pakistan. In 1996 the Taliban took over most of Afghanistan and imposed a strict Islamic fundamentalism that horrified the world. But they created some semblance of order, which is why many Afghans supported them.

The Americans, their grandiose goals attained, immediately withdrew their money, resources, and interest. "It was a great victory," the former director of the CIA noted in his memoir published in 1996. "Now the Afghans could resume fighting among themselves—and hardly anyone cared."[20] Without realizing it at the time, Washington too had fallen into the trap it had set for the Soviets. Islamic fundamentalism was now immensely strengthened, its military competence and resources had increased immeasurably, and hatred of the United States and the regimes it supported became its overriding obsession.

There were other crises and areas for Washington to consider, of course, given its unlimited global ambitions and ultimate willingness to intervene in any part of the globe. But neither time, nor manpower, nor physical and monetary resources permitted it to cope with a vast unsettled world that was becoming far more challenging and unpredictable, not to mention far better armed, once communism ceased to exist. The Korean and Vietnam Wars had revealed that politicians would lose elections if wars went badly. Although Americans appeared willing to support the executive branch's foreign initiatives in the short and even medium term, it was precisely such interventions, all of which were supposed to be relatively brief and manageable, that repeatedly caused the United States to lose sight of its priorities. Its hubris made impossible a coherent foreign and military policy and the selective management of its ultimately finite resources. By the early 1990s the United States no longer had clearly identifiable rivals, and in this crucial regard the world was very different than it had been over the past century or longer. The question of war and peace was largely linked to US objectives and actions in the new era and whether it would accept the status quo, as sloppy and unpredictable as it was. Communism disappeared but wars continued, and the same myopia that had brought ruin to the world over preceding centuries still existed among US leaders. The new enemy was far more amorphous, and it was largely the product of the United States' own making, as its friends and those it had supported and aided became its enemies.

Communism Capsizes

Had there not been a vast bloodletting between 1914 and 1918, it is inconceivable that Vladimir Ilich Lenin would have ended as more than an obscure crank. Bolshevism's health and very existence always depended on the profound irrationality of the status quo. The same was true of the Chinese variant of the Russian experience, which needed a Japanese invasion to galvanize the otherwise dormant peasantry. By itself communism had neither vitality, nor intellectual coherence, nor justification, and it began to weaken internally once it succeeded and state systems were created to administer it. There were many reasons for this, ranging from the fact that communists came to power in much of Eastern Europe because the Soviet army installed them and many party leaders were increasingly ambitious bureaucrats hardly any different than their peers in capitalist countries. Both were system managers, fascinated by power on any terms and ideological only in the vaguest sense. Theoretically, bolshevism was weak to begin with; time only made it more fragile.

Throughout the 1970s and later, there were officials in Washington who were aware of the Soviet Union's weaknesses and its inherent conservatism, developments I discuss earlier in this book, and George Kennan had predicted in the late 1940s that communism would eventually change and become increasingly benign. The CIA had always had senior analysts who focused on the fragility of the Soviet Union, as well as its growing determination to avoid conflict with the United States and the North Atlantic Treaty Organization (NATO). But the Pentagon and its allies in Congress could scarcely justify increasing arms expenditures with the CIA's objective assessments and managed to bury most of them, often conjuring crises simply to justify larger budgets. Henry Kissinger and other national security advisers thought they were better able to judge Soviet capacities and intentions, and some CIA directors had their own political and action agendas and paid no heed to what their analysts were telling them. Indeed, as Iraq showed, politicians ignore the CIA if it tells them what they do not wish to hear. After 1976, as a former senior CIA official later recounted, "It was no longer a rational research and analytic process, but a political-bureaucratic arena dominated by the military services and anti-Communist ideologues."[21]

Still, there had not been a war with the Soviet Union, and deterrence had kept a long if sometimes uneasy peace between nuclear-armed adversaries. By the late 1980s, ideologues notwithstanding, there were many key decisionmakers in Washington who admitted that, as Deputy Secretary of State Lawrence Eagleburger put it in September 1989, "For all its risks and uncertainties, the Cold War was characterized by a remarkably stable and predictable set of relationships among the great powers." There were those who wanted Mikhail Gorbachev's reforms to succeed and the process of change in the Soviet Union to be gradual and even those who wanted Soviet troops to prevent Romania or Georgia from breaking up in ways that might lead to civil war. President George H. W. Bush and most of his key advisers wanted the Soviet Union to survive in some form and for its constituent republics to remain united. "We have an interest in the stability of the Soviet Union," declared Brent Scowcroft, Bush's National Security assistant, and that was the consensus in Washington until the Soviet Union broke up before and after August 1991.[22] Above all, they feared an all-powerful Germany, reunited in Europe again and unwilling to accept the borders imposed upon it in 1945 or subservience to the dictates of a US-dominated NATO. Indeed, German internal politics were as unpredictable as politics anywhere, and what its politicians might say or do to gain votes made its power that much more ominous to Washington.

Fear of communism had ultimately been the US-led alliance's most enduring cement. "Historical enemies" would be "less constrained by the bipolar Superpower alignments," the US Joint Chiefs of Staff predicted in 1991. Now there was "international deregulation," as a top US planner admitted, and "even at the height of US-Soviet geopolitical competition, the Kremlin could normally be counted upon not to allow the rivalry of clients to escalate to the point that direct US-Soviet confrontation became a possibility." The Soviet Union's "increasingly constructive role" and its prudence after 1945 had now ended. Europe and Japan no longer needed the United States and would not follow its lead, key US leaders worried, and the alliances the United States had formed were therefore at risk.[23] Nations were increasingly likely to go their own ways. The only inhibitions on US conduct were the inherent difficulties of the task itself and domestic public opinion, which had opposed the Gulf War of 1990–1991 until the last moment and then voted the president responsible for it out of office.

As President Bush declared in February 1990, "the enemy is *unpredictability.* The enemy is *instability.*"[24] Unpredictability and instability had existed throughout the twentieth century, but there had been a significant respite during the Cold War, as long as the Soviet Union existed and held sway over other nations and parties. Communism was the reflection rather than the cause of the larger structural and historical factors that had produced wars and conflict throughout the world for over a century, even some senior US officials now conceded. As a result of the Soviet Union's collapse, there was now an enormous void in the world. Mounting hazards ranged from the proliferation of weapons of all sorts to the rapid growth of diverse and far less controllable noncommunist movements, from Islamic fundamentalists to the Brazilian Workers Party, all seeking to replace governments in which the United States had major stakes. What were intended as small interventions, as in Iraq and Afghanistan, soon loomed as major challenges to the United States, but only because it chose to regard them as such. More than at any time in the modern period, after 1990 unpredictability and instability were inherent in the way the world operated and the hallmark of the age of perpetual war in which we now live.

3

The World Comes Apart: The 1990s

THE DISINTEGRATION OF THE SOVIET BLOC COMPLETELY TRANSFORMED the tense but predictable stability that had permitted Europe after 1945 to experience forty-five years without wars. US decisionmakers' fears that the demise of the Soviet Union would produce uncertainty and grave new dangers were almost instantly realized. But it was the overweening ambition of the United States to continue to play an activist role in the world that created much of this unpredictability. Communism's demise had little to do with causing the unexpected, for it was never the origins of the world's crises that Cold Warriors alleged. Communism was simply the reflection of all the atavistic illusions and factors that had led to World War I and beyond. The problem was that US leaders remained just as eager to attain their elusive goals, notwithstanding the fact that all their earlier great military adventures, above all Vietnam, had revealed the limits of their power. The United States possessed an unlimited readiness to fight yet more local conflicts, and its vast military expenditures precluded the admission that its weapons might be finite, if not useless. But the world has proven far too complex and elusive for it, and the period after 1990 has been much more violent than the decades before it.

Both in its goals or by objective measures of real power—military and economic might—the United States had always been the superior of the Soviet Union. Now it seemed there were no longer any barriers to realizing its ambitions, as if it was simply Moscow or Beijing that had stood in the way of its successes. The demise of the major communist power removed inhibitions that might have constrained the United States, a point that was explicitly acknowledged in the Middle East context but was equally true elsewhere. "For the first time in 40 years we can conduct military operations in the Middle East without worrying about triggering World War III," a State Department official observed in 1990.[1]

After 1991, Europe was again the scene of protracted wars. Germany and Japan reemerged potentially more powerful than ever. But although strong states capsized, the spread of technologies of mass destruction revolutionized the nature of warfare, transforming and ultimately equalizing the potential ability of more and more countries, both the economically weak and strong alike, to inflict terrible ruin on their enemies. What did not change throughout the twentieth century, despite the basic transformation of the weapons that nations command, is the way that many of the world's most important leaders—above all, those of the United States—think and act. The same myopic and dangerous assumptions about power and diplomacy that led to World War I and its sequel remain no less influential today. There are civil wars and conflicts between neighboring states in Africa, South Asia, and Europe, and threats of wars are more numerous than ever. Above all, the United States is involved in wars in Afghanistan and Iraq, and it has asserted its right and obligation to intervene anywhere.

The Dilemma of US Political Strategy and Military Power

The breakup of the Soviet Union only intensified the official US confusion, since no one could any longer explain problems by referring to nefarious forces in the Kremlin. Indeed, as the Soviets ceased to play their inhibiting and essentially conservative role, the world became more dangerous than ever. But the Pentagon's strategy and military equipment were oriented primarily toward Soviet targets and Eastern European conditions, and now they were irrelevant. The US National Security Agency, the world's biggest and technologically most sophisticated spy agency, for the first time since its founding in 1952 had far less to do with its billions of dollars of equipment.[2] A visible enemy and alleged dangers had been both extremely useful and essential for Washington's leaders after 1945, if only because they could often convince an occasionally reticent Congress and American public that more arms spending was justified. Communist parties were now of no consequence, but change still occurred, indeed more rapidly and unpredictably than ever, and myriad political groups of other ideological persuasions were just as active. To emphasize a crucial point I made earlier, Washington belatedly acknowledged the role that the Soviets played after 1945 in discouraging radicalism throughout the world and admitted that the Western European parties most under their control were essentially docile members of ruling political coalitions. In China, especially, Moscow urged the communists to pursue a much more moderate line, laying the basis for the subsequent break with Mao Zedong. The original justification for the virtually hegemonic global leadership pretensions of the United States—with its bases and massive military hardware virtually everywhere—was now gone.

After the dissolution of the Soviet Union, the United States believed it was the only superpower, but in reality it was also more vulnerable. It could not predict the origins of future challenges to it or even the identity of its new enemies, and it only increased the risks it now took with the welfare and security of its own people. Like the world before 1914, when all the leading great powers miscalculated the potential consequences of their actions, illusion and reality became intertwined. The world looked simpler, but it was more complex than it had ever been.

How to assess, much less respond to, the inevitable social and political consequences of deeply rooted trends in many nations without experiencing another debacle like Vietnam remained a fundamental challenge for the United States. Even in the twenty-first century, Washington still engaged in the quixotic search for a military doctrine that offered it the assurance of victory in the Third World. The prospects for confrontations and crises were even greater after communism's demise because the opposition to the political and social regimes the United States sought to sustain in so many countries had became increasingly diverse and decentralized. These groups ranged from conservative nationalist and Islamic movements to the indigenous left that inexorably reemerged in some nations. Now the United States had many enemies, often unknown to it, fighting in incredibly diverse ways for which its military was quite unprepared.

Charting its way through the complex world that followed in the wake of the collapse of communism has proven an enormous challenge to the United States, its perceptions, its economic and military power, and its ambitions. By and large, it had failed after 1945 in its never-ending quest to find a coherent strategic theory that allowed it to attain success—as had all other overly ambitious nations before it—but events after 1990 were even more disastrous for it, as its military power was again incapable of overcoming the political realities it faced in almost every corner of the globe. Nowhere did its military triumphs—as in Afghanistan or Iraq—allow it to gain political victories, and wherever it fought it left behind troubled, unstable, and violent countries.

After 1991 the United States assumed that its objectives and desires, backed by its growing military armada, could increasingly guide change in any region it chose to intervene in. That is why the United States defines, for better or worse, the nature and course of international affairs in the future. The extent to which it acts rationally is, as with other nations throughout modern times, to a great degree dependent on the accuracy of its intelligence and the extent it uses information to guide its actions. But collective illusions have characterized the leaders of most nations since time immemorial. They have substituted their desires, ambitions, and interests for accurate estimates of what may occur from their actions. At best, intelligence organizations gather data of tactical rather than strategic utility. An infrastructure of ambitious people exists to reinforce the leaders' preconceptions, in part because they too are socialized to believe what often proves to be illusion. But bearers of bad tidings are, by and large, unwelcome and prevented from reaching the higher ranks of most political orders. It is extremely difficult for nations to behave rationally, which means accepting the limits of their power, and what is called intelligence has to confront the institutional biases and inhibitions of each social system. Thus deductive, symbolic reactions become much more likely, notwithstanding the immense risks of their being wrong. The US war in Iraq and the geopolitical folly of its larger strategy in the Persian Gulf is but one recent example of it.

It is all too rare that states overcome illusions, and the United States is no more an exception than Germany, Italy, England, or France before it. The function of intelligence anywhere is far less to encourage rational behavior—although sometimes that occurs—than to justify a nation's illusions, and it is the false expectations that conventional wisdom encourages that make wars more likely, a pattern that has only increased since the early twentieth century. By and large, US, Soviet, and British strategic intelligence since 1945 has been inaccurate and often misleading, and although it accumulated pieces of information that were useful, the leaders of these nations failed to grasp the inherent dangers of their overall policies. When accurate, such intelligence has been ignored most of the time if there were overriding preconceptions or bureaucratic reasons for doing so.

The Gulf War and Its Aftermath

Kuwait began demanding repayment of its huge loans to Iraq as soon as the latter's war with Iran ended; even more provocative, Kuwait greatly exceeded its Organization of Petroleum Exporting Countries (OPEC) oil quota, reducing the world price of oil and Iraq's major source of hard currency. Worst of all, it demanded that Iraq abandon its border claims on it. In response, the Iraqi army invaded Kuwait on August 2, 1990. The administration of George H. W. Bush was utterly surprised; it had never conceived such a war was possible, and it was unprepared—it had no up-to-date maps, desert camouflage netting, and the like. The United States, Kuwait, and Saudi Arabia for a decade had pursued a political strategy in the Persian Gulf that had backfired in a way that was disastrous. Saddam Hussein erroneously assumed that the United States was his ally and that its overriding concern was Iran. But the Bush administration believed that US credibility was at stake, as was—in the president's words—"the dependability of America's commitment to its friends and allies."[3] That group no longer included Hussein. Washington had financed and supported Iraq as a balance to Iran, and destroying Hussein's forces produced the very outcome US policy had sought to avoid: Iran became—and remains—the dominant power in the oil-rich Gulf region. The US response to Iraq's actions produced a vacuum, ensuring that Iran would remain the principal long-term threat to US interests. Hussein had calculated rationally—but incorrectly.

The war with Iraq began January 17, 1991. Saddam followed the rules of conventional warfare and proved an astonishingly stupid enemy. Over forty-seven days of air power largely decimated his army, especially his elite Republican Guard, and Iraq's modern equipment. The 240,000 US soldiers plus 140,000 allied forces were used against 183,000 Iraqis in Kuwait alone; military victory came very quickly. Only the Kuwaitis favored the US-led forces driving all the way to Baghdad, which they could have easily done, but its coalition would have disintegrated. Fear of Iranian regional domination kept Hussein in power, despite UN sanctions and US and British air attacks, until March 2003.

Civilian deaths caused by the US-led war against Iraq and sanctions throughout the 1990s differ radically. As many as 33,000 civilians died during the short 1991 war and the Kurdish and Shiite rebellions that followed, and estimates of the number of civilians who died over the next decade as a result of UN sanctions (which the United States enforced more strongly than any nation) on absolutely vital imports of food and medicine range from 100,000 to 500,000. These figures, as shocking as they are, are still much lower than the casualties Iraq inflicted upon Iran with indispensable Kuwaiti, Saudi, and US backing.

The brief US war with Iraq—made so easy because Hussein was an incompetent military strategist—ended the occupation of Kuwait but created more difficulties for the victors, above all Saudi Arabia. That nation is troubled and increasingly unstable, having been ruled since 1744 by an alliance between the al-Saud family, which has held political power since, and the al-Wahhab family, which runs what is the state religion along exceedingly conservative, puritanical lines and is in charge of Islam's holiest sites. This hereditary arrangement is a gross anachronism. The vast majority of locals, including the growing number of educated men (women have no rights whatsoever and cannot freely work or even drive), are politically impotent. There have been increasingly vocal attempts to challenge the monarchy's absolute power, but erstwhile reforms during the 1990s in the form of consultative bodies changed nothing. The ruling family itself (which numbers about 7,000) is divided, the succession unclear, and some family members live ostentatiously abroad, whereas others support fundamentalist dissidents, including bin Laden. Most workers are foreigners (7 million out of 22 million people) who have no rights, but the majority are Muslim. Because of the drop in oil revenues, per capita income has fallen by almost two-thirds since the early 1980s, which has also fueled criticism. Class distinctions are sharper than ever.

There is growing dissatisfaction with the basic political structure, much of which has taken religious forms. Indeed, opposition in the guise of religion is the only legally tolerated form of dissent in much of the Arab world, and Islamic extremism reflects this fact. There is now an alternate clergy, but Wahhabism still remains a charismatic religion. In this unstable context, bin Laden was highly successful in recruiting followers and raising money. With the encouragement of all religious tendencies, at least 12,000 young Saudis went to Afghanistan to fight Soviet troops during the 1980s. Bin Laden, also a member of the elite, began his career there.

The Central Intelligence Agency (CIA) worked closely with the Saudis during the 1980s to fund the war against the Soviets in Afghanistan. Many of bin Laden's wealthy Saudi contacts, motivated by similar religious convictions, a sense of guilt, or the like, continued to fund him in the 1990s. They included members of the extended royal family unhappy with current trends and the possible succession. The United States encouraged Islamic movements—except those in Iran—as an antidote to secular leftists, whom they feared would work with the Soviets, just as it preferred the shah in Iran to secular middle-class nationalists. Saudi Arabia and Pakistan, ardent Muslim nations, were its most important allies in this decades-old strategy, but scarcely the only ones. To fight communism, the Americans strengthened Islamic fundamentalism—and terrorism.[4]

Alliances and Coalitions: US Dilemmas

The Balkans have been a source of Europe's most bitter nationalist and irredentist rivalries for centuries, and it was no coincidence that events in Bosnia-Herzegovina triggered World War I. The most recent crisis in Yugoslavia began in 1990, when the Yugoslav federal republic began to disintegrate and Croatia seceded without negotiating the status of the significant Serb minority within its borders. The violent sequence that followed led to a sustained ethnic war that killed and wounded many thousands of people; about 3 million people become refugees—most permanently. The UN-led armed force that entered the region in early 1992 has remained since then, managing to halt the violence only in November 1995. By any criterion, the UN's first effort was a political, human, and economic failure, and the entire former Yugoslavia remains fraught with profound ethnic discord.

Because the Yugoslav tragedy defied all solutions and US intelligence throughout the 1990s also detailed the Balkans' internecine political challenges, Washington hesitated to get deeply involved in the ordeal's first phase. From an international juridical viewpoint, Kosovo is an integral part of Yugoslavia. But Yugoslavia was to become yet one more example of leaders ignoring information that does not reinforce their policy preferences.

The crisis intensified in Kosovo in 1998 because Albanian extremists resorted to arms to secede, and it arose at a time that Washington imperatively needed an opportunity to impose its leadership over the North Atlantic Treaty Organization (NATO) as well as to justify its ambitious role in Europe. The actual political events that produced the tragedy were secondary to this overriding organizational goal.

The 1999 war in Kosovo taught the United States a lesson it was determined not to repeat. There were many unpleasant surprises. As was typical of nearly all wars, things went badly wrong. President Bill Clinton thought the bombing might "be over within a couple of days" once Yugoslavia's leader, Slobodan Milosevic, saw the alliance was united.[5] But the air war lasted seventy-eight days and was the principal cause of the humanitarian crises that occurred, including population displacement. The Pentagon, of course, shared the faith of those in power that using high-technology weapons and overwhelming firepower was the best way to relate to an increasingly complex world—despite the fact that the United States had lost its two most ambitious wars since 1945 to enemies who understood that decentralization made bombing and technology far less effective. Tactical aviation—over 1,000 planes were involved—

became the main military instrument of the war, but the Americans added strategic carpet bombing as the war became protracted and used it in ways for which it was not designed, causing many Serbs to rally to Milosevic for purely patriotic reasons. Airpower was often inaccurate and killed many innocent people, and rather than preventing the expulsion of Kosovo's ethnic Albanians, bombing accelerated it. Although his fellow Serbs drove Milosevic from power and he ended up in The Hague on charges of war crimes, the region is more destabilized than ever. As predicted by many, Albanian irredentism, which is largely Muslim, spread to Macedonia, where a sporadic civil war now festers. Indeed, many of those the United States aided as "freedom fighters" in the region were also involved in flourishing criminal activities, and these elements became increasingly important, so that Kosovo today is largely in the control of the Albanian mafia, who have driven out most of the non-Albanian population.

The Kosovo war, NATO's first encounter with combat, transformed it from a defensive alliance against the Soviet Union into an offensive coalition. Although it projected US power and ambitions into Eastern Europe as never before, it also involved a frustrating, time-consuming need to consult NATO's nineteen members about targets and much else. As the Pentagon later commented, "gaining consensus among 19 democratic nations is not easy and can only be achieved through discussion and compromise." But Wesley Clark, the American general who was NATO's supreme commander, regarded the whole experience as a nightmare—in his relations with both the Pentagon and NATO's members. "Working within the NATO alliance," US generals complained, "unduly constrained US military forces from getting the job done quickly and effectively."[6]

US political and military leaders resolved never again to fight wars this way; after 1999, NATO had a much smaller role in their military planning. For practical purposes, indeed, as NATO expanded, it became increasingly marginalized, and Washington was ready to use it only on its own terms. The implications for the European security system were potentially disastrous, and politics remained the Achilles heel of US policy, both in regard to the former Yugoslavia and especially in the nominal coalition it had created in Europe. Key US decisions to become more unilateralist were made well before the 2000 presidential election.

But the Pentagon itself was wracked by disagreements, from small matters such as tactical decisions to fundamental issues such as should the United States be tied up in the Balkans in the first place. Many senior officers believed that the Persian Gulf and North Korea were too important to get distracted in Yugoslavia, for these were the only places they were prepared to fight effectively. What they could not concede is that they were addicted to preconceived plans, that world politics could not be predicted, and therefore their strategies and careful calculations were inherently meaningless.

After using NATO forces in Kosovo, the United States fought its war against the Taliban in Afghanistan without NATO's inhibiting presence, even though many of its members sent token forces and resented being excluded from planning. The British initially attempted to confine the campaign against terrorism to Afghanistan alone, and the Germans and French were strongly opposed to giving the Americans carte blanche to fighting elsewhere. After the Kosovo war Washington believed that alliances are constraints, and the fewer it had the better. It still paid obeisance to them, principally as a means of controlling the policies of other nations, especially Germany and France. In Afghanistan it simply defined for its European allies what they could do on a take-it-or-leave-it basis.

Once it initiated the air war over Yugoslavia, the United States was resolved to vindicate the credibility of its military power. What was also at stake for the United States, and it alone, was the limits of its arms and the consequences of its being stalemated or even defeated in warfare. Such calculations caused it to make the initial political goals of its interventions secondary or even to forget them altogether. But its increasing reliance on airpower inevitably meant that it would strike civilian targets and populations. At no time has the United States entered a war aware of the time, material, and human costs demanded of itself or others.

In Kosovo, for example, the United States accepted the high risk of politically destabilizing the entire region when it encouraged and armed the Kosovo Liberation Army (KLA)—Muslim fanatics closely tied to bin Laden. The United States detested Yugoslavia's rulers, but earlier it had condemned the KLA, whose sporadic terrorism after 1996 greatly intensified Serb repression and triggered a cycle of violence. It has always strongly opposed the KLA's irredentist goals of an independent state leading to the creation of a Greater Albania that would redraw the region's boundaries. The State Department in 1998 had listed the KLA as terrorists. But in Bosnia, notwithstanding some reticence in Washington about such marriages of convenience, an alliance with it was inevitable as soon as the United States placed a much higher premium on a quick military victory and destroying targets than attaining political results that were far more compatible with a durable peace. The KLA correctly saw foreign intervention as the essential precondition of dismembering the existing state, and its members got it. But peace has yet to return to the former Yugoslavia, and Kosovo remains a troubled, violent region with severe unemployment and a crippled economy that in many areas is controlled by organized crime—its ultimate political status, whether an independent state or Serbian province, remains unresolved. About 20,000 NATO troops were still there in 2004, and in March of that year Albanians attacked the Serb minority, killing nineteen and causing more than 4,000 to flee their homes.

The war in the former Yugoslavia raised again the open and potentially highly destabilizing question of Russia's future relations to Europe. Although NATO agreed not to consider expansion until 2002, Slovenia, Romania, and Bulgaria were very useful allies during the Yugoslav conflict, and they were in due course admitted to NATO—creating a de facto cordon sanitaire on Russia's borders and revising European geopolitics fundamentally. The attacks on the World Trade Center on September 11, 2001, temporarily reversed this worsening trend in Russian-US relations because Russia's cooperation was important to the war effort. No sooner had Washington's incentives disappeared, however, than so too did its relatively conciliatory stance toward Moscow—above all on the 1972 Treaty Between the United States and the Union of Soviet Socialist Republics on the Limitation of Anti–Ballistic Missile Systems, which the United States renounced in December 2001. Meanwhile, NATO remained confused and disunited about how to handle Russia, giving the United States additional incentives to turn it into a largely ceremonial organization with no important role. Russia's economic problems caused it to tolerate the realities imposed upon it, but it did not like many of them, and its concessions were temporary. It was still a military superpower.

Surprises: The Outcome of War in Yugoslavia

The first and most obvious result of the war in the former Yugoslavia was to undermine NATO as a credible, efficient, military, and political coalition. Politically, its nineteen members immediately disagreed on its diplomatic objectives and military policies, differences that grew deeper as the war dragged on. The ruling political coalitions in two states, Italy and Germany, risked collapse if they pursued the conflict to the ultimate limits, and public opinion in both these crucial nations and in the United States, especially the Congress, immediately emerged as a decisive constraining factor. NATO leaders spent much of their time attempting to reconcile basic disputes. In coalition warfare in political democracies, the lowest common denominator prevails. When there is no working consensus on political and diplomatic goals, the alliance functions badly. Nothing in NATO's strategic calculations since it was created prepared it to cope with such unpredictable and overriding realities.

Before the air war began, no one in NATO doubted that massive technology and firepower would produce Serb acquiescence almost immediately. By forcing Serb forces to leave Kosovo, NATO made the KLA's obduracy, if not its eventual political triumph, much more likely, guaranteeing that a destabilized Balkans would remain a source of crises for years. Worse yet from the US viewpoint, its ability to dictate the political outcome of wars—and its credibility—were diminished greatly.

The United States and its allies eventually attained their immediate military objectives but also cast grave skepticism on NATO's effectiveness as an organization. NATO's first military effort reiterated the basic lesson of all wars in the twentieth century: military success leaving a political vacuum is tantamount to defeat. Washington emerged from Kosovo more adrift, more devoid than ever before of a coherent and attainable vision of its role in Europe and its relationship to the rest of the world.

As the United States learned in both Korea and Vietnam, massive airpower against decentralized armies has decisive limits. Planes designed to deliver nuclear bombs and strike cities and concentrated military targets failed to destroy the larger part of the Serb army. It withdrew from Kosovo only after intense negotiations over terms, which included Yugoslavia's ultimate sovereignty over Kosovo. In the end, NATO increasingly attacked essentially stationary civilian targets—waterworks, transportation, and energy—with the disingenuous argument, used in past wars, that the population would compel Yugoslavia's authoritarian leaders to accede to NATO's terms. The air war did not produce a political triumph but only another imbroglio waiting to reemerge. Only a land war could have compelled the Serbs to capitulate without conditions, and NATO was neither able nor willing to mount one. The 1999 war in the former Yugoslavia was a Pyrrhic victory. Everyone lost it.

For the same reasons that prevented the public's approval of political objectives within key member countries, NATO's members fought their first war wracked by serious differences. Initially, they could not agree on bomb targets, which were subject to extensive negotiations. A ground war itself, an immense risk inherent in the very act of initiating a conflict, was virtually impossible, even for the United States. Germany, Italy, and Greece firmly opposed a land war that might have lasted a very long time and involved thousands of NATO casualties. The United States recognized finally that its allies' domestic politics were far more important than nominal alliance obligations. But its European allies also realized that any future war the Americans initiated, whether on the Continent or even beyond, was very likely to be fought without extensive US ground forces. Neither Congress nor the public, still deeply traumatized by Vietnam, was prepared to give the White House much leeway on such a decisive matter.

In the end, the 1999 war in the former Yugoslavia shattered the illusion of NATO as a practical instrument for confronting crises in Europe—much less elsewhere. It could survive in theory so long as Europe was stable and there was no war, and that was largely the result until 1990 of both Soviet intentions and a universal dread of a nuclear holocaust. NATO was not disbanded, but the Yugoslav war made it passé. In practice, NATO failed: politically, the former Yugoslavia and the Balkans are more precarious than ever; militarily, despite the immense damage it inflicted on Yugoslavia's civilian economy, its enormous superiority of arms failed to win an unequivocal victory. Most important of all, leaders in a sufficient number of key NATO nations, the US included, finally realized that their populations would refuse to sanction wars of any substantial size or duration and that if they failed to heed this overriding political reality, they would risk their careers. For practical purposes, NATO was dead before George W. Bush's accession to power in January 2001.

The Kosovo war brought to a head worrisome US anxieties about Europe's future military structure and especially Germany's role in it. Washington and its nominal European allies disagree on two major issues: whether a projected and expanded European Union military force—which the United States nominally favors—will be independent of NATO (and a US veto); and Europe's opposition to a US missile defense system, which many nations as early as 1999 regarded as destabilizing and unilateralist. This projected missile shield and the US Senate's rejection of a test ban treaty in 2002 caused many important Europeans to conclude that the Americans preferred overwhelming military superiority to arms control. The Clinton administration had already indicated that "NATO could become a relic" if Europe created a military force parallel rather than subordinate to NATO's, which it has since done.[7] The Bush administration took exactly the same position but failed to act on it.

The Enigma of Germany

A reunited Germany is the crux of the great enigma—and challenge—confronting the United States, and Berlin was initially undecided what its future military role would be: either as a part of a European alliance or as a power in its own right. Germany's use of its economic power to restore its historically dominant role in Eastern Europe; its aggressive advocacy of Czech, Hungarian, and Polish membership in the European Union and NATO; and especially its successful effort in 1991 to obtain international recognition of Slovenian and Croatian independence before a mandatory effort was made to settle the borders of a disintegrating Yugoslavia, all had immense political and military repercussions. Germany, if it chooses, can circumscribe US influence in Europe. Its role was complicated after 1991 by its own deep uncertainty about the extent it wished to cooperate militarily and politically with the United States in Europe, but Bush's unilateral actions on Iraq after 2003 compelled Germany to resolve its ambivalence and pursue a far more independent foreign policy.

Both the British and French fear that Germany's military power could equal its dominant economic power in Europe, but Germany has begun to define a role for itself. The Schroeder government supported the war in Kosovo and took the military lead in Macedonia, despite the fact that only a small proportion of Germans supported sending troops there. Although a majority of Germans favored the US war on terrorism in Afghanistan, and the government offered 4,000 soldiers for use in that war, they were adamantly against sending forces to Iraq. Germany has yet to determine the full extent of its future course, save that it desires considerably greater prominence in European and world affairs, but it is moving in the direction of assuming a far larger role than it has in the past. Germany is translating its industrial power into political power. The outcome of this change has fundamental consequences for all its neighbors—with whom it has fought two wars in the past century—and the United States. It was precisely these kinds of fundamental geopolitical questions that US officials had worried about in the late 1980s, when the Soviet Union began disintegrating.

These basic issues have immense implications for Europe's future, and they began to undermine post-1945 alliances and friendships soon after Germany reunited and communism disappeared. The US-led war against Iraq beginning in March 2003 compelled Germany and France to pursue far more independent foreign policies. The Cold War is dead, at least in appearance, but what will replace it? The dissolution of the

Soviet Union in Europe destroyed the nominal raison d'être of NATO and forty years of alliances, and Europe itself is changing rapidly both diplomatically and economically. Today, nothing is settled.

The Pentagon Searches for a Strategy: Confusion in High Places

The self-confident optimism that characterized the Pentagon's efforts after the mid-1950s is now largely gone. Counterinsurgency and a reliance on massive firepower failed in Vietnam, and even though the military had plenty of theorists who could concoct assorted doctrines, in fact US policies since then have been ad hoc and incremental, including a botched Iranian hostage rescue debacle in April 1980, barely concealed "covert" aid to the contras in Nicaragua and or mujahidin in Afghanistan during the 1980s, the outright use of US troops in Grenada in 1983, and the like. After 1981 the Reagan administration favored a massive arms buildup. Although it articulated the Weinberger Doctrine in November 1984 to warn that it would utilize all its military power should it fight again—and was sufficiently vague to frighten the Russians with visions of the United States using its nuclear weapons in a first strike—in fact, the doctrine must also be seen as the military's decisive limiting preconditions on ill-conceived action. The American public, its initial martial impulses notwithstanding, was extremely fickle during the Vietnam War, and no one was more aware of that than officers in the Pentagon. The Joint Chiefs of Staff were now usually less pugnacious and more conscious of what might go wrong than the White House. Weinberger's was a doctrine that left more questions unanswered than resolved.

In practice, however, US responses to military challenges were never consistent or coherent, and the Weinberger doctrine became just one of many ideas that Washington has concocted—and then usually forgot. The search for a winning strategy never occurred in a static context but usually as decisions were taken during a new crisis, as in El Salvador, Nicaragua, Angola, and many other places. Washington's strategy was generally quite sloppy and unsuccessful. Moreover, the reality of competing military services, each with distinctive tactics and rival interests that reinforced their doctrines and claims in the bitter struggles for a share of the total military budget, persisted unabated then and now as a fundamental, extremely costly aspect of both the definition and application of US military power. The Iranian hostage rescue debacle of April 1980, the invasion of Grenada in October 1983—a classic case of confusion and inherent complexity as the rival services attempted to fight together—or the 1990–1991 Gulf War all revealed the lack of communication and coordination inherent in the military's schismatic institutional context, which made an effective, affordable US military doctrine and strategy no more likely as the twentieth century ended than it was after the Korean War. Such a goal remains as much a chimera for the United States as it has been for every other aspiring power in modern times.

Despite its past failures, the United States has persisted in its futile search for a doctrinally coherent and convincing justification for employing its massive military power. Many grand strategies were concocted, but most reflected service justifications for their budgets and were quickly forgotten. None gave the United States the doctrines it needed to win wars that were to be fought in very different conditions—from the urban Third World to jungles or deserts everywhere. There was no end to these futile searches, but as Vietnam proved and innumerable failures since then have confirmed, they reflected weakness rather than strength. Above all they called into question the reliance on technology, on which countless US arms producers and their workers depended for prosperity, rather than on accurate assessments of the political, social, and ideological bases of crises. What the United States refused to do is heed the lessons that all the follies of the preceding centuries taught, for to do so would be the abandon the vainglorious dream of controlling the world's destiny—and the immense expenses of keeping these dreams alive. As the twentieth century closed, it appeared to be the sole nation wealthy enough to ignore its failures and absorb the economic and political costs of its accumulated defeats. It remained ready to make war in other nations, but would it accept that violence could come to it on its own soil?

US leaders, whether Republicans or Democrats, failed to understand the negative long-term political, economic, and ideological consequences of their country's policies. That was their fatal oversight, to misunderstand that the world is so complicated that weapons cannot solve its problems. Countless US interventions have been counterproductive and earned the United States the hatred of those who were once its friends—or at least not hostile to it.

The United States has almost always succeeded in its military efforts, whether covert or overt, where its enemies were weak and foolish. It won, at least in the short run. In Cuba it failed because its proxies were venal and its efforts incompetent. There is some basis for its overweening self-confidence, but its victories rarely nullify the longer-term negative political and ideological consequences of what seemed to be successes. Moreover, US losses in Vietnam and Korea were crucial because they revealed how finite its military power was when it confronted able enemies ready to make the most of the terrain and space, enemies able to neutralize its firepower and concentrated forces. Military technology notwithstanding, advanced industrial powers do not often win wars against decentralized and determined enemies—and the United States is no exception. Few, if any, leaders in Washington seriously analyzed these defeats. "Across thirteen years of frequent military actions," a former senior US intelligence official wrote in 2004, "we have not once definitively and finally defeated the force—military, paramilitary, or armed rabble—we defined as the foes. . . . US officials and political leaders no longer define victory in precise quantitative or qualitative terms, but by whatever can be gained by the military in a tight time frame set by domestic political strategists who estimate how long and costly a war American voters will tolerate."[8] The period after 1950, and certainly the wars in Korea and Vietnam, were no different because politics remain decisive and today staying in power is more important to successive administrations in Washington than the nominal military victories the Pentagon hopes to achieve quickly.

A Balance Sheet: War at the End of the Twentieth Century

As fear of the Soviet Union that had unified the US-led alliance disappeared in 1991, Washington attempted to define a new international framework, one it could control more easily to better confront the perplexing multitude of new challenges facing it. The Soviet bloc's disintegration intensified what still remains its elusive, increasingly frustrating search. The crisis in the world economy after mid-1997 further intensified the bitter debate among former allies regarding trade blocs, Europe's and especially Germany's pursuit of a more autonomous political and economic strategy on the Continent, and Japanese and Chinese economic and military power. The problems confronting Washington were astonishingly complex. Even much more than at the beginning of the twentieth century, real and threatened nationalist and atavistic conflicts, both between nations and within them—in Africa, Afghanistan, the Middle East, the former Yugoslavia, and many other places—confirmed that the spread of increasingly deadly weaponry today makes wars in all their forms the most imperative problem facing humankind.

The situation the United States confronted after 1990 was far more perplexing than Korea or Vietnam because there was no longer an easily definable enemy on which to focus both its armed forces and diplomacy. Its policy in the Middle East had been a disaster and was instrumental in producing terrorism on a much larger scale than had ever been known. The very absence of a single adversary in concentrated places threatened to neutralize its vast arsenal, undermine the principal justification for its burgeoning defense budget, and destabilize its foreign policy. Indeed, Washington's inability to reliably predict future crises made it much more difficult for it to articulate priorities to orient its ultimately finite resources.

Notwithstanding the dilemmas faced by the United States, it remained more convinced than ever at the end of the twentieth century that it had the ability, the right, and the moral imperative to guide the world's political and economic affairs whenever or wherever it chose to do so. The protracted economic crisis that began in the summer of 1997 in East Asia made the attainment of what it described as a new "architecture" in the world economy especially imperative. But it also remained more obsessed than ever with maintaining the credibility of its armed might. This fixation on the symbolism of its military power had become an end in itself in Vietnam, and it is just as compelling today. Such reasoning makes the credibility of its arms an overriding goal that dictates which political and military options are considered when challenges arise. In a word, the new crisis in US foreign policy began when the Soviet Union disappeared, long before George W. Bush became president.

The Future of the Alliance System

In late 1998, Washington found the Germans, but particularly the French, reticent about its still vague ideas for transforming NATO into an alliance whose functions might also extend beyond Europe's immediate borders. The United States also envisioned this coalition as an opportunity to impose a new political and military arrangement on a postcommunist Europe that would preempt the emergence of a truly independent European security system with its own foreign policies.

The US project for NATO at the end of 1998 was also a response to its conflict with Iraq, which was about to resume. Above all, its proposals reflected the fact that there was no longer a Soviet strategic military threat for NATO to confront. As Washington envisaged it, dealing with terrorism, the spread of chemical and biological weapons, and nuclear proliferation were all to become crucial to NATO. Both its new geographical scope and potential military role were left obscure, but they might extend to "rogue states" wherever they existed. More important, the United States wanted the new NATO to act, if necessary, without first obtaining the approval of the United Nations, where Security Council vetoes could paralyze it. In effect, the United States aspired to create an organization with a potentially unlimited mandate, immune to the cumbersome political rules that had governed the world after 1945, when communism ostensibly posed a fatal danger. NATO was to be transformed from a staid defensive alliance into an ambitious offensive one.

At the beginning of 1999, the unprecedented turmoil in the world economy was aggravating Washington's relations with many of its allies; European states and especially Japan frequently publicly criticized the international economic role of the United States. Attempts to reduce US mastery over the International Monetary Fund (IMF) and World Bank appeared imminent, and the launching of a common European currency in 1999 immediately challenged the dollar's dominant role in the world economy since 1945. This global economic environment and the disputes it generated created an inauspicious context both for US ambitions for NATO and for its pretensions to lead the world. France in particular attacked its unilateral and hegemonic political objectives.

Although the United States no longer considered Russia as a threat to Europe, a view that the parlous state of its economy and political life fully justified, it still remained a nuclear superpower whose interests could not be casually dismissed. Officially, Washington desired friendly ties with Russia and a constructive "engagement" with China, even though the Pentagon's November 1998 strategy statement for East Asia implied that China remained the single most important justification for keeping its armed forces in the region. After 1991 Washington could either cooperate with Russia or continue to constrain it, and despite comforting words, its actions were the only meaningful test of its intentions. The Clinton administration's crucial decision in the summer of 1995 to enlarge NATO to include Poland, Hungary, and the Czech Republic created a predictable nationalist upsurge in Russia and was a major reason for the communist-led bloc emerging as the strongest in the Russian Duma in elections at the end of 1995. This decision, which was expanded to include the Baltic states in 2004, moved NATO 500 kilometers closer to Moscow, and whatever their politics, all Russians opposed NATO's "encroachment."

Wanted: Credible Enemies

The Clinton administration (1993–2000), like its predecessors, offered no innovations that might solve the mounting and increasingly awesome diplomatic and military problems bequeathed to it by a succession of Democratic and Republican presidents. The Pentagon moved away somewhat from the US preoccupation with Europe and focused far more on the Persian Gulf and especially East Asia and China, but these changes were of degree rather than kind. The "uninhibited access to key markets, energy supplies, and strategic resources," to cite the Pentagon's 1996 annual defense report, was crucial even if it could not identify who could resist its "unilateral use of military power" to protect US "vital national interests." There were also mystical elements in the vaguely defined US mission to reform the way the world has existed and operated, but at its core such documents always identify the world's interests and those of the United States as one and the same. But enlarging the number of free-market nations, too, was no longer a problem; both China and Vietnam now believed passionately in the market and were well on their way to becoming capitalist in all but name. The writers of the report thought an "unpredictable" and "uncertain future" was likely and stated that the world "remains a complex, dynamic, and dangerous place," but they could not pin down the reasons for these anxieties now that communism had virtually ceased to exist. The report referred to "failed states" and "dangerous technologies" that were proliferating, but it was painfully silent on where and how all this was occurring. What was plainly clear is that the US military wanted to justify the budget that would allow it to modernize, "to retain military superiority."[9] But if nuclear power is the criterion, it had that already and no longer needed to spend prodigiously. Growing doubt was the hallmark of US thinking on its strategy and foreign policy after 1991.

Although NATO emerged more united than divided on the war in Kosovo, whatever goodwill remained among its members was largely dissipated by the anti–ballistic missile (ABM) shield Washington talked of building to protect the North American continent from an attack by technically sophisticated adversaries. Such a shield has been on the drawing boards for decades. Successive administrations mentioned North Korea, Iran, and Iraq as the possible culprits, but no nation possesses the technical capacity to inflict sufficient damage before it is utterly devastated by a US riposte. Deterrence had kept the peace with the Soviet Union, and exactly the same logic applied elsewhere. An arms race exists in South Asia and the Middle East, but it is intended for regional enemies and scarcely a threat to the United States, with its overwhelming nuclear supremacy. The Pentagon implied that the real enemy was China and perhaps others, but it was too impolitic to state this openly. Moreover, should the ABM shield work, then mutual deterrence, the basis of US strategic nuclear theory for decades, would end; it could strike any nation with impunity first, with conventional or nuclear weapons, and destroy any riposte. The only credible nuclear power would be the nation with an ABM shield—the United States. The shield would make its military adventures much more feasible and therefore all the more likely.

The prospect of the United States building the ABM had created deep dissension within the NATO alliance, alienated Russia (its 1972 anti–ballistic missile treaty with the United States would have to be annulled), and spread suspicion in every direction by early 2000. But such a system became a football in US politics and a gargantuan plum for defense contractors. It was all liabilities, and although its research had cost at least $71 billion as of 1999, it was technically and politically a very bad idea—except for the contractors building it.

US allies thought the idea dangerous, and so did the Russians. RAND experts concluded it would be "practical and economical" for Russia to overcome the US system, but nominally Russia was no longer an enemy.[10] But the Congressional Budget Office in April 2000 wrote that even a limited system would cost $60 billion—and it might not work. Indeed, the system was potentially open-ended in terms of expenses, and every phase of it had to be technically perfect. At worst, RAND experts warned, a partial system would create all liabilities, offer no protection, and waste money. That is exactly what has happened. In 2004 the missile defense system failed both of its tests.

The ABM was first proposed by Ronald Reagan in 1983 and has yet to be proven feasible. But its astonishing persistence to this day reflects the Pentagon's fascination with supersophisticated technology, the extent to which it can be impervious to the obvious political implications of its fads, and its immense attraction for defense contractors. These contractors, especially Lockheed Martin and Boeing, were crucial in eventually reversing the CIA's technical assessment in the mid-1990s that Iran, North Korea, and other "rogue states" were incapable of building a credible missile delivery system in the foreseeable future. Technically, the ABM system the Clinton administration proposed could not distinguish between real warheads and decoys, and its advocates were accused of rigging its tests—by 2000 there were also increasingly strong opponents of the ABM within the Pentagon, who thought it a waste of funds better spent in other ways. By late 2000, most of the Joint Chiefs of Staff were among them.

US-Russian relations were also increasingly damaged by this issue. Russian prime minister Vladimir Putin proposed new European defense arrangements and went to North Korea in July 2000 in the hope of getting sufficient verbal assurances from Kim Jong Il to stop Washington from pursuing the ABM system. US friends in Europe saw it as an example of its emerging unilateralism, and even Defense Secretary William S. Cohen, the ABM's strongest advocate within the Clinton administration, confessed that he was uncertain of the vast, expensive enterprise's technological premises—"That remains to be determined." An "act of terrorism taking place on the United States is more likely than [an] intercontinental ballistic missile," he conceded, and the US intelligence agencies concurred that weapons of mass destruction are more likely to be delivered by some means—boats, airplanes, and the like—against which the ABM is utterly useless.[11] The administration had alienated its allies in Europe, muddied relations with Russia, and caused China to worry it was really the ABM's principal target. In fact, the Clinton administration also wanted to help Vice President Al Gore get elected, and so it favored the ABM to make it appear as if the Democrats were as bellicose on military spending as their opponents.

The Dilemma of a World with Elusive Enemies

What was gone, as one general told a Senate committee in January 1998, was "the bi-polar nature of superpower competition [that] allowed for substantial continuity in US defense planning and force development."[12] Variations of these themes suffuse all Pentagon justifications for higher budgets. In the five years ending in fiscal 2005, the Pentagon asked for $1.6 trillion. It wanted more modern weapons—nuclear, conventional, anything—against unnamed enemies and targets. In reality, there are no longer credible enemies for its vast armada of advanced technology to destroy, but no US administration will concede what is obvious.

President Bill Clinton admitted in principle that terrorism might become more of a threat than wars as they had been fought for centuries, but he encouraged the insatiable Pentagon demands for conventional hardware. In January 2000—with an eye on the November 2000 presidential election—military planners added $115 billion to the Pentagon's projected five-year Future Years Defense Plan, extending to 2005, far more than what Republicans were calling for. The Clinton administration refused to sign the Ottawa Landmines Treaty, fought many of the terms of a proposed treaty controlling the small arms trade that the National Rifle Association disliked, and strongly opposed linking burgeoning US arms exports to criteria on a nation's human rights and democracy record. The already dominant US share of the world arms market grew even larger—from 32 percent of the world trade in weapons in 1987 to 43 percent by 1997. By 2004 it had fallen to 34 percent. Of the 140 nations it gave or sold arms to in 1995, 90 percent were not democracies or abused human rights. Not counting the ABM system, at the beginning of 2001 the Pentagon had over $500 billion in major weapons systems in the pipeline, all of which the Clinton administration had approved. In 1995 the Pentagon's budget accounted for nearly two-thirds of the world's spending on military research and development. In reality, there was no foreign military threat to even remotely justify these expenditures, only politically powerful contractors who would fight cutbacks.

By the time the Clinton administration left office, even establishment critics believed its military and diplomatic priorities were profoundly awry. A few former top officers said as much publicly. There simply was no inhibition on US ambitions, even though it had shown time and again that it was physically unable to do everything it was committed to attaining. Its repeated political failures only confirmed that the world had problems about which the United States could do nothing and it was to everyone's interest that it avoid getting involved in them. The Pentagon has even tacitly admitted that past priorities and perceived political threats were essentially wrong and that the basic assumptions that guided US grand strategy since 1946 were erroneous.

The most important area of US operations was in the Middle East and especially the Persian Gulf, which possesses the larger part of the world's oil reserves. Bin Laden made this concern all the more certain by turning on the absolutist, authoritarian Saudi elite that had initially sponsored him. The half-million infidels who entered the kingdom in 1991 to reverse the August 1990 Iraqi invasion of Kuwait and the approximately 5,000 US troops who remain until this day (plus a larger group of civilians who are connected with the military) compelled him to become an enemy of the Saudi regime in the name of Islam. He still retains very important friends and sympathizers within the elite, although in 1994 the Saudi government stripped him of his citizenship. Saudi Arabia was one of only three nations to recognize the Taliban regime in Afghanistan, and there exists a close affinity between the two forms of Islam—which has made the Saudis extremely unreliable allies for the United States. Were people who agree with bin Laden to come to power there, it would create immense problems for Washington in a region absolutely vital to US economic and strategic interests.

Terrorism Comes of Age

The mood of crisis that has engulfed the United States since the awesome September 11, 2001, attacks on Wall Street and the Pentagon has its roots in a history that goes back nearly a half-century. It was virtually inevitable.

Terrorism has no rules. In war there is success or failure; there are winners or losers; and if the stakes are high and one side has few weapons, then they employ what their enemies describe as terrorist methods. It is the weapon of the weak against the strong, of the poor against the highly organized, and its victims are, overwhelmingly, ordinary and quite innocent people. Many use terrorist methods, and a few terrorist leaders are successful and achieve power, becoming respectable politicians. Some, indeed, eventually denounce those who get in their way as terrorists. If we examine the organizations once accused of terrorism—the Irgun and Stern Gang in Palestine, the African National Congress in South Africa, and innumerable other nations—we also compile a who's who of successful political movements over the past century. The political causes that give rise to terrorism are integral to the way in which our world is organized. It existed in various forms a century ago and terrorism, in various guises, will continue.

There are, however, other forms of terrorism than that used to gain political power; the police and the military have used torture and arbitrary arrests in Chile, Iran, Uzbekistan, Argentina, Indonesia, and countless other states where human rights violations occurred routinely. Such state-sponsored terrorism is much more extensive and expensive than the desperate and essentially random acts of violence that Al-Qaida and comparable groups engage in. Since 1950 the United States has funded, trained, and supplied dozens of state-terrorist organisms to sustain not only regimes that were described as anticommunist but also groups—like the contras in Nicaragua during the 1980s—that employed violence to overthrow established governments. Today the United States has bases in many states that violate human rights routinely, and it funds others. I do not deal with this much more common and deadly form of terrorism in this book, but US sponsorship of this form of state terrorism is one of the crucial reasons it now confronts violence on its own soil. More important, the United States has advised as well as fought many wars everywhere in the world since 1947: two major conflicts in Korea and Vietnam, but dozens of others, covert as well public. It has more enemies, by far, than any other nation. The surprise is not that it was finally massively attacked on its own soil but that it took so long to occur.

Examples of this form of warfare against the United States, of the weak against the strong, began to appear in the 1990s. The bombing of the World Trade Center underground garage in February 1993, in which six people died and hundreds were injured, presaged the future: terrorism against Americans on their own soil became a reality. Throughout the 1990s the federal government conducted hundreds of planning exercises, the large majority of which involved chemical and biological attacks, even though some of its experts argued that low-tech hijackings or bombs against symbolic targets were much more likely. Innumerable reports, documents, and policy directives on terrorism dating back to the 1980s revealed that Washington had an acute consciousness—at least on paper—of the dangers terrorism posed for the United States itself. The bombings of the US base in Saudi Arabia in June 1996, in which nineteen US personnel were killed and 240 wounded, and its embassies in Kenya and Tanzania in August 1998, which killed over 200 people, reinforced a widely shared belief in official circles that terrorism was a clear and present danger.

The Roots of Terrorism

Terrorism has many causes, but the primary one is economic: persistent poverty, unemployment, and economic instability in the Third World are the indispensable reasons for its growth. I have already discussed how the structural causes of discontent—and terrorism—intensified in the 1970s and 1980s, but in many regards they became worse after the fall of communism. Joseph E. Stiglitz, chairman of the President's Council of Economic Advisers from 1993 to 1997, has described the Clinton administration's intensification of the "hegemonic legacy" in the world economy. The 1990s were a "decade of unparalleled American influence over the global economy in which one economic crisis seemed to follow another." The United States created trade barriers and gave large subsidies to its own agribusiness, but countries in financial straits were often compelled to cut spending on the poor and "adopt policies that were markedly different from those that we ourselves had adopted."[13] No nation was more influential in shaping the contours—and consequences—of the world economy. The United States gained; others lost badly.

The world was far more troubled economically in the 1990s, however one measures it—and therefore politically also. Increasingly unequal income distribution in much of the Third World explains most of the persistence of discontent, and grossly inadequate economic growth much of the remainder. In Russia and Eastern Europe this inequality, stagnant and declining economies, and the abolition of virtually all forms of social protection added greatly to the world's poverty and human and social problems. IMF insistence on poor nations balancing their budgets caused many countries to reduce the proportion of their gross domestic product (GDP) allocated to health and education, and what spending there was on education, health, and transfer programs in developing nations did not reverse growing income inequality and often benefited mainly upper-income groups. Latin America fared especially badly, with utterly inadequate social safety nets. In some nations during the 1990s the gains made in preceding decades were reversed, and despite economic progress in a number of places, in many countries economic and social conditions fed the supply of terrorists.

The number of hungry people in the world fell by 37 million during the first half of the 1990s, only to increase by 18 million during the second half—acquired immune deficiency syndrome (AIDS), civil wars, and drought helped to reverse the decline. There were 842 million under-nourished people in 1999–2001. Regionally, only Latin America and the Caribbean, as well as China, succeeded in reducing the number of hungry in the late 1990s. But in 2004 nearly half of Latin America's half-billion population were still deemed poor. Even the optimistic assessments agree that economic changes have been minimal and in some regions conditions have gotten worse. Indeed, the gap in health care standards between the rich and poor nations has widened since the mid-1990s, and in some countries, especially in Africa, the HIV epidemic and civil wars have reversed medical progress made since 1970.

In all, fifty-four nations with 12 percent of the world's population had negative economic growth from 1990 to 2001—especially in sub-Saharan Africa and Eastern Europe—and another seventy-one nations with 26 percent of the world's population had zero to low growth and often failed to keep up with population increases. The per capita income of only sixteen developing nations grew at more than 3 percent annually between 1985 and 2000, and mean per capita global GDP growth in the decade ending in 2003 was about one-third of the 1961–1968 increase. China accounts for most of the recent statistical progress that has occurred in East Asia and the entire world, but the per capita GDP gap between the twenty richest and twenty poorest nations has more than doubled between 1960–1962 and 2000–2002—with the richest nations now having an average per capita income 121 times that of the poorest nations, up from fifty-four times as much. Yet another measure is basic sanitation: in 2004 the World Health Organization reported that more than 1 billion people drink unsafe water and over 2.6 billion, or about 40 percent of the world population, have no access to basic sanitation. Diarrhea kills about 1.8 million people annually, mainly children under age five.

For all the less-developed countries (LDCs) combined, the percentage of the population living on less than $1 a day grew from 48 percent of the population in 1965–1969 to 50 percent during 1995–1999, meaning that the number of people living in extreme poverty more than doubled during that period, from 138 to 307 million people. The International Labour Organization, however, estimates the number of working people in 2002 living on $1 a day or less at 550 million—and adding the unemployed would make that figure far higher. The ILO believes that 1.237 billion people lived in absolute poverty in 1990 and 1.1 billion in 2000, but China and India accounted for much of that progress. In seventy countries the ILO surveyed, forty-eight of them—containing 59 percent of the population of the sample—had rising income inequality from the 1960s to the 1990s and sixteen had stable inequality. In only nine—with 5 percent of the population—was inequality declining.

The problem of hunger is linked to the persistence of unemployment and underemployment, which has been growing despite the growth of world GDP. In 1993 there were 141 million people worldwide unemployed and looking for work, but there were 186 million in 2003. Reliable figures on underemployment do not exist, but it is an immense problem. Unemployment is greatest in the Middle East and North Africa, reaching 26 percent in 2003 among youth in those regions— with inevitable political results in the form of extremism.[14]

The outcome of trends such as these is that an increasing number of men and women become desperate—and terrorists. There is little doubt that the economic causes of terrorism have grown substantially, and the collapse of the left has meant that there are no secular answers to hunger, poor health, or unemployment. One cannot assign a precise weight to economics as a cause, but informed observers think it a crucial and perhaps the most important factor. The failure of globalization to bring a modicum of prosperity to an important part of the Third World has greatly increased the number of people ready to become terrorists. Many who turn to Islamic extremism do so for the same economic reasons that people once became secular revolutionaries, and to a great extent the rise of such groups is due to capitalism's failure to bring prosperity to poorer countries—which pits them not only against foreigners but also against their own rulers.

An Increasingly Unstable World

Economic, social, and political transformations since 1980 have made instability part of the modern historical experience. The US government acknowledges the structural causes of grave discontent but still advocates the policies that perpetuate them, ranging from support for socially dysfunctional IMF policies to subsidies for its own cotton, rice, and commodity producers that prevent Third World farmers from earning more for the crops on which they are dependent. These choices maintain the unequal relationship between rich and poor nations. The United States helped destroy most of the secular options in the Middle East and aided Islamic fundamentalists whenever they were useful. Above all, it has given Israel large amounts of economic and military aid and supported many of its most aggressive policies, until Israel became its proxy, further alienating the Muslim world. Now there is a storm of revenge—"blowback"—fanning terrorism in ways that simply were not the case in the 1970s. Terrorism is the weapon of the weak and discontented, and they are more numerous than ever.

The difficulty, as the US Army admitted in discussing terrorism in May 1999, was that "these threats are much less predictable" than when communism existed, but the focus in official circles was overwhelmingly on chemical and biological weapons, or even nuclear bombs in suitcases. Before the collapse of the Soviet bloc the United States had one clearly defined enemy. At the turn of the twenty-first century it had many, often unknown to it, fighting in incredibly diverse ways for which its military was simply unprepared. When in December 2000 the CIA sought to predict global trends for the next fifteen years, it too emphasized WMD but predicted they would be used "against the United States itself," not only against its bases and companies operating abroad.[15] The problem for the United States was that having an amorphous enemy complicated its capacity both for deterring an attack and retaliating once it had occurred. Indeed, this situation left its justification for an anti–ballistic missile system in shambles.

A US destroyer was attacked in Yemen in October 2000, killing seventeen sailors. By 2001 the federal government was spending nearly $800 million in predicting and preparing for terrorism—efforts that ranged from abstractly calculating possible terrorist attacks to stockpiling essential equipment. Indirectly, it spent ten times that sum in combating terrorism, or what the Pentagon also clinically dubbed as "asymmetrical methods." There were many predictions that terrorism against the US homeland itself was inevitable, but few—perhaps no one in power—quite believed them.

The combined intelligence agencies' annual budget in 2001 was $30 billion, but they had no inkling whatsoever of an impending attack on Wall Street or the Pentagon. The monumental events of September 11, 2001, were a profound shock, both symbolically and physically, to the United States. If in principle a terror attack, somewhere and at some time, was fully expected, in reality no one was prepared for the magnitude or the location of these attacks. Surprise, the ultimate ingredient in successful terrorism as well as warfare, was total. Nothing in recent memory, perhaps since the Civil War, so seared the American people's consciousness; for the first time since 1865, war's front line had arrived on the US mainland. Despite its immense efforts since 1945, it was more insecure than ever.

*   *   *

The 1999 war in Yugoslavia marked the beginning of a fundamental new phase in international relations. It was the beginning of the end of NATO, a gradual but irresistible process that President George W. Bush accelerated but that began under the Clinton administration. Geopolitics reemerged without ideological illusions to obfuscate US intentions and interests. The basic US priorities throughout the world and its future relations with Russia and China now had to be reassessed—including by the leaders of those two nuclear powers and all the major nations that had been US allies after 1945. Its growing commitment to playing a more overtly independent role in the world, to unilateralism, was now plain for all to see, and was clearly defined in the minds of Washington's decisionmakers. The world was moving, again gradually but irresistibly, toward multipolarism, a process that Bush's actions greatly accelerated but that were the logical outcome of the Balkans, Israel-Palestine, and other post-Soviet crises. Above all, civil conflicts in and near Europe shattered the region's unprecedented long peace and exposed NATO's decisive limits as the Continent's only security system. Indeed, the war in Yugoslavia compelled very influential US strategic thinkers—including those who had once been ardent advocates of its Cold War missions—to conclude that it was a grave error for the United States to become entangled in third-tier issues and nations at the sacrifice of its vital relations with Japan and its former communist enemies, its domestic responsibilities, and much else. They had finally to concede that the US impulse to intervene virtually everywhere in the world had led to an incoherent foreign policy that confronted many more challenges than it could resolve.

At the end of the twentieth century, the way the United States viewed the world and its commanding role in it, along with its core assumptions about the means and institutions it possessed for attaining its goals, were seriously confused. Neither the United Nations nor NATO offered the political or military mechanisms for it to attain its ambitions, and existing international rules and institutions were an increasingly frustrating hindrance. But no viable alternatives were emerging to replace them. Its aspirations far exceeded its capacity to achieve its ultimate objective of leading the world wherever its vast ambitions pointed, whether in Europe or the Third World. Politics, above all, remained the Achilles heel of US ambitions. The world, with its inordinately complex and diverse political and social realities, continued to elude it, just as it had frustrated all those powerful European nations that over preceding centuries had aspired to assume the mantle of the world's leader.

The dilemma was not only its persistent definition of global priorities that exceeded its military and political resources, but also the fact that many of the places in which the United States had intervened in the past remained continuing obligations, leaving an accumulation of troublesome legacies to potentially challenge it in the future. Some nations, such as Afghanistan or Haiti, appeared relatively dormant for a while but eventually flared up again. Nearly a half-century after the Korean War ended, the United States still had 37,000 military personnel stationed there. A decade after the Gulf War, US airpower and boats continued to operate in the Gulf, and it will remain in Afghanistan and Iraq indefinitely, probably many decades. It became entangled in the Balkans well over a decade ago, and in 2004 there were still 20,000 NATO soldiers in Kosovo, about one-third of them Americans.

Its virtually uncontrollable impulse to intervene in crises in all the corners of the world and to articulate lofty justifications for doing so required the United States also to sacrifice those larger objectives and interests that are fundamentally more important both to itself and to world peace. The mere fact that the 1999 war in Yugoslavia alienated both Russia and China deeply, making some form of strategic alliance between them increasingly probable, meant that the reemergence of bipolar confrontation and a return to the Cold War in another, nonideological form—essentially the classic conflict of national interests—will also affect future international relations profoundly.

When the twentieth century ended, the United States still could not master most of the world's complex political problems. On the contrary, its attempts to do so only aggravated them. Its universal pretensions and obsessions, which began during World War I and matured after 1945, were more dangerous than ever—both to itself and to the complex world.

War was no longer a question of conflicts between states that were roughly equal, as it had been for the first four decades of the twentieth century, but increasingly a matter of US interventions, whether for rational economic or simply idiosyncratic reasons. War has increasingly become synonymous with the problem of the United States, its ambitions and pretensions, its intellectual moods, and its supercomplex military equipment, and to solve the problem of war one had to address this presumptuous nation in all its dimensions.

Only the United States today has the will to have a global foreign policy, to believe that every part of the world was potentially important to it and that it has both the right and the obligation to be as active as it thinks necessary everywhere. It possesses a spectrum of strategies that premise an activist role for itself, and they allow it to regulate each and every continent's fate. It believes it has the military resources or will obtain more lethal versions of them, that its economy can afford interventionism and maintain prosperity domestically, and that the American public will support whatever intervention is necessary to set the affairs of some country or region on the political and economic path it deems essential. This grandiose mission was always bipartisan, and there is a fundamental consensus that the two parties share, however much they disagree—mainly for temporary election purposes—on details.

The United States did not acknowledge after Korea and Vietnam that its ambitions and strategies had limits. It could not abandon its hubris, its sense of destiny, or the assumption that the answer to political complexities was simply to spend more money on more military equipment. Apart from the fact it would have been a calamity to the military-dependent industries, there was the question of an overweening sense of mission that dated back to the nineteenth century.

What US leaders could not internalize fully, though abstractly they conceded it might happen, was that US global pretensions would make it a magnet for trouble and that the war might come to its own shores. September 11, 2001, corrected that myopia: the consequences of its foreign policies finally came home with a vengeance.

4

The Twenty-First Century: The United States and War on the World

NO NATION HAS EVER FOUGHT A WAR IN THE MANNER IT PREDICTED, and the United States is scarcely an exception. Its grand military strategy always contained an important element of wishful thinking; but as it became more ambitious, the unexpected surprises increased. Its defeat in Vietnam revealed that although the United States had a great deal of fire-power, it utterly lacked the essential political understanding needed to avoid more failures. Its strategy has also been, in large part, defined by the three major Pentagon services advocating rival approaches to justify as large a share of the military budget as possible. This meant a much greater emphasis on highly sophisticated weaponry and, above all, on air-power capable of delivering nuclear weapons. But as Vietnam proved, when its military goals and technology met unanticipated challenges, the United States escalated step-by-step, and its initial war strategy and political objectives became counterproductive. Indeed, affirming the credibility of its military power soon transformed its original aims.

Worse yet, the United States has also prepared to fight future wars with assumptions that have proved completely erroneous. It armed for fifty years to destroy the Soviet Union with nuclear weapons and by sending its ultramodern military forces across Eastern Europe's relatively congenial terrain, notwithstanding the CIA's consistent opinion—which was ignored—that it was unlikely that such a conflict would ever be necessary. But now the Soviet Union no longer exists, and its other real and potential adversaries have few concentrated, urbanized targets. Its vast armada of missiles and planes is largely useless.

What the United States does best is spend money as if weapons provide solutions to political and social problems, and because it is so rich it has not learned anything fundamental from its past errors. Arms can destroy people, including its enemies, but they cannot solve the core reasons why most crises occur in various nations in the first place—reasons that are overwhelmingly political and economic. The United States lost the war in Vietnam for reasons such as these. Even in strictly military terms, its technology and its basic strategy are unsuited to the physical and economic realities of much of the Third World, which is the only place since 1945 it has fought major wars. Since then, the United States has never won unconditional victories in its major wars in which its own troops were involved for a sustained period. In the Gulf War of 1990–1991 against Iraq—which lasted only forty-seven days—it easily drove Iraqi forces out of Kuwait, but for political reasons it allowed Saddam Hussein to remain in power for over a decade. Today the Persian Gulf area is more politically destabilized than ever, and Iran is the dominant and growing power in the region. The United States can mount spectacular forays against weak nations, and some are successful, like those against the tiny states of Grenada in October 1983 or Panama in December 1989, but even its attempt to free hostages in Iran in April 1980 or its commando raid in Mogadishu, Somalia, in September 1993 (eighteen Americans were killed and scores wounded) were spectacular failures. The US-initiated wars in Afghanistan in late 2001 and Iraq after March 2003 will perhaps be nominal military victories, but even now they appear to be political failures—which means they will be lost insofar as the original US goals are concerned.

US leaders have ignored whatever lessons their repeatedly futile wars should have taught them, for defeat is not an option for them, and they have paid even less attention to the dismal fate of other imperial powers. The United States has been alone in its readiness since 1947 to intervene with its own overt or covert military power virtually anywhere in the world. US leaders have refused to believe their own intelligence, as in Vietnam, when it told them that they were failing. Even good news, like the grave weaknesses that led to the collapse of the Soviet Union, was given scant heed because it undermined the political agendas of various administrations and their appeals for greater military spending. Most of the recent major crises the United States has confronted, even some senior Pentagon officials now confess, were unforeseen. But their solution to this problem is "to build capabilities for the future which aren't oriented toward a specific conflict or a specific war plan," as if the same weapons and simply killing people fit all possible challenges. "The whole last century is littered with failures of prediction," Paul D. Wolfowitz presciently observed in June 2001, and then ignored his own words.[1] The Bush administration's disastrous failure to anticipate the September 11 calamity, much less to find weapons of mass destruction in Iraq or receive the glorious welcome it predicted it would receive there, reiterated that it was not the adequacy of its intelligence but basic policy that is responsible for the basic US errors.

The Myopia of Leadership

For many reasons, most leaders do not act rationally in political, diplomatic, or human affairs in general. Ignorance of, or blindness to, facts is surely a major cause, and this myopia comes from their belief in the core premises of their nation's conventional wisdom—a quality absolutely essential for ambitious people. This very precondition of success also makes errors likely but is an unavoidable result of careerism. There is, of course, also the cynical mouthing of conventional positions because ambitious people know that they are much more likely to advance if they are reliable ideologically and politically. But the notion that intelligence, in the sense of objective, impersonal information, influences basic policy is largely quixotic. These core assumptions frequently ignore reality but far more often than not guide a state's policies. That is why the same errors are made again and again. Their contradictions accumulate and, depending on the nation, result in everything from leaders being voted out of office to revolutions. This process has occurred in all nations most of the time over the past centuries, and is scarcely unique to the United States. What is special to the United States since at least 1947 is that its myopia, because of the sheer scale of its military power and its readiness to use it, has had exceedingly harmful consequences.

The people who have run the Pentagon are beset by grave doubts, and some of its senior officers have freely assessed its various dilemmas. Although the four services spent much of their energy after 1947 fighting each other for a larger share of the military budget, which was overgenerous by any criterion, a much larger consensus bound them together. Their common fixation on Soviet power was the main core of their irrelevance. Comprehending why it lost the Vietnam War remained exceedingly troublesome for the United States, and it responded to this catastrophe with congenital US optimism and new weapons and doctrines rather than focusing on erroneous policies. Failure is not in the politicians' or military's vocabulary, which led to yet more relatively minor adventures—some successful and others not. But the US refusal to acknowledge the limits of its power is also the principal cause of why war has ultimately reached the US homeland.

Ambition and Military Power

The United States decided early in the 1990s that it would seek a decisive preeminence in any future war against a modern enemy, especially control of the skies and all forms of communications. It still wishes, notwithstanding earlier major failures, to use force to accomplish its goals, whether quite minor or vast. In practice, it expected the Europeans to play a substantially greater role in keeping the peace on the Continent and to accept and aid its initiatives elsewhere, and it hopes that military aid and training will suffice in most places—as in Colombia. Although it would prefer to avoid overcommitting US troops, and the Pentagon is still extremely sensitive to how the Vietnam War eventually became highly unpopular with the American public, it does not exclude ground warfare. The Pentagon is aware that it will not be given unlimited time to fight wars, and able foes can deprive it of quick military success. But its statements in the *Quadrennial Defense Review Report* of September 2001 and earlier make it perfectly clear that it desires military supremacy in every corner of the globe. "America's security role in the world is unique. . . . The United States has interests, responsibilities, and commitments that span the world."[2] But attaining them is quite another matter.

Apart from much of the world coming to dislike the United States, its self-appointed global mission enabled irresponsible and increasingly dangerous Americans to gain power. Although the style of Washington's present leaders seems bizarre to those with no knowledge of history, quirks and idiosyncrasies among its presidents and leaders has been the case for well over a half century—and the substance of policy and responses to challenges has not varied over that time. Harry Truman was not overly clever, James Forrestal was paranoid and committed suicide, and John Foster Dulles was deeply religious; foibles and eccentricities are almost the rule among those in power. The British government, for example, worried in 1950 that the United States would embark on a preventive nuclear war against the Soviet Union. In the late summer of 1961 the Kennedy administration considered a range of nuclear first strikes against the Soviet Union, and it even drew up the necessary plans. Much more crucial is the fact that US leaders have only the flimsiest analytic base for applying what is a great deal of power: they think they should use it regardless of the political context or consequences. Folly is scarcely a US monopoly, and the assumptions supporting its leaders' policies have plagued history for centuries. After 1945 there were crucial misconceptions of the nature of communism and the Soviet Union, and when it disappeared without war, revolution, or even a whimper after 1990, it was testimony to the fundamental myopia of the entire Cold War leadership. George W. Bush is simply an average US president, no better or worse.

The US obsession with power and its failure to create the world order it idealizes has been its defining characteristic for at least a half-century, and the problems—and dangers—with the Bush administration emerge directly from those that preceded it. All presidents, whether Democrats or Republicans, have sought to shape the contours of politics worldwide. This global mission and fascination with military power has entangled its priorities and stretched its resources over and over again. Differences between US administrations are of degree but not kind, of style but not substance. The perceived dangers of communism have all but disappeared but the dangers confronting the United States—both imagined and real—are greater than ever. But in very large part the goals and challenges facing the United States predated and transcended the existence of communism. The United States has always believed that it had a global destiny. Some of its advocates expressed these ideas with elegance, whereas others were crude, simple nationalists, but the conviction that the United States has a universal calling and the economic and military power to fulfill it is a notion with deep historical roots. That other nations have in the past also believed they were predestined for imperialist missions only confirms that the United States is not the only imprudent country in the world; but it has been much slower than others to learn from its errors and adjust to reality.

The Bush Presidency's Ambitions

When George W. Bush became president in January 2001 he inherited a vast legacy of contradictions and errors, but he did not create these dilemmas. Anyone who looks at the 1990s closely will recognize all of Bush's conundrums and his responses. The unilateral direction he took had already been set by his predecessors, who were far more diplomatic in expressing it but after the same goals. All of his foreign policy statements, and certainly the doctrine of preemption, were very much a part of the history of US foreign policy dating back to World War II. Still, the administration's unique, blunt style created an image of wild irresponsibility—which it deserved.

The new president agreed with Donald H. Rumsfeld, his new secretary of defense, that the nation's credibility would be weakened unless military power were used to deal with any threat to US interests. Bush, like most presidents before him, promised to rationalize the Pentagon's

organization and to do more for less cost, increasing military spending if necessary, while balancing the budget at the same time. An aggressive foreign policy was preordained, but its location was subject to the pressures and differences that always exist in the ranks of decisionmakers in any powerful state. Where the United States would be most active was far from resolved before September 11, 2001. The spectacular destruction of the World Trade Center and a part of the Pentagon, the most cherished symbols of US power, decided that.

Here the role of the neoconservatives in the Bush Administration's ranks—Paul D. Wolfowitz, the deputy secretary of defense until spring 2005, Douglas Feith, Pentagon undersecretary for policy until mid-2005, and Richard Perle of the Defense Policy Board are the best known of many—deserves consideration, if only to set an essential context for US actions after Bush became president on January 2001. The neocons have been influential about where to apply power, but most of the frustrations that the United States experienced after Bush came to office were due to the basic assumptions he shared with his predecessors. Had the neocons not existed, the policy would have been essentially the same, although the arguments in its favor would have been different and perhaps less grandiose.

The neocons have been a crucial but not a decisive factor. Ideologically, there is no originality in neocon ideas, and the more abstract notions they advocate on the national purpose and uses of power are quite traditional. The contention that a nation has military power and should use it in the belief that things will fall into place politically has been asserted in various ways by many countries for over a century, but it is far more elegant when it comes from intellectuals than from politicians. There have always been foreign policy establishments in the United States and elsewhere, singular or plural; the neocons are merely another. Neocon persistence and influence was based not on their intellectual originality or cogency but on the fact they were a mafia, close friends and social soul-mates for decades. They are largely academics and intellectuals who think deductively and put ideology before reality; they are oblivious to history altogether. Attacking Iraq and perhaps other states in the Middle East and somehow creating a presumably more congenial environment for Israel in the region was at the top of their agenda by the mid-1990s, although some were also aware of growing Chinese power and eager to confront it. But the United States was pro-Israel three or more decades before the neocons had any influence whatsoever over policy; it is historically more accurate to stress the foreign policy consensus between Republicans and Democrats than assume there is something qualitatively different in the Bush administration's designs. There is not.

The neocons surely played a key role in the decision to make war on Iraq, but they were not decisive by themselves. There were many individuals who were at least as belligerent, Democrats as well as Republicans, over the preceding half-century. The problem, in brief, is not personalities but policy, and to focus on the neocons as if they are unique or distinctively causal is highly misleading. Their role does not explain US policy in that region, which became dangerous much earlier. The Bush administration would have been bellicose regardless of the region of the world, but that it wanted to recast the balance of forces and ideology in the Middle East was very important.

The neocons gained influence because of Defense Secretary Donald Rumsfeld and Vice President Dick Cheney, who found the neocons' visceral impulses and their skills useful. Cheney and Rumsfeld and the eclectic hawks in Bush's administration were oblivious to the consequences of their recommendations or to the way they shocked US overseas friends. They possess aggressive, geopolitical visions that assume the ability of overwhelming US military and economic power to attain these goals. Eccentric interpretations of holy scripture—which a number of presidents have also shared—inspire yet others, including Bush himself. That the United States proclaims it wishes to alter the influence of Islamic fundamentalism in shaping politics in numerous countries, converting Muslims to secularism, only confirms that it is utterly confused ideologically. Some members of the Bush administration are born-again Christians who believe the United States has a divine mission to reorder the world. Most of these crusaders employ an amorphous nationalist and messianic rhetoric that makes it impossible to predict exactly how Bush will mediate between very diverse, often quirky influences, though he is partial to advocates of the wanton use of US military might throughout the world. No one close to the president acknowledges the limits of its power—limits that are political and, as Korea and Vietnam proved, military too.

The neocons are much more a reflection of the triumph of dangerous men and ideas rather than a cause of foreign policies that are oblivious to the limits of power. Bush, Cheney, and Rumsfeld came to power determined to pursue a very muscular foreign policy, "robust" and "forward-leaning" as they describe it, with China on the list of three highest priority problems.[3] The neocons simply exploited the opportunity that September 11 created to redirect the focus to an aggressive foreign policy in a way that was compatible with Israel's interests in the Middle East. But correlation is not causation, and that this mafia was in the right places and the right time is not, ultimately, the source of the crisis. They are hawks in the largest sense, ideologically as well as specifically, just as aggressive on Far Eastern questions as Middle Eastern, and that is why they got their jobs. In the final analysis, all the analytical and more practical problems that the United States now has can be traced back a half-century or so, through Democratic and Republican administrations and long before the seeming triumph of the neocons. That is certainly the case with breaking alliances. The inspirational notion of the United States as a "city on the hill" is centuries old, and it was the devout Calvinist professor, President Woodrow Wilson, who over eighty years ago articulated the idea of the United States transforming global politics, including the economic and political foundations of nation-states. Comparable groups, with elegant philosophies on the efficacy of military power, have existed in other nations.

Much the same can be said for the Christian evangelicals and fundamentalists, although most of them—with notable exceptions—lack the aptitudes and skills required for high policymaking offices. They have constituencies far larger than the Jewish neocons and are powerful because of their voting strength, but they are neither causal nor original in the ways and purposes of foreign policy. Quirky justifications and advocates notwithstanding, there is a long historical continuity in thinking that far transcends these bizarre eccentrics. Religion has always been very important in American life and politics. For example, Prohibition (1918–1933) was enacted largely for religious reasons. The problems and responses of US leaders are quite predictable, and the second President Bush is no exception. In the final analysis, there is nothing original in his actions anywhere in the world, and no one should blame neocons or evangelicals for any of them.

A World Full of New Dangers

What the US government lacked after the demise of the Soviet Union was a credible enemy, one that could unite the Congress and public. A sense of danger and fear was essential to the US effort to maintain its hegemony over its allies and justify immense military funding from a Congress unwilling to accept deficit financing and higher taxes. Without it, the United States had to find much more convincing justifications for its policies and actions, and not only was it loath to do so, but it could not. The Pentagon and government searched for a reason to justify maintaining bases and manpower overseas and spending huge sums, and they found it in East Asia, which by the end of the 1990s was deemed the place where the United States would be most involved over the coming decade. About 100,000 men would remain stationed in the region to implement a policy of "robust engagement." With whom? This question has not been answered for obvious reasons: no nation in the region will risk confronting the United States because it has nuclear weapons and has declared its readiness to use them. But the administration painted as gloomy a picture as possible of the challenges facing the United States, implying it had many enemies—old and new. As its Nuclear Posture Review made clear to Congress in January 2002, Syria and Libya are "immediate" dangers, and China and even Russia "remain a concern."[4] The "axis of evil," which the president excoriated in a speech to Congress the same month, includes Iran, Iraq, and North Korea.

From the beginning of 2001 until September 11 of that year, China was the US potential threat of choice and was crucial to the justification for its extravagant spending policies. Terrorism, especially by Osama bin Laden, and the proliferation of weapons of mass destruction throughout the world were also grave challenges, but no nations, not even Iraq, were identified by name—save one. China was opposed to the anti–ballistic missile (ABM) system, but so were many of the oldest US allies. "We are competitors," Secretary Rumsfeld observed in January 2001. "They are seeking influence in the region, and we are in the region. We see their defense budget increasing by double digits every year."[5] Rumsfeld's enormously complex task of reorienting the Pentagon, both to make it more efficient and to prepare it for the most likely political and military challenges, was immensely simplified if China replaced the Soviet Union—terrorism was too nebulous to justify the changes and huge military outlays he planned. The expensive technology the services seek is irrelevant against terrorists and suitable only for war against states; China fills the bill.

Like most defense secretaries over the past half-century, Rumsfeld set himself the grandiose goal of making US military budget and strategy much more rational and effective; overcoming vested interests, including vicious service infighting and parochialism; and creating order out of chaos. The *Quadrennial Defense Review Report (QDRR)*, which was presented at the end of September 2001, was the place he could outline his ideas for reforms. This four-year survey is a regular Pentagon institution and has, so far at least, changed nothing. Since 1947, when the Department of Defense was created, the military services have struggled with each other for shares of the escalating budget, which has moved irresistibly toward increasingly expensive high-tech weapons and reductions in manpower and operational costs to pay for their acquisition and maintenance. A great number of jobs are at stake in building hardware, and both contractors and members of Congress influence decisions about funding. What is called "strategy" is the haphazard outcome of a mercurial process that really has little to do with the real world and the quite unpredictable nature of warfare.

The problems Rumsfeld confronted were compounded because since 1990, no one could be certain who the main US adversary would be, but for convenience's sake the review appeared to stress a threat from China. There were many neocons in crucial posts who had long wished that the United States would turn its attention to the Middle East, in particular to remove Saddam Hussein from power in Iraq one way or another, but before September 11 their influence was far from decisive. They were united on the "robust" use of US power, but there was as yet no consensus among the neocons on where to employ it. Rumsfeld's key adviser, Andrew Marshall, the head of the Pentagon's internal think tank in charge of the review, was a long-time advocate of the alleged China menace. He favored shifting much of the military's assets from Europe, where US vital interests were no longer challenged, to Asia. In July 2001, Rumsfeld stated, "My view of China is that its future is not written, and it is being written." Its succession process was unpredictable, and the military might jockey civilians out of power. China was unstable and unpredictable, "an authoritarian system, a communist dictatorship," but also increasingly powerful. In a statement certain to make its leaders fear the new administration, at the end of August Wolfowitz declared that "over the long run the Chinese political system is going to have to change."[6] The United States simply did not trust China, which in turn has been seeking to make defensive accords with Russia and the former Soviet Central Asian republics.

China, as well as perhaps North Korea, has a limited number of nuclear weapons, and the means to deliver them is a definite deterrent to US action. The tension on the Korean peninsula seemed in 2001 to be nearing resolution, if only because the North Korean economy was a disaster and it was merely a question of time before the south—either de facto or even formally—took over what is a basket case economy. In 1999 North Korea was being portrayed as perhaps the leading "rogue" state, but by mid-2000 it had agreed to cease testing missiles, which eliminated the main justification for the ABM project. Only China has the capacity and, allegedly, the will to become the "peer competitor" to the United States. It has some 400 nuclear weapons, as well as missiles, including about thirty intercontinental missiles that can reach the United States, and although the Pentagon has talked of confidence building with it, it also stated that "the gap that exists in [China's] strategic visions" could lead to "military accidents and miscalculations."[7] China's military budget is growing at a rate of some 12 percent annually, and it has increasingly modern equipment, developed itself and built mostly in Russia. Some comes from Israel, however, which has legally and not so legally obtained some of the best US hardware.

China is an immense challenge for the United States, for US power in East Asia is being eclipsed. China is already a major power and rapidly growing, and the way the United States relates to it will determine the prospects for war and peace in the future. In 2004 it produced more finished steel than any other nation, over twice the US output, and its enormous demand for raw materials now gives the South Americans as well as others an alternative to dependence on the US import market. It is now the major export outlet for Australia, and it is South Korea's major trading partner. By 2010 its economy will be double the size of Germany's—now the world's third largest—and by 2020 it is projected to surpass Japan. All its Asian neighbors have a vested interest in accommodating its dynamic growth, and the Bush administration has openly complained that China's aggressive diplomacy is the handmaiden to its burgeoning economic power. Its geopolitical influence is largely reflective of this economic dynamism. Washington has alternated between treating China as a friend and as a foe: it is, in fact, already a peer competitor to the United States because of its strength. Whether or not it wishes to play that role, China increasingly overshadows US power in East Asia, an area the United States dominated for the three decades after 1945. China denounced massive US naval maneuvers in the Taiwan Strait in July 2004 as provocative and responded by mounting its own war exercises. The United States must make fundamental geopolitical decisions regarding China's inevitable political, economic, and military power, and it will drive a wedge between itself and most of Europe and much of industrialized East Asia if it cannot accommodate the Chinese reality.

The one problem, as its own experts put it, was that China was by the end of the 1990s eager to embrace "multilateralism" and had effectively given up socialism in all but name. Objectively, China is a capitalist economy: its income distribution is more unequal than that of the United States, it is quickly abandoning the state economic sector, and the Communist Party's decision in mid-2001 to allow businesspeople to join transformed it into a much broader instrument of the economic as well as political ruling class. The party is nominally communist, but it has been taken over by very able technocrats, many from prosperous families once characterized as "bad elements," and they are committed to the property rights that have brought a very high annual rate of economic growth and prosperity.[8] During the 1980s, China helped the

Americans to finance and arm the Afghan mujahidin to fight the Soviets. And although the bombing of the Chinese embassy in Belgrade in May 1999 and the accidental crash of US and Chinese planes over Hainan Island while the former was on an intelligence mission in April 2001 brought out a great deal of latent Chinese anti-Americanism and nationalism, its rulers are experts in stifling dissent.

China's leaders want to do business, and their highest priorities by far are economic; their membership in the World Trade Organization is the surest indication they seek to be integrated into a capitalist world economy. China was encouraged to develop a stake in the system and did so, becoming far stronger industrially and a great economic power in the process. There is still a Chinese military establishment, and like many nations—above all the United States—it sells weapons wherever there is a market. In addition, China still claims Taiwan as a province, but the Taiwanese have invested heavily in China, and this very old dispute is hardly a cause for serious worry. The fact is that the problem the United States has with China transcends its nominal Marxist ideology, which ceased long ago to be a motive of Beijing's actions. It is a question of power and influence only, for even a conservative China is a threat to US ambitions—not just in East Asia but in South America as well. Despite its efforts and desires to be a part of the global economy on the terms the United States had defined and let ideological bygones be bygones, by mid-2004 China was compelled to abandon its economically oriented passivity and moved toward much stronger criticism of the irrational US colossus.

It is neither possible nor in its interests for the United States to remain the dominant power in East Asia, but it will not accept the reality of Chinese influence in the region. China will not disappear, and it defies both geography and facts to treat it as a "peer competitor" and risk conflict with it. China is a nuclear power, and war between it and the United States is likely to be nuclear. Despite occasional statements to the contrary, Washington is in favor of Taiwan's autonomy and is hostile to Chinese interests and ambitions most of the time. Its planned movement of its European bases and troops closer to China is part of an effort to contain it. All this augurs badly for the future, unless events intercede and drive the Americans elsewhere. But their global pretensions and ambitions remain, even if their immediate priorities shift—as they often have—to other parts of the world. US interest in maintaining its hegemony in East Asia is a reflection of its worldview—its psychology and dangerous pretension. In an age of nuclear weapons and missiles, it is also consummate folly.

The War to End Terrorism: September 11

September 11, 2001, confirmed that the US homeland itself was vulnerable to the consequences of its foreign policies and that determined enemies could attack and inflict horrendous damage upon US cities. Of the four hijacked planes, three smashed into the ultimate symbols of US power—the Pentagon and Wall Street—killing about 3,000 people and causing at least $35 billion of damage. It was, by far, the greatest loss of lives within the United States itself since the Civil War. The debate over strategy, China, money, and much else was resolved, at least temporarily, by the stunning new circumstances. Terrorism replaced communism as the source of fear and loathing. The war the United States has been fighting abroad since 1947 had finally reached its shores.

President Bush immediately declared a "war on terrorism" and warned that "more than sixty" countries might be called to account: "The war on terror begins with al-Qaeda, but it does not end there. It will not end until every terrorist group of global reach has been found, stopped, and defeated." There would not be one battle "but a lengthy campaign." "From this day forward," Bush stated, "any nation that continues to harbor or support terrorism will be regarded by the United States as a hostile regime"—an illusion to Iraq, which many of the neocons urged be attacked first even though there was no evidence whatsoever that ties or sympathy existed between the fundamentalist Al-Qaida and the secular Saddam Hussein. The war against terrorism, Cheney predicted, "may never end. At least, not in our lifetime." The Al-Qaida network was worldwide, and it would continue to exist even if bin Laden were captured or killed. When pressed, the White House admitted that Al-Qaida's links with other global terrorist organizations were "amorphous." In that case, which groups and which nations were involved, and what constituted linkages?[9] What would or could the United States do to so many nations, and was Bush referring to Ireland, Colombia, the Philippines, or Russia when he mentioned the countries that might be involved? Neither the president, nor his spokespeople, nor the Pentagon was explicit. The Pentagon's civilian hawks, led by Wolfowitz, immediately advocated extending the war to Iraq and even set their sights on Somalia, Syria, and Iran. Rumsfeld and Cheney agreed with the principle but not the timing, and theirs was the decision that counted; their opponents were Secretary of State Colin Powell, most generals, and the Central Intelligence Agency (CIA), a division that generally persisted subsequently on most issues. Ultimately, the president decided, but during his first term he supported the hawks most frequently.

Al-Qaida was "just one of the networks" in forty or fifty countries, as the defense secretary argued, and although the war in Afghanistan was "important to the credibility" of US efforts, it by no means ended the Pentagon's ambition to root out terrorism. Even if bin Laden were killed, terrorism would continue. Al-Qaida has not only emerged largely intact from this crisis, but it is more powerful than ever; its credibility has been enhanced, and since it trained about 20,000 men in Afghanistan alone over the past decade, it now exists in many countries. And there are many Islamic jihad groups everywhere that have no direct connection with it—only their aims are identical. Meanwhile, Rumsfeld was asked how the American people were "to prepare for the next threat without knowing what the next threat is," and he replied that "I wish I had a good, simple, easy answer that fit on a bumper sticker," but that there were many new, unfathomable dangers—in the air or water, for example—that required "a sense of heightened awareness," an apprehension and fear. "The other thing we can do is to support a government that's decided that's not the way we want to live."[10] It is a vision that has potentially unlimited consequences and is certain to shatter old and new alliances.

In the weeks after September 11 the Bush administration warned that more attacks were highly likely. What the president called "a second wave of terrorist attacks" began in late September, but the perpetrator was probably a white middle-class American, indistinguishable from the vast mass of ordinary citizens, who had access to the Pentagon's own high-grade biological weapons. He or she was wholly independent of those who crashed planes on September 11 and was never caught. This person caused a few cases of anthrax, killing five in Washington, New York, and other locations in the United States, and paralyzed a significant part of the federal government for at least two months, costing immeasurable amounts of time and money. Most of all, these attacks gave credibility to the president's warnings.[11] Psychologically, the anthrax scare generated an immense amount of fear and affected many more people, making them profoundly insecure.

The press devoted extensive coverage to the nation's vulnerability to various forms of nuclear attack, ranging from spent nuclear power fuel being mixed with dynamite and exploded in urban areas to nuclear power plants being destroyed and their materials released. Indeed, no form of terrorist destruction on US soil—nerve gas and germ warfare included—was left unmentioned, and the very magnitude and horror of the September 11 attacks made them all sound plausible. Moreover, the United States is not well prepared for most such scenarios. Successive administrations have predicted terrorist attacks within the United States and elsewhere for years, but the US intelligence apparatus was surprised on September 11, and although there was twelve minutes' notice that a hijacked airliner was heading toward Washington, D.C., before it crashed into the Pentagon and killed nearly 200 people, nothing was done to stop it. All the warnings before September 11 were ignored, and it is very much an open question whether the US government will do any better the next time terrorists set out to inflict mortal harm on it.

The War Presidency and Politics

A number of things were clear, however. George W. Bush assumed the presidency under a cloud, with the slimmest margin in a much-disputed vote in Florida, where his brother was governor, which was subject to protracted litigation. His rhetoric and responses to the attacks were excruciatingly vague but immensely popular. The president's approval ratings went from 55 percent just before September 11, with "somewhat" approval being about equal to "strongly," to about 90 percent in the months after the attack, most of which was now strong approval. He even had the public's support for sending Americans "into a long war with large numbers of US troops killed or injured" and for military action against other countries that assist or aid terrorists.[12] But although he had no intention of taking this risk immediately, war in Iraq was only a matter of time. His strategy in Afghanistan depended on airpower and very minimal exposure of American soldiers to danger and possible death. The Democrats in Congress supported President Bush from the inception and tried to compel the administration to spend a great deal more for homeland defense and rebuilding New York City. Bush had campaigned in 2000 as a critic of "big government," but after September 11 he became an "imperial" president with new draconian powers over civil liberties, he sought congressional advice much less, and his administration sharply restricted the war news.

What was also clear was that US foreign and military strategy and plans defined after 1990 were now topsy-turvy and it had again lost control of its nominal priorities. "The things that were at the top of our list we're no longer paying much attention to," said Brent Scowcroft, who advised Bush's father when he was president.[13] The Bush administration made foreign policy proposals that were breathtaking and open-ended, painfully and obviously vague projects and commitments whose ultimate consequences in most cases could scarcely be predicted. There were new promises but also new dangers.

The official Bush administration line is that the origins of terrorism do not have to be comprehended or that its existence at this time is no mere coincidence, but that terrorists hate the United States and wish to do it injury because of its countless virtues—above all, its "freedom." It is an evil incarnate, based on hatred pure and simple. Moreover, such an interpretation is a gross misreading of the Islamic basis for the attitudes of those the United States deems terrorists, much less the numerous political issues that have made extremism flourish—the Palestine issue being the most important.

This enemy is highly decentralized, and the weaponry suited for combat in Europe is useless against people without uniforms hidden in houses and caves and spread out over impenetrable vast deserts and mountainous terrain. The logistical problems of fighting enemies of this sort are far greater, least of all because no one is fully certain who the enemy is or even what they look like. Worse yet, the very process of seeking out such amorphous enemies creates even more of them. At least 70,000 and perhaps as many as 120,000 people have been trained by Al-Qaida over time, a significant number during the US-backed war against the Soviets in Afghanistan in the 1980s, and they exist all over: Bosnia, Indonesia, Chechnya, the Philippines, Iraq, and many other Muslim nations. Many of their leaders have been captured or killed, but they have an impressive regenerative capacity, and they have adapted, mainly by decentralization. Their philosophy—and terrorism—is more charismatic and powerful among alienated Muslims than ever. Most of bin Laden's inner circle was not caught, and he is still free—and far more popular in the Arab world than ever. The Iraq War was a catalyst. Indeed, by late 2004 bin Laden had ceased to be a leader of a specific organization and had become a symbol of an international jihad to preserve the Muslim faith by fighting US imperialism.

Even if Al-Qaida's leaders are eliminated, the structural causes of terrorism virtually guarantee they will be replaced. There are now many organizations, some with links and others autonomous, more diffuse and dangerous than they were in 2001. Jihad has grown larger and become more attractive. Islam is being radicalized, according to a leading CIA expert, and the struggle with it will endure for years because the faith itself is being challenged. What the Americans call terrorism is for Muslims a struggle for the very survival of their religion. The struggle has nothing to do, as President Bush has often claimed, with bin Laden's hatred of American freedom; it has everything to do with US policies and actions in the Muslim world—above all, its support of Israel.

Al-Qaida's "resiliency and their ability to reconstitute is truly remarkable," a senior US counterterrorism official admitted.[14] "Today, we lack metrics to know if we are winning or losing the global war on terror," Rumsfeld wrote in a private memo on October 16, 2003, creating a storm when it was made public.[15] "It is pretty clear that the coalition can win in Afghanistan and Iraq in one way or another, but it will be a long, hard slog." Some US Army strategists predicted that "for decades to come" there would be counterterrorism missions for it to perform.[16] In mid-2004 the State Department admitted that the number of "international" terrorist episodes in 2003 rose to 208 from 205 in 2002, and the number of injuries increased by half. But US officials conceded that these numbers are arbitrary and involve only attacks against citizens of other nationalities; if citizens of the same country are attacked, they are not counted. The war on terror, now the principal US international mission, is just beginning, and the chances of losing such a nebulous, decentralized conflict are much worse than earlier wars in Korea and Vietnam.

Hardly any US ground forces were necessary in Afghanistan—about 50,000 US military personnel and over 400 aircraft were deployed from the Red Sea to the Indian Ocean, about mid-November 2001. "There are no beaches to storm, there are no islands to conquer, there are no battle lines to be drawn" in the future, the president said, but the military was more essential than ever, the risks much more subtle but greater than ever. Even if bin Laden were killed and the Taliban defeated, Defense Secretary Rumsfeld warned in mid-November 2001, Al-Qaida would "be carrying on and managing those networks in a way that would be deadly to lots of people in the world." Americans now live in a "new country," President Bush warned in mid-October, and terrorism could strike them directly. The war, obviously, had reached US shores as never before in its entire history, and the president assured its people it would continue. He gave no time limit: "this is a difficult struggle, of uncertain duration."[17] He gave no price tag either, but much of the Pentagon's most modern equipment was designed to fight on very different terrain than mountains and deserts. The war on terrorism was potentially very expensive in both manpower and money—open-ended and unpredictable, the preconditions of futility such as have plagued all warriors since time immemorial.

The Vague Colossus

What kind of war, how great a danger does it pose, and is it worth it? Why, indeed, after the collapse of communism, is the United States in greater danger than ever? The Bush administration implied it had a plan or design, but in reality it improvised as it searched for concrete responses to the attacks of September 11. It was—and remained—profoundly ignorant of terrorists, their motives, and their alleged networks.

The studiously vague US war on terror introduced an element of irrationality in the international order that did not exist until the mid-1990s. The dilemma is that its enemies cannot be precisely identified; its targets are ephemeral, distributed over a vast part of the world; and much of the Pentagon's sophisticated technology is either useless or intended for very different conditions. The war on terror is not only manpower-intensive to an extent that knows no precedent since 1945, but its logistical demands are insurmountable. The war in Iraq will probably be the most expensive in US history. Precisely because the enemy cannot be easily identified and located and the Bush administration has itself stressed that the enemy may be everywhere and anyone and fight "asymmetrical warfare"—to use a favored Pentagon phrase—with relatively small and cheap weapons that give it a crucial advantage of surprise, the war on terror went badly from its inception. After Afghanistan and Iraq there is scarcely any nation for the United States to focus on, unless it is ready for a potentially debilitating and protracted conflict. The "axis of evil" is a convenient expression, but jihadists are much more likely to come from states with which the United States is nominally friendly and dependent—Saudi Arabia and Pakistan being the most obvious.

The war against terrorism was open-ended and potentially very expensive, and its scope and duration defied predictions. But Washington once believed that attaining a military victory in Afghanistan over the Taliban regime and bin Laden posed few time-consuming challenges—after all, they were a scruffy band of essentially irregular forces based on clans and warlords of largely dubious loyalty, and they lacked the logistical preconditions for fighting the world's preeminent military power very long. "It may take more than two years," the president stated in mid-October 2001, to attain the administration's still-amorphous goals of uprooting terrorist networks in an indefinite number of countries.[18] But the war in Afghanistan continues, and potential terrorists are today, if anything, stronger and more widespread than ever.

The Afghan War: Military Victories and Political Failures

Initially, the United States sought Pakistan's cooperation, and so it encouraged defections from the Taliban in the hope it could prevent the sort of vacuum of power and political chaos that followed the withdrawal of the Soviets in 1989, but this cumbersome effort took too much time and was largely abandoned. The use of airpower, including B-52 carpet bombing, military pressure from the Northern Alliance, and even cash and promises to the opportunistic Pashtun chieftains and warlords within the Taliban coalition were all tried. But the Taliban violated the basic principles of guerrilla warfare that had brought them success against the Soviets. Although they were always a largely rural movement, during the first weeks of the war they attempted to hold most of the cities against Northern Alliance forces, including in non-Pashtun regions, thereby enabling US aircraft to decimate them. And rather than send in large numbers of its own ground forces, the United States reluctantly decided to help the fractious Northern Alliance conquer as much territory as it could, which meant they and other anti-Taliban, non-Pashtun forces quickly took the cities. The Pentagon ended by relying almost exclusively on them, providing the Northern Alliance with guns, funds, and horrific air cover. As in Vietnam, the United States believed its credibility was at stake.

But the Northern Alliance's principal sponsors after the mid-1990s were Iran and Russia, and the forces that comprise it have often fought each other. Indeed, in the last analysis, no one controls these tribes, with their profound linguistic and ethnic loyalties and only Islamic tradition in common. Although they take money and arms from Americans and others, they hate foreigners as much as they detest each other. Politically, reality made the US mission to create a united country and modicum of order to fill the Taliban vacuum quixotic from the inception— as events since 2001 have shown.

As the wars of the past century have proved repeatedly, military victories do not bring peace. At most they produce interludes, and if the right political settlements are not attained, then violence resumes, or there is political disorder. The United States has rarely, if ever, seen politics as the primary objective of making war, and it invariably seeks to win military engagements as if there is some independent justification for doing so.

In Kosovo the United States utilized the Kosovo Liberation Army (KLA), which it had earlier denounced as terrorist, because it sought to win battles, and the KLA—criminals, terrorists, and all—was deemed indispensable. In Afghanistan it did the same: it fought the Soviets by depending heavily on Islamic fundamentalists, who came from all over the Middle East, and then it fought the fundamentalists by relying on the warlords, who are loyal only to their own constituencies. Success in both places was measured in military terms, and that was a recipe for ultimate failure.

Afghan politics are inordinately complex by any criterion, for although it is legally a nation, in reality it is divided by ethnicity, warlords and clans, clientelist structures, brands of Islam, and countless other factors. Afghan society on a local level is to a large extent organized around these cohesive mutual aid societies, and the people are fiercely loyal to them. The Northern Alliance reflects this disparate reality: some of its warlords, chieftains, and factions took arms and money from Iran and others from the Soviet Union and Russia, which at one time was its major backer; even India has aided it because of its hostility to Pakistan. Some of its most important leaders fought for the Soviet forces during the 1980s, but others opposed them, and in the fall of 2001 the Northern Alliance even hired some dozens of former Soviet soldiers to advise them. Opportunism is the rule among those who lead it. Without the Northern Alliance, the United States would have been compelled to use a far larger number of its own soldiers, exactly as the Soviets had done. Much of the Northern Alliance's success after 2001 was due to defections from the Taliban.

The Taliban were opposed to opium cultivation and reduced it in areas they controlled to virtually nothing by 2001, but the Northern Alliance has refused to touch it—indeed, its opium revenue tripled between 1999 and 2001, and the United States has reluctantly tolerated it for fear that destruction of the opium-based economy will stoke the flames of opposition in every form. By 2004, with reconstruction confined largely to cities and corruption rampant, the vast rural areas were largely untouched, and Afghanistan's opium output was the highest it has ever been. Until recently, well over half of the world's opium supply came from Afghanistan; by 2004 it was 87 percent. Opium gives local warlords immense revenues. Drug exports are increasingly funneled across Afghanistan's long frontier with Pakistan, whose intelligence service helps smugglers.

The methods the US military used to remove the Taliban in 2001 immediately became an insurmountable political obstacle. With US-supplied weapons and money, the warlord-led militias that drove out the Taliban remained largely intact but much stronger. Fair elections were impossible, and holding them prematurely in October 2004—to meet Washington's demands so that the administration could claim a political victory—only increased ethnic and tribal dissension and instability, threatening more civil war. There is no real central authority, and the armed units under Kabul's command are too small and weak to make a decisive difference. In the early 1990s, when the Northern Alliance took power in most cities, its factions fought each other, and the reign of violence, terror, and chaos that ensued was the major reason the Taliban came to power. No sooner had the Northern Alliance captured Kabul in

November 2001 than its factions again began to fight each other, a pattern that has subsequently been repeated elsewhere—usually for spoils and control over revenues. The only thing they have in common now is their hatred of the Taliban—and Pakistan. Their policy toward women is as bad as the Taliban's.

Many of the groups and soldiers that comprise the Northern Alliance are unreliable and perfectly capable of switching sides; some of their leaders have done so in the past. As soldiers they are, at best, mediocre; fraternization and commerce between them and Taliban forces was fairly common. For many, fighting is a way of life. After failing to find options, military imperatives caused Washington to rely increasingly upon this disparate, scruffy coalition. If there was ever to be political stability in this war-torn nation, they were a poor choice to work with, and US officials always knew it. When honest elections were held in September 2005, over half of those chosen for the lower house of the parliament were Islamic conservatives, former mujahidin who had opposed the Russians and even—in a few cases—Taliban who had fought the Americans. Warlords and corruption were more entrenched than ever.

The United States was exceedingly unhappy with the marriage of convenience it made with the Northern Alliance, and Pakistan regards it as a sworn enemy. But to an extent that cannot be predicted, Pervez Musharraf's power is linked to alleged US assurances that the Northern Alliance would not be permitted to reach Pakistan's border. And although Pakistan occasionally responds to US demands it fight the Islamic fundamentalists, the Taliban along the border are again growing in numbers and power. The Pakistanis often claim ignorance of their existence, but in fact Musharraf largely overlooks what goes on in the tribal areas bordering Afghanistan because the Islamic extremists are stronger than ever and he needs their tolerance, if not support, to retain power when promised presidential elections are held in 2007. The Northern Alliance argued, quite accurately, that Pakistan put the Taliban in power and still seeks to dominate the nation. The US commission investigating September 11 concluded that Pakistan aided the Taliban and bin Laden from at least 1996 onward and that the latter had close ties with Pakistani intelligence dating back to the early 1980s. Indeed, by the end of 2004 the Taliban had begun to return to the southern and eastern parts of the country, where Pashtuns are strongest, and the presence of 18,000 US troops has not stemmed the nation's descent into civil war, its rapidly growing dependence on opium cultivation, and discord. By the end of 2005, four years after it entered the country and proclaimed victory, the Americans believed that bin Laden and his closest aides were still directing increasingly murderous attacks on their forces. "I don't think we're close at all" to defeating the insurgents, the operational commander of the US-led military confessed in September 2004.[19]

Pakistan represents a serious dilemma for Washington. Musharraf is its nominal ally but is utterly unpredictable save in one regard: he wants to retain the power he took when he led a military coup in 1999. In the last analysis, he must have the army and its intelligence service's support, and they constrain his policies. He is allied with Islamic parties and in 2002 kept secular leaders from running in parliamentary elections. He promised Washington in late 2001 to control the 13,000 religious schools, many of which inculcate radical ideas about Islam, but he has yet to do so. He has partially cracked down on the numerous Al-Qaida cells, leading to some terrorism in Pakistan, but they are still very powerful. Pakistan was and probably remains the leading nuclear bomb technology proliferator, and it cooperates with China on military technology. The closer the United States becomes to India—which it seeks to do more and more—the less US leaders can rely on Musharraf. In September 2005 President Bush's national security adviser complained that both Pakistan and Afghanistan were not cooperating enough with the United States in the war on terrorism.

Without the agreement of both Pakistan and Iran, a durable peace in Afghanistan is very unlikely, but polls show that US unpopularity in Pakistan has consistently grown—despite Washington's economic and political favors since September 2001—and the political liabilities of doing US bidding are now much greater. Weaving its way through these shoals has been difficult for the United States. At first it even accepted the possibility of some Taliban factions remaining in power, as Pakistan desired, but it gradually abandoned the idea. There is scarcely any constancy in its views on the future of Afghan politics. The Pentagon was insistent it would withdraw US soldiers entirely when the fighting ended and when they captured or killed the Taliban and Al-Qaida leaders on their list, which they never did. Bin Laden is still free, as are most of his key aides. And although the United States was ready to see an international peacekeeping force in Kabul under the British and Germans, it was also reluctant to see it established before fighting ended. To complicate the situation, the Northern Alliance opposes any extensive foreign peacekeeping force. Russia believes the Northern Alliance alone is the legitimate government, and its best-known warlord, Abdul Rashid Dostum, is a corrupt leader who fought for the Soviets for nearly a decade. Iran agrees with it. At the end of 2001 Dostum also became the Pentagon's military vehicle, but he (as well as other crucial Northern Alliance leaders) refused initially to accept the interim agreement the anti-Taliban parties reached in Bonn in December 2001. Thus the US military opportunism in supporting the Northern Alliance turned out to be consummate political folly.

Nation building was not US business, the Pentagon argued, and it has prevailed because the complexity of Afghan politics makes a political settlement acceptable to all major factions virtually impossible to attain. The United States has encouraged the United Nations to deal with the disputatious factions, but the UN personnel with the longest experience there express varying degrees of pessimism. The delayed presidential elections held in late 2004 resolved little, and President Hamid Karzai's authority is exceedingly limited. Efforts to create political accords between the main factions have largely failed, and Afghanistan emerged from this war as divided as it was in the early 1990s, creating the same corruption and chaos that was crucial to the Taliban coming to power in the first place. Warlords retained about 50,000 of their 60,000 armed militia, and crime and corruption have become more and more prevalent as they abuse the people. Karzai has accommodated them and the opium mafias because they are too powerful for him to confront. The control of the nation reflects the outcome of warfare—those who possess the militia command the ground and define politics, creating a de facto partition of what is only nominally one nation.

The war for the countryside, however, has not ended. The Taliban lost a great deal of matériel, manpower, and morale in the crucial first weeks of the war. But they still hold a substantial amount of Pashtun territory, a region full of mountains and caves that the non-Pashtun warlords are loath to enter, and the Taliban can fight guerrilla warfare there much more effectively. Because a considerable nostalgia for the security of the Taliban years has reemerged, it has rebuilt its base in the south and southeast. But it now has supporters in every area, attracting money and manpower from the entire Islamic world—including some who have been to Iraq and have a mastery of deadly tactics. By August 2005 the US death toll in Afghanistan was already the highest it had been since 2001.

The ultimate political aim of creating a stable nation no longer under the domination of Islamic fanatics is infinitely more difficult than prevailing on battlefields. The sheer equation of military power assured that the United States won battles fought essentially on its terms. But it was the overwhelming destructiveness of this power and the speed with which it succeeded, at least in the cities, that created the very political outcome that the United States, Britain, and Pakistan initially sought to avoid. The election in October 2004 resolved nothing, since all US support and, more important, money went to elect Hamid Karzai in a context where traditional tribal loyalties were decisive and polls meant very little. Karzai himself has worked in every way with the opium interests, appointing some of them to cabinet posts, especially those connected with the Northern Alliance. Reconstruction—which had cost the United States nearly $5 billion by mid-2005—was a failure, and narcotics were the backbone of the economy; acreage planted with opium poppy increased 64 percent in 2004 over the preceding year, and about 60 percent of the country's gross domestic product (GDP) came from the production and trafficking of opium. In 2004, an estimated 87 percent of the world's opium and heroin supply came from Afghanistan. Afghanistan is today a narco-state, living off drugs. India favored Karzai's efforts to create a unified state, but Pakistan prefers to see something like the Taliban reemerge and impose order on tribalist chaos before it infects its own tribal region to the north, a view shared by its critical Islamicist, Pashtun minority. Warlords rule Afghanistan, and the Taliban are again a growing force.

Destabilizing the Islamic World

The wars the United States is fighting in Afghanistan and Iraq further destabilized Pakistan and weakened the ruling family in Saudi Arabia. Any upheavals in either of these two crucial nations are likely to bring to power men essentially sympathetic to one or another brand of Islamic fundamentalism. The situation in the entire Islamic world was already increasingly unstable before the United States took on the mission of transforming it. To win the war on terror militarily but lose it politically would be a disaster for the United States, one it is very likely to have to confront sooner or later.

Pakistan is not merely a major power in the South Asia region but also a nuclear state; there are a number of ways it could be shaken to its core, and Washington was aware of these dangers but decided to play a very dangerous game with high risks. Today there is a strong chance it will see the worst case realized. Some of these issues are very old, involving Pakistan's fundamental interests in seeing a friendly regime rule Afghanistan, and will continue in the future regardless of whether General Pervez Musharraf remains in power. Until the fighting was resolved in Afghanistan, Pakistan had a great deal more leverage in dealing with the United States, but the moment the fighting ended, it lost most of it. Pakistani public sentiment was from the inception hostile to Musharraf's alliance with the United States. In mid-October 2001, public opinion was 87 percent opposed to the US attacks on Afghanistan, and nearly two-thirds were pro-Taliban. Thousands of Pakistani men— Pashtuns—went to Afghanistan to fight for the Taliban. In mid-2004, the Taliban were still using Pakistani border areas as a refuge and logistical base, and elements of Musharraf's pro-Islamicist intelligence service continued to defy him. Pakistan's sale of nuclear technology to foreign nations, which continued on throughout the 1990s, is dangerous to US military power. Pakistan is and was a politically fragile partner, and to base US strategy in the region on it was folly. It would be the worst of all worlds to destabilize it, leading to Islamic fundamentalists taking power—for the nation to be "Talibanized," as one former Pakistani senior official put it.[20]

No one could foresee the sequence of events that brought India and Pakistan at the end of 2001 to the brink of their fourth war since 1947. In October 2001 Pakistan-supported Kashmiri terrorists attacked the parliament in Indian-controlled Srinagar in Kashmir and killed thirty-eight people. Then on December 13, 2001, they assaulted India's parliament in Delhi itself, causing fourteen deaths. Fighting with conventional weapons erupted along the cease-fire line in Kashmir, a line that was established in this largely Muslim province in 1948 and gave India about two-thirds of the disputed territory. India's military mobilization was the largest in its history, showing a willingness to make war. Both India and Pakistan readied their nuclear bombs. India chose to attempt to finally resolve the principal dispute that has caused at least 33,000 deaths and blighted relations between the two states for over a half-century.

The frightening Pakistan-India confrontation, which ended only because Pakistan made significant concessions, revealed that US actions have further destabilized the precarious South Asian geopolitical balance. Pakistan now confronts Indian demands it end its claims on Indian-controlled Kashmir and cease supporting guerrillas there. Any government in Islamabad that does so risks being overthrown.

Washington officials sought to gain the support of both Pakistan and India for the war in Afghanistan, but the Indians correctly pointed out that the Taliban regime and Al-Qaida trained many of the separatist guerrillas in Indian-held Kashmir; over half of those killed there since 2000 were of foreign nationality—mainly Pakistanis but also Arabs, some of whom gained experience while fighting Soviet troops in Afghanistan. Pakistan has been the principal source of aid for these guerrillas since 1990; it calls them freedom fighters, but many are Islamic extremists recruited by pro-Taliban Islamic groups in Pakistan and now largely controlled by Pakistan's intelligence. No one, Musharraf made clear in his ostensible peace overture to India at the beginning of 2002, would be handed over to foreign authorities, including those involved in the attack on India's parliament. But he closed training camps for Kashmiri guerrillas in Pakistan at the beginning of 2002 to placate India, detained over 1,400 people, and said he would impose controls over the Islamic schools from which the Taliban emerged. That pro-Taliban tribes represent a relatively small minority is less consequential than the fact that they are concentrated along the vast northern border of Pakistan, providing Taliban forces with a refuge they use to this day. By breaking with Islamic extremists, as India and Washington demand he do as part of the war on terrorism, Musharraf also risks undermining his Kashmir policy and the support of the military.

Musharraf simply cannot afford to turn the Islamicists and their allies in the military against him, and in January 2002, even when on the brink of war with India over Kashmir, he stated he would not cut Pakistan's aid to those indigenous Kashmiris fighting India's control of the disputed province. He has continued to nurture the military as his power base, and he has been prudent in dealing with Islamic extremists—some of whom tried during 2004 to assassinate him. In so doing he has given the United States far less than it has desired in fighting Al-Qaida and extremist elements in the remote northern regions. He has sought to prevent another war with India, but he also vaguely declared that Pakistan was still deeply committed to the Kashmiri cause. He does not have the power or will to end support to the Pakistan-based terrorists who are India's principal foes in Kashmir. There is an independent dynamic in Kashmir and too many unpredictable factors to assume that the contentious problems there will be settled soon. Equally dangerous, Pakistan has been selling its nuclear weapons technology to Iran, Libya, and other nations, and its relationship to the Saudis—who generously financed its quest for nuclear weapons and missiles in the first place—is clouded in mystery. But they both belong to the same branch of Islam and have common motives and enemies, and the Saudis have a great deal of influence in Islamabad. Friends have become enemies, and enemies have become friends, and everything Washington has done in the vast arc stretching across the Islamic world has increasingly destabilized an already incredibly dangerous situation.

The geopolitical consequences of its wars in Afghanistan and Iraq are unpredictable to everyone, including US leaders. They are likely to be far-reaching. At no time over the past century have the rulers of the world thought about the implications of their actions and follies. For now there will be acute, frightening tension between India and Pakistan, nations that have often fought each other. What the Kashmir crisis does confirm, regardless of any short-term settlements that may be reached, is that any dispute between nuclear powers can threaten the peace and stability of entire regions. As more nations acquire these weapons, the world will become even more dangerous—and hence rational political solutions, compromises, and arms control become more imperative.

Pakistan is more important than India to the United States only as long as the United States fights in Afghanistan, but Pakistan's tradition of coups—which is how General Musharraf came to power in October 1999—makes it all the more unstable and troublesome to the Bush administration. Washington has sought to reassure India, which rightly believed that the United States had tilted toward Pakistan. The United States now confronts a geopolitical dilemma in South Asia that it cannot solve.

Of prime importance to Pakistan are its relations with India and the Kashmir question, and linked to them is its nuclear arsenal of forty to fifty warheads and the missiles to deliver them. It also has a very great security interest in seeing a friendly Afghanistan on its long northern border, which means Pashtuns must control it. Afghanistan is very likely to remain Pakistan's fractious, unstable neighbor; its security interests have now been imperiled. Musharraf lost his gamble there—badly. "A strategic debacle," a "quagmire," is how senior Pakistanis described the situation at the end of November 2001, even before the crisis with India erupted.[21] If the remnants of the Taliban or Pashtuns are successful in their fight against the Karzai government, nominally elected in October 2004, then Pakistan will be under great pressure to get involved in some way, ranging from opening its borders to supplying the regime's opponents. It has done so in the past, often.

However remote it may seem, Pakistan's nuclear arsenal may fall into the hands of Islamic extremists, a possibility that will exist as long as a significant part of the military and intelligence—estimates run between 25 and 30 percent—are devout Islamicists. The Pakistanis claim that they have firm control over their bombs, and they also briefly detained several of their leading nuclear scientists who are Islamic fundamentalists and friendly to the Taliban. But such risks are also inherent in the proliferation of nuclear weapons. South Asia is much more dangerous than ever before, but so is the world in the twenty-first century.

Many of Pakistan's officers and intelligence were hostile to the US war in Afghanistan because they remembered the political turmoil that followed the Soviet defeat and how that enabled the Pashtun-based Taliban to gain power in 1996 (although with the Inter-Services Intelligence's [ISI's] help). Pakistan fears that the Americans will abandon the region as they did after the Soviets withdrew in 1988 and that it will again have to confront a political vacuum and chaos in Afghanistan. The Pashtuns are the most important ethnic group living along Pakistan's nearly 1,000-mile-long border with Afghanistan, and that and ISI connivance explain not only why the Taliban received a considerable amount of food and vital materials from Pakistan at the war's outset but why the

ISI is helping Al-Qaida and Taliban fighters now that the Taliban have been defeated. Musharraf confronts opposition from these people, and although he has purged some Islamic hard-liners, Pakistan's historic geopolitical interests, both in Afghanistan since the fall of 2001 and then in Kashmir and in its relations with India, are a reality that potentially undermines his government. Pakistan cannot militarily confront tension along its borders with Afghanistan and India at the same time. For reasons such as these, many in the intelligence service and military regard Musharraf's concessions to the United States as a disaster.

The ISI continues to be crucial in Pakistani politics; Musharraf would not have come to power without it. The crisis in relations with India means that he must have as wide a base of support as possible, from the Islamic groups to the secular democrats. In the final analysis, however, his power base is the military, and he watches over its interests. Should Musharraf be replaced, the successor government might include Islamic fundamentalists. That nuclear weapons would fall into their hands is speculation, but it is much more likely this way than any other—and that would greatly increase the dangers in South Asia. If Musharraf is overthrown because he has been too close to the United States, then Pakistan would be far more hostile to the US role and interests in the region. Unfortunately for Musharraf, the United States was neither in a position or mood to help him install friends of Pakistan in Kabul when the war ended: Karzai has played the India card against them.

The United States has insoluble dilemmas in Afghanistan. It has not found political or ethnic elements with whom Pakistan can live, and at the same time it badly needs the few bases the Pakistanis gave its forces and whatever intelligence the ISI provides. The ISI gave far less information than the Pentagon desired or needed, and it was accused of being pro-Taliban. Militarily, the United States greatly aided the Northern Alliance, over which it had very little control, because it did not find alternatives. Musharraf's position at home was weakened, and time will tell if Pakistan has been destabilized fatally. If so, then US problems will become far greater—and much more dangerous—and it may very well be preoccupied with the fragile region for much longer than it expected or intended. What was a tactical victory in Afghanistan will then become a strategic debacle in South Asia.

The Conundrum of Saudi Arabia

Washington's increasingly difficult relations with Pakistan are matched by its problems with Saudi Arabia, which has become a much more unstable country due to various factors, of which the US role in the region is one of the most important. Both nations are crucial to US goals, and were one of them, much less both, destabilized, then the geopolitical and military problems confronting the United States would be far greater. The Bush administration's war in Afghanistan created risks, but its war in Iraq has increased them immensely, if only because it removed Iraq as a barrier to Iranian domination of the entire region. The United States must now improvise responses to crises in Pakistan and Saudi Arabia that are wholly of its own making, but the form its actions might take are unpredictable. There have been mainstream media accounts of future Pentagon-led efforts to destabilize Iran and even other nations. Despite the political failures of its two main wars on terrorism, much less the financial costs, the Bush administration is still quite capable of escalating and embarking on new adventures. If it does not, then Iran will exercise controlling power over the entire Persian Gulf, and the future of Saudi Arabia—and control of oil—will be much more in doubt.

Bin Laden has greater influence and financial contacts in Saudi Arabia than in any other country. The Saudis were vital in supplying money and men during the CIA-led war against the Soviets in Afghanistan, and bin Laden's role was crucial. He knows many Saudis who are still important in the nation's politics. But bin Laden's appeal is especially great among younger, better-educated men—precisely the kind who flew the planes on September 11—because of the nation's political and social instability. Many of them consider bin Laden a hero and a dedicated Muslim. Since 1996, when a bomb killed nineteen US servicemen, the Saudis have given the United States far less cooperation in tracking down "terrorists" than it desired.

Saudi Arabia's rulers did not stake their own futures on the US wars in Afghanistan and Iraq. They are reluctant allies, trying to placate both the Americans and irate Saudis. In mid-October 2001 prominent Muslim clerics urged Muslims to wage a jihad against Americans within the kingdom, and they came close to identifying the royal family as apostates. The regime did not allow US planes to bomb Afghanistan from Saudi bases, and nominally opposed a renewed full-scale war against Iraq. Saudi public opinion, especially among the better educated, was very hostile to the war in Afghanistan and to the United States in general. One prominent Saudi political commentator declared in late October 2001 that the United States "doesn't realize that if the government cooperates more they will jeopardize their own security." But Washington did not want to test already hostile Saudi public opinion and is aware of the immense risks if the regime is replaced. "Saudi Arabia is a pivotal country and our presence in the Gulf is strategically vital to us," as one US official succinctly put it.[22] Yet US actions in the region made the position of the royal dynasty, already precarious and internally divided, that much more unstable. The wars in Afghanistan and Iraq raised the geopolitical ante in the oil-rich and strategic arc ranging from South Asia to the Middle East. The longer the wars and their politically unstable aftermath last, the greater the risks. Were Saudi Arabia destabilized, then the United States would confront strategic and economic challenges of immense magnitude, both in the region and with regard to its petroleum supply.

The End of the European Alliance and the Return of Tension with Russia

Tension between the United States and its former close allies built throughout the 1990s, not simply regarding the disappearance of communism but also trade rivalries, economic questions, and policy differences on innumerable political matters, especially Palestine-Israel relations. The North Atlantic Treaty Organization (NATO), to repeat a point I made before, was less a military alliance than Washington's way of coping with the reemergence of German power and of preventing Europe from pursuing Charles de Gaulle's and Winston Churchill's dream of a Western European bloc to assert the region's interests independent of the United States. The United States, especially after the Kosovo war in 1999, had resolved to pursue its aims more aggressively and be less bound by alliance constraints, and it began moving in a unilateralist direction on arms, environmental, and numerous other questions before the Bush administration came to power. The Pentagon's objectives and the budgets to sustain them were defined during the Clinton years, and that the United States should retain overwhelming military, economic, and political power in the international system was always an explicit assumption in Washington, whoever was in office. But style is the essence of diplomacy, and brashness from Bush administration spokespeople muddied relations with innumerable foreign nations, not because its policies differed from those of earlier administrations but because it was consummately inept in almost everything it did.

For Washington, the problem of NATO has always been linked to the future of Germany, which since 1990 has been undecided about the extent to which it wishes to work through that organization or, more importantly, to conform to US initiatives in Eastern Europe. Germany's eagerness to recognize Croatia in December 1991 was crucial in leading to the war in Bosnia and revealed its potentially dangerous and destabilizing capacity for autonomous action. Its power over the European Monetary Union and European Union understandably causes other Europeans to fear the revival of German domination. But for the United States, the issue of Germany is also a question of the extent to which it can constrain US ability to play the same decisive role in Europe in the future as it has in the past. Such grand geopolitical questions have been brewing since the early 1990s.

From the day the Bush administration took office, it sounded unilateralist and was proud of it. Examples abound, from renouncing the Kyoto Protocol on global warming and the Biological Weapons Convention to publicly downgrading the role of the United Nations in world affairs. But nothing better illustrates this tendency than its relations with Russia, its former enemy and nuclear superpower. It showed that however large the ideological consensus between the nuclear powers on "market" economics, their national interests still transcend such abstractions. As soon as the Bush administration took office, it indicated that the 1972 Treaty Between the United States and the Union of Soviet Socialist Republics on the Limitation of Anti–Ballistic Missile Systems would soon be nullified and it stated that it wanted Lithuania, Latvia, and Estonia admitted to NATO, taking it right to Russia's borders. The nations along Russia's borders regard NATO purely as protection against Russia. The new administration wanted to annul the ban on underground nuclear testing, which was essential to arms control. Bush also greatly accelerated the development of an anti–ballistic missile system, which would (if it worked) give the United States a first-strike capacity and which China and Russia justifiably regard as threatening to renew the nuclear arms race. In March 2001 the Americans expelled fifty Russian diplomats from the United States—an action intended to show that the president was committed to a new "realism" with its former enemy. "We are on a collision course" with the Russians regarding the 1972 accord on nuclear arms control, Wolfowitz told the Senate in July 2001.[23]

September 11 temporarily changed this growing public hostility toward Russia, although in private many administration officials remain deeply skeptical of that country. The administration immediately shifted on Russia's brutal policy toward Chechnya because it is an Islamic rebellion and bin Laden's followers are deeply involved in it. But the United States needed Russia's cooperation in the war on terror, and that gave President Vladimir Putin important leverage.

The United States wanted access to Russian airspace to fight the war in Afghanistan, but it was denied permission to fly warplanes over Russia. Much more important, the United States was compelled to rely principally on the Northern Alliance in Afghanistan to provide the ground forces without which the Taliban would not have been driven out of the cities. The Russians had covertly armed major components of the Northern Alliance after 1996 (many of whose leaders had earlier worked with the Soviets) in the hope it would create a buffer along its borders and prevent Islamic extremism from spreading to the now independent former Soviet republics. After September 11 they supplied the Northern Alliance with a new infusion of tanks, artillery, and other heavy equipment. If the Northern Alliance is oriented to any foreign nation, it is Russia.

Washington and Moscow disagree on several issues, the end of the Cold War notwithstanding. For example, Russia wants to sell arms to Iran, which it stopped doing in 1995, and build another nuclear power reactor there. And although the United States at the end of 2001 simply renounced the 1972 accord, Russia did indicate it was amenable to some changes. But among the many troubling questions in US-Russian relations are influence in the former Soviet republics of Uzbekistan and Tajikistan and gas pipelines that may eventually run from Turkmenistan—another former Soviet republic—which possesses 30 percent of the world's known gas reserves.

The United States is now seeking to establish its power in Central Asia only because the breakup of the Soviet Union made it possible for it to begin to play the "Great Game" for influence there. The issues are both geopolitical and economic, and neither Russia nor China are allowing the Americans to establish hegemony on their very borders. The basic question regards influence over the fate of a vast, rich area. There is now a contest in that area, expressed through military bases, gas and oil concessions, pipelines, and similar manifestations of power. Uzbekistan signed an accord with the United States in October 2001 that brought it up to $150 million in loans and grants and unknown security guarantees, for which the United States got undisclosed operational base rights. But in 2005 its rulers let the Americans know they wanted them to leave soon, and at the end of the year they agreed to do so. Tajikistan was even more important as a potential staging ground for US forces, but there is a risk of a resumption of a Muslim-based guerrilla struggle; there are about 20,000 Russian troops on its soil who operate the bases. The Tajiks have to tread a fine line and like the Uzbeks tied some onerous conditions to treaties. Turkmenistan, the region's most valuable prize, is strictly neutral and even refused to allow the United States to use its airspace. And so the Pentagon chose Kyrgyzstan as the least complicated place to build a large air base capable of acting as a transport hub for the entire region, but the treaty between the two nations is valid for only a year at a time. The United

States established thirteen new bases in nine countries, and it had no presence in most of them before September 11. At least four of these states are Islamic and unstable; it is a recipe for new resentments and potential troubles for the United States.

The Russians and Chinese have gone to great pains to make certain they will play a role in the region's gas and pipelines business. And Russia's generals strongly oppose US bases and influence in a Central Asian region that was once a part of the Soviet Union; Putin needs their support. Both nations have the will and the money to exert their power, and the local rulers are exploiting this lucrative rivalry. In August 2005, partly as a message to Washington, Russia and China held joint military maneuvers, and they have formed a common front—at least for now—against US ambitions in the vast region.

The United States is now deeply entangled in an area full of great promise and terrible problems. Every one of the five former Soviet republics in Central Asia suffers from varying degrees of corruption, poverty, and authoritarianism, a fertile breeding ground for Islamic extremism. At the beginning of 2002 the Bush administration let it be known that human rights would no longer be a consideration in its relations with these nations.[24] But it has been compelled by blatant infringements of civil rights and rigged elections to return to "human rights" in a lukewarm fashion when it could not avoid taking a stand on some gross infraction of them—thereby alienating the rulers who are useful to it. Its policies in the region have been erratic save in one overriding regard: it seeks to become the dominant power in that vast area. The ultimate risk is that it will intervene to save a regime it considers an ally, entangling itself even further in an inherently unstable zone.

The problem in the US relationship with Russia is that the latter, although economically weaker, is still a military superpower capable of destroying the United States. Upon entering office, the Bush administration almost immediately turned what appeared in the mid-1990s to be a blossoming friendship with the former Soviet Union into an increasingly tense relationship. Despite a 1997 nonbinding US pledge not to station substantial numbers of combat troops in the territories of new members, NATO has incorporated seven Eastern European nations and is now on Russia's very borders. Moscow regards the Caucasus and Central Asia as its sphere of influence, and it has plans for economically reintegrating the former components of the Soviet Union—of which the Ukraine is the most important. At the end of 2004, in the Ukraine presidential election, it was threatened with an opposition that had US support at every stage and endorses membership in NATO. Russia has stated repeatedly that its encirclement by the United States requires that it remain a military superpower, and it is modernizing its nuclear delivery systems so that they reach their targets regardless of the Pentagon's increasingly expensive and ambitious missile defense system. It has at least 5,286 nuclear warheads and 2,922 intercontinental missiles, all operational. A dangerous and costly renewal of the arms race has begun, and US relations with Russia have progressively worsened.

The Great Game in Central Asia

By installing bases in small or weak Eastern European and Central Asian nations, the United States is not so much engaged in "power projection" against an amorphously defined terrorism as again confronting Russia and China in an open-ended context. Such confrontations may have profoundly serious and protracted consequences that neither US allies nor its own people have any inclination to support.

Such bases are integral to the geopolitical game that is now being played out with China and Russia. But Central Asia also holds fabulous quantities of gas and oil, borders that have yet to be delineated, and extremely repressive regimes. More than 1,000 Americans poured into Uzbekistan to build bases there, and although three years later Defense Secretary Rumsfeld called them "expeditionary" bases, they might still become permanent. Even some Pentagon strategists saw the bases as a trap that might lead the United States to intervene in Central Asia or the Caucasus. In the process of maintaining client regimes that are also failed states, the United States would risk exhausting its finite military resources.

Russia is strongly determined to protect its historical interests against US penetration. The United States is already deeply involved in the heady, complicated geopolitics of the region. Human rights in Uzbekistan are especially bad, a political crisis is wracking it, and in mid-2004 a small sum of US aid to it was suspended because the dictator there refused to implement the human rights reforms he had promised. But the State Department minimized the gesture, and the head of the Joint Chiefs of Staff immediately visited it and made it clear that bases there were "enormously important."[25]

In this context, the new US bases and its political interest in Central Asia threaten both China and Russia. In 2004 Russia said the bases were no longer required to fight terrorism in Afghanistan and should be dismantled. China is also a US rival in Central Asia, and the states there have significant and growing economic ties with China, which also wishes to prevent their becoming havens for Uighur Islamic separatists.

Russia exports military equipment to China, which in turn exports missiles to Pakistan, and the Russians may indeed prefer that China play a larger role at US expense in the vast, rich, and very complex region. China and Russia are de facto strategic partners and might be willing to create a more formal alliance uniting them.

But Washington's activities in Eastern Europe are even more important to Russia. In February 2004 Russia threatened to pull out of the crucial Conventional Forces in Europe treaty, which has yet to enter into force, because it regards US ambitions in the former Soviet bloc as provocation. "I would like to remind the representatives of [NATO]," Defense Minister Sergei Ivanov told a security conference in Munich in February 2004, "that with its expansion they are beginning to operate in the zone of vitally important interests of our country." And by increasingly acting unilaterally without United Nations authority, where Russia's seat on the Security Council gives it a veto power that—in Ivanov's words—is one of the "major factors for ensuring global stability," the United States has made international relations "very dangerous."[26] Russia, which is now stronger economically than it was in the 1990s, does not accept US nuclear or political hegemony—nor does it have to.

Russia had stated repeatedly that it must depend on its nuclear forces in the event of a future war, and it regards NATO expansion and the Pentagon's project to build an anti–ballistic missile system as highly provocative. Although communism has disappeared, the US ambition to define the balance of power in a region of Europe where it has no significant national interests has caused serious tensions with Russia to reemerge. Washington sought to reassure Moscow that NATO was only a defensive alliance while mobilizing the nations around it into a cordon sanitaire. It was of the greatest national importance to both the United States and Europe's nations that Russia consider them friendly states with which it could continue mutual nuclear weapons reduction agreements. Under no circumstances should Russia and China be provoked into perceiving US plans as a menace to their national security. Otherwise, notwithstanding the disappearance of conflicting ideologies, a return to many of the Cold War's tensions and risks is inevitable.

The United States Goes It Alone: Ending the Alliance

The events of September 11 compelled the United States to minimize the rhetoric that accompanied its march toward unilateralism, but the president and his key advisers still believe that overwhelming US military capability justifies its acting alone if necessary. In late 2001, however, the United States sought to attain the same objectives with more subtlety but without sacrificing its goal of greater freedom in its foreign and military policies. The sudden upsurge of its references to new coalitions was improvised and mostly ad hoc. Essentially, it embarked on a public relations campaign, but that only strengthened the impression among its allies that this administration is both unstable and unreliable. It also raised some basic questions within the Pentagon and its own ranks.

The United States informed its European allies that they could offer troops and equipment as individual states but that the United States would be the sole judge of how, and if, it wished to use them. NATO per se was excluded. The French, Germans, Italians, and others offered to send small numbers of forces to Afghanistan because of initial public sympathy for the US losses, internal politics, and their image of themselves as world-class powers. Initially the United States did not want them, but it accepted these offers when it became clear the war, especially its aftermath, would take longer than the Pentagon expected. But it did not consult European states at all on military matters and treated them with indifference and disdain on political and legal questions, ranging from how and where alleged terrorists were to be tried, to the composition of the new regime in Afghanistan, to possible expansion of the war to Iraq and elsewhere—frightening most of its important NATO allies. The war in Afghanistan was fought without NATO but on US terms by a "floating" coalition "of the willing," a model for future conflicts "that will," according to Rumsfeld, "evolve and change over time depending on the activity and circumstances of the country."[27]

The president told Congress on September 20, 2001, that the United States would decide which state was providing terrorism "aid or a safe haven" and "pursue" it. A year later, in what may be described as a more grandiose statement of objectives and means—a doctrine—Bush declared that the United States would fight "preemptive" wars if necessary. "Rogue states" with weapons of mass destruction would be attacked before they could inflict damage on others, and a new era in international relations existed. But his rhetoric could mean anything, for the practice of preemption was a century old in the Western Hemisphere. It was common after 1947 for the United States to install and bolster friendly tyrants, covertly or sending its own troops if necessary, to determine the political destinies of innumerable nations everywhere. Not only Iraq was mentioned as the next possibly to feel US wrath. Sudan, Somalia, and even Indonesia and the Philippines would also somehow have to confront US military power in some undefined way.

In October 2001 the United States sent a letter to the United Nations stating that it reserved the right to take military action against countries other than Afghanistan. War would begin, not end, there.

Meanwhile, the impression of US instability and belligerence was reinforced by official references to "floating coalitions," "revolving coalitions," and the like, as if nations had no enduring interests and could or would make ephemeral alliances to suit Washington's fancy to fight what it termed "a new kind of war."[28] But the very concept is obviously superficial, can mean anything, and is merely a mask for US unilateralism. In essence, the Bush administration finally did what was inevitable after 1990 and especially after the Kosovo War in 1999: it ignored and broke up the alliances the United States had inherited from over forty years of the Cold War, reshaping relations with the powerful nations of Europe and the future of the world. The Iraq War became the focus of this profound shift in the world's power alignments, but it was both expected and long overdue. The prospect of war in Iraq, and then the conflict itself after March 2003, was the breaking point for the United States and its former allies. The nations that had followed the US lead had new potential domestic political dangers and constraints, but the origins of the schism went back at least a decade and were due to the fact the Cold War was over.

In much of the world, public opinion had been turning against the United States even before Bush came to power, and before September 11 it was seen as selfishly unilateralist and anti-European—over 70 percent of Britain, Germany, and France felt this way in August 2001. The events of September 11 caused a groundswell of sympathy for the United States, and the war in Afghanistan was genuinely popular in Europe only temporarily, but the critical mood returned as soon as Bush declared war on the vaguely defined "axis of evil" and stressed his unilateralism, commitment to preemption, and simplistic philosophy. Whatever informal coalition on the war against terrorism had existed in late 2001 began to disintegrate as US policy became far more ambitious. In the Middle East and especially Turkey, people became convinced—with ample reason—that the United States was out to transform the entire region and all of Islam. Even in the largest Latin American nations, growing animosity toward the United States came to a head as the war against Iraq was debated widely. In 2002, although the United States retained friends in Japan, the Philippines, and a number of countries, opinion in most places was increasingly critical—in twenty of twenty-seven nations, including Germany, Pakistan, Turkey, Italy, and Great Britain, the "image" of the United States had fallen. The war in Iraq began in March 2003, and by May in five of seven NATO nations surveyed, the populace supported a foreign policy more inde-pendent of the United States—from 57 percent of the Germans to 76 percent of the French. When comprehensive polls were released in September 2004, the percentage of Europeans who disapproved of a US foreign policy based on strong leadership had increased 20 percent in two years and reached 76 percent. Public opinion in Islamic nations was already highly critical, and although Western European opinion of the United States in 2005 remained stable—it could hardly get more nega-tive—more Europeans wanted their countries to pursue a more indepen-dent foreign policy. The United States was isolated more than ever.[29]

After April 2003 Americans became markedly more critical as the fighting in Iraq continued, but a majority still supported the war in June 2004, and, of course, Bush was reelected, although the rest of the world overwhelmingly preferred his opponent. International cooperation exists principally when there is a menace that nations can agree upon, and the polls showed it. As the war with Iraq was debated, whatever consensus had existed after 1990 dissolved, and many of Washington's traditional allies now feared its unilateralism more than they did terrorism. The coalition against terrorism was vanishing, and so was the Cold War's organizational legacies.

But Europe's leaders knew that opinion was shifting and sending or leaving their troops in Iraq might cost them elections. Europe had fewer domestic problems in 2004 than at any time in over a century, and its leaders wanted no part of the vague US ambition to transform the world, beginning with the Middle East. Alliances with the United States, espe-cially NATO, were no longer in Europe's interest. Essentially, the Bush administration agreed.

*   *   *

Beginning with the presidency of George W. Bush, there have been innumerable crises between the United States and its former allies and friends. Although such dramatic shifts have been common enough in the past, they occurred with increasing frequency after 2001, until now the entire international system is being shaken to its foundations. The pre-dictability that existed before 1990 has disappeared, and the US claims to leadership no longer have justification. The dilemma its former part-ners confronted was made plain by the protracted discussion throughout 2002 of a possible US attack on Saddam Hussein's Iraq and other coun-tries. Not only did NATO split, becoming functionally useless, but nations that had once been friendly to the United States, like Turkey, effectively asserted their independence, and world public opinion became alienated by US plans and then its action. To an extent that had never been the case before, whether political leaders followed Washington's dictates or maintained their independence became decisive in elections. The Iraq War was not the major turning point, which had begun to occur a decade or so earlier. It was, however, a threshold that isolated a unilateralist megapower to an extent that had no precedent, that brought together festering issues and ended an era, ushering in the new world of unpredictability and conflict in which we now live.

Alliances have been a major cause of wars throughout modern history, removing inhibitions that might otherwise have caused Germany, France, and countless other nations to reflect much more cautiously before embarking on death and destruction. The dissolution of all alliances is a crucial precondition of a world without wars.

US strength, to an important extent, has rested on its ability to convince other nations that it was in their vital interests to see the United States prevail in its global role. With the loss of that ability will come a fundamental change in the international system, a change whose implications and consequences may ultimately be as far-reaching as the dissolution of the Soviet bloc. The unlimited scope of the US world role is now far more dangerous and ambitious than when communism existed, if only because it believes there is no power that can thwart it. But it was fear of the Soviet Union alone that gave NATO its raison d'être and provided Washington with the justification for its global pretensions. Enemies have disappeared, and new ones—many once former allies and congenial states—have taken their places. The United States, to a degree to which it is itself uncertain, needs alliances. But even friendly nations are less likely than ever to be bound into complaisant "coalitions of the willing."

Preemptive Action in an Era of Instability

Nothing in President Bush's extraordinarily vague doctrine, promulgated on September 19, 2002, of fighting "preemptive" wars, unilaterally if necessary, was a fundamental new departure from previous US policy. His vision extends far beyond the constraints inherent in alliances, much less agreeing to conform to the decisions of the United Nations. This "new" era in international relations, with momentous implications for war and world peace, in fact began long before 2002, but it was inevitable that the unilateralists in charge of US foreign policy would bring it to its logical conclusion. Genuine dialogue or consultation with its NATO allies was out of the question, and all Bush did was make that policy more explicit. Bush's policies, notwithstanding the brutal way in which they have been expressed or implemented, follow directly and logically from the crucial decisions made after the war with the former Yugoslavia in 1999. NATO members' refusal to contribute the soldiers and equipment essential to end warlordism and allow fair elections to be held in Afghanistan (it sent five times as many troops to Kosovo in 1999) is the logical result of US disdain for the alliance.

The world today is increasingly dangerous for the United States. Since communism's demise destroyed the core premises of the post-1945 alliance system, more nations have obtained nuclear weapons and the means of delivering them; destructive small arms are much more abundant; there are more local and civil wars than ever, especially in regions like Eastern Europe that had not experienced any for nearly a half-century; and there is terrorism—the poor and weak man's ultimate weapon—on a scale that never before existed. The political, economic, and cultural causes of instability and conflict are growing, and expensive weapons are irrelevant—save to the balance sheets of those who make them.

So long as the future is to a large degree—to paraphrase Defense Secretary Rumsfeld—"unknowable," it is not in the national interest of traditional US allies to perpetuate the relationships created from 1945 to 1990. Through ineptness and a vague ideology of US power that acknowledges no limits on its global ambitions, the Bush administration has lunged into unilateralist initiatives and adventurism that discount consultations with its friends, much less the United Nations. The outcome has been serious erosion of the alliance system upon which US foreign policy from 1947 onward was based. With the proliferation of destructive weaponry and growing political instability, the world is becoming increasingly dangerous—and so is membership in alliances.

Bush's reelection in 2004 meant that the international order will likely be very different in 2008 than it is today, let alone 1999. No objective assessments of the costs and consequences of its actions are likely to alter US foreign policy priorities in the near future. The CIA has attempted for decades to offer them, and it has always been rebuffed. Senator John Kerry was an ambitious patrician educated in elite schools but was neither articulate nor impressive as a candidate, much less as someone able to formulate an alternative to Bush's foreign and defense policies. They still have far more in common with Clinton's than either would care to admit. Differences existed, but mainly in style, not substance. There is important bipartisan support for resurrecting the Atlanticism that Bush is in the process of smashing and to reconstruct the alliance system as it existed before the 1999 war in the former Yugoslavia, when the Clinton administration turned against the veto powers built into NATO's structure. Traditional elites are desperate to see NATO and the Atlantic system restored to their former glory. But their vision is premised on the expansionist assumptions that have guided US foreign policy since 1945, for very different conditions and power alignments than now exist. Such a traditional Democratic vision is far more dangerous than that of the inept, eccentric mélange now guiding US foreign policy, but Kerry's defeat means there is scant chance it will be revived. Instead, the Bush administration's falsehoods, rudeness, and preemptory demands will continue to destroy an alliance system that should have been abolished long ago.

The Stakes for the World

The United States still desires to regain the mastery over Europe it had during the peak of the Cold War, but it is also determined not to be bound by European desires—or indeed by the overwhelming European public opposition to the war with Iraq. US relations with its former allies have become somewhat more civil in tone only, but essentially most of the nations that banded together after 1947 now have very different strategic visions. Genuine dialogue or consultation with its NATO allies is out of the question for the United States. There have been fundamental changes in the existing alliance systems, in large part because US leaders believe they are more powerful without alliance constraints. Although this process will take a little longer to complete, there should be no doubt that the Cold War geopolitical legacies are ending and a new configuration of nations is in the process of being created.

There is no way to predict what emergencies will arise or what commitments alliances now entail, either for the United States or its allies. As Iraq proved after 2003 and Vietnam long before it, US intelligence on the capabilities and intentions of possible enemies it declares its readiness to "preempt" is utterly irrelevant, less because it is inaccurate than because policymakers ignore it unless it confirms their preconceived ideas. Iraq was the breaking point for US allies, and all the accumulating concerns and reasons not to be allied with the United States came to a head. There was also a major shift in public opinion, with decisive political repercussions, that had been building since 2001 and now made it foolhardy for politicians to follow Washington's lead uncritically. Without accurate information, a state can believe and do anything, and this is the predicament the Bush administration's allies are in. It is simply not in their national interest, much less in the political interests of those now in power, to pursue foreign policies based on a blind, uncritical acceptance of fictions or flamboyant adventurism. Such acceptance is far too open-ended, both in terms of the potential time and the political costs involved. US allies and friends are increasingly compelled to confront such stark choices, a process that will redefine and probably shatter existing alliances. Many nations, including the larger, powerful ones, will embark on independent, realistic foreign policies, and the Spanish election in 2004 has reinforced this likelihood. France and Germany are now far too powerful economically to be treated as obsequious dependents. They also believe in sovereignty, as does every nation that is strong enough to exercise it, and they are now able to insist that the United States both listen to and take their views seriously. It was precisely this danger that the United States sought to forestall when it created NATO over fifty years ago.

The current crisis in NATO was both overdue and inevitable. Its timing and the ostensible reason for it were far less important than the underlying reason it occurred: the growing US realization after the early 1990s that although NATO was a growing military liability, it still remained a political asset. The United Nations and Security Council was strained in ways that proved decisive, but the United States never assigned the UN the same crucial role as it did its alliance in Europe. Even if its organizational structures continue to exist in name, the Iraq War was the final step in NATO's demise.

5

Things Go Wrong: The United States Confronts a Complex World

THE UNITED STATES HAS NEVER FOUGHT THE WARS THAT IT EXPECTED to fight, much less foreseen the political and social outcomes of its interventions. Some of its friends became enemies, enemies became friends, and its proxies have often been venal and unreliable. Some wars lasted far longer than expected and required, as in Korea, large numbers of US forces decades after they nominally end. Military victories generally fail to solve political problems, and interventions often create more of them. The grand military strategy of the United States has combined wishful thinking and its unintended step-by-step escalation to meet unanticipated challenges. Strategy has also been the product of the major Pentagon services urging competitive approaches that rationalize their obtaining as large a share of the military budget as they can. The result is a much greater emphasis on complex, expensive military technology and especially on means of delivering nuclear weapons, above all airpower and submarines.

The United States has never been more confused or dangerous, both to itself and the world, than at the present moment. Unpredictable crises deluged the Bush administration at the very time the Pentagon was chimerically formulating a strategy in which the United States would rationalize expanding the military to combat unknown and largely unnamed enemies. Starting with September 11, reality doomed Defense Secretary Donald H. Rumsfeld to the same failures as his predecessors. But the Iraq War greatly accelerated the breakup of traditional US-led alliances, above all the North Atlantic Treaty Organization (NATO), and raised the specter of protracted war and the defeat of US technology and power—the destruction of the dreams that the president and, above all, his coterie had at the beginning of 2001. Both in manpower and costs,

Iraq was a disaster for the United States. Like most rulers in most places before them, US leaders deluded themselves, and virtually the only thing that was predictable in their behavior is that they would commit folly one way or another.

The Pentagon initially defined for itself one fundamental problem: before September 11 it had long planned to move its abundant but ultimately finite resources toward the East Asia–Pacific region, which it argued remains relatively unstable but also has growing economic importance. Politically this was not an appealing shift of emphasis, but it gave the United States tangible potential enemies—China and North Korea—and the area's great wealth justified its choice. A tremendous amount of effort went into defining a fundamental strategy that did not abandon Europe or the Persian Gulf but was an orderly redeployment elsewhere consistent with its priorities and resources. Rumsfeld endorsed this shift before September 11. That this planning reorientation was just another delusion in the US confrontation with the world's real problems is immaterial—it happened.

When the United States went pell-mell to Afghanistan, it was uncertain what the president and some of his advisers might do next. But not only its allies thought it was confused. So too did some very important people in the Pentagon, who believed that an Afghan war risked destabilizing Pakistan and completely upsetting the region's geopolitics, with unknown but potentially calamitous consequences. Whatever the tactical gains from victory in Afghanistan, the US strategic problems could end up being far greater and open-ended, and it was unprepared for many, if not most of them. "Our actions so far," one general said at the end of October 2001, "show only short term thinking." Rumsfeld attempted to muzzle officers criticizing him, and so their opinions were made in private, but some of the Pentagon's outside consultants were quite open about their misgivings. The secretary was asked about this undercurrent, ignoring entirely all of his effusively optimistic statements on military planning the preceding nine months. "I watch people's behavior, my senior staff and the military, and I'll stop them and say look, that makes a lot of sense before September 11th. How do you feel about the priority now? And yet they go along a track. We all do. We're human beings. . . . We need a lot of transformation in this building. There's no question."[1]

The Elusive Search for Mastery

Strategic confusion has plagued the Pentagon for years, and it failed to attain victory in its two longest wars, Korea and Vietnam. Designating

China the principal (but surely not exclusive) potential enemy was only part of the pending review conducted before September 11. Weapons and firepower still hypnotized it, but it had lost some of its confidence in axiomatic victories following from high technology. The Pentagon should have been much more critical of its well-worn premises than it was, but Rumsfeld and his colleagues were prepared, up to a point, to examine the military's responsibilities. The press was full of leaks on their contemplated report. Rumsfeld especially wanted to change the way that military branches were organized, ostensibly to make them more functional; there would be a "capability-based strategy" cutting across existing service boundaries.

The many attempts since 1947 to reform the services have floundered because of intense service opposition to all changes that reduced the size of their forces, equipment, and budgets. All efforts to rationalize the military establishment have failed. There are over 200 bases in the United States, many of them plums to friendly members of Congress, and they cannot be closed easily, for they too represent vested interests from past strategies, most of which are now irrelevant. Much costly equipment designed to confront the Soviet Union, such as the B-1 bomber, is still maintained. About a quarter of the existing "infrastructure" is superfluous, but by the end of 2001 the administration got Congress to agree to close a few bases in 2005, two years later than Rumsfeld wished but long enough to allow members of Congress ample time to save them. And despite a few successes, most expensive and largely superfluous weapons that should have been abandoned were still slated for purchase because the producers had allies in Congress. Rumsfeld wanted more missile defenses, ultramodern equipment, and flexibility in how to utilize the military services—and he met ferocious resistance. He is very clever and even able, but he was extremely naive about the magnitude of the task and the ability of his enemies to use the press, Congress, and other means to derail his changes. It was essential to save money via internal changes as well as obtain more from Congress. The services merely deluged him with their wish lists of futuristic and extremely expensive weapons, many concocted by aspiring weapons producers and with 2020 as the target for most. The US Army's tab alone came to $100 billion to start with, including air and unmanned vehicles of every type, but the army admitted it could not fund both its "old" weapons and develop the required technology for the new contraptions. "This is by far the most disorganized effort I've ever seen," one general told a reporter. In strategic terms, the military now planned to win one rather than two major wars, for the Kosovo war proved that an obdurate, well-entrenched enemy was a much greater challenge than expected and might take far longer to defeat. More crucial, the Pentagon's specific conflict and war plan was now, as Paul D. Wolfowitz put it, "somewhat hazier."[2] At the end of June 2002, Rumsfeld admitted that the forthcoming review would only partially alter the Pentagon's expensive habits; at least another year would be required before his reforms were completed. In the end, Rumsfeld encountered the same military resistance that has for decades frustrated all efforts to make the Pentagon more efficient and economical.

In 2004 Rumsfeld was still talking about reform, now stretched out over ten years and in smaller increments, but he had overwhelming opposition to confront. Some were services eager to preserve their favored weapons and the biggest slices of the Pentagon budget possible, and as allies they could count on the firms that made these useless but expensive devices as well as members of Congress in the districts in which these firms were located. Rumsfeld was reluctant to accept the fact that any waste of taxpayers' money was someone's profit, but his ambitious schemes for reforming the Pentagon were defeated.

September 11 altered a great deal, but not everything, and those writing the highly touted review were told to forget their many months of labor and to start again, to "think outside the box." The attacks on the World Trade Center provided them with an excuse to avoid the embarrassing compromises and discontent they had appeared destined to produce. China instantly ceased to be the most likely enemy of the United States. Indeed, when the *Quadrennial Defense Review Report* was issued at the end of September 2001, as scheduled, allusions to China were buried in rhetoric. "Maintaining a stable balance in Asia will be a complex task. The possibility exists that a military competitor with a formidable resource base will emerge in the region" was as close as it came to mentioning it.[3] That problem, at least, had temporarily disappeared. But if China was really a threat to the United States before September 11, it was still a threat after that date, unless the very proposition was highly irresponsible, dangerous Pentagon rhetoric to justify its budget requests. China's military budget is about one-eighth of the Pentagon's, and it has roughly 150 strategic nuclear weapons—compared to over 6,000 in the US arsenal. In fact, China's nuclear posture was a minimum deterrent only—at the beginning of 2002 they had a maximum of thirty intercontinental ballistic missiles—and although the number will increase over the coming years, there was no reason to assume they would be any more likely than the Soviets to take adventurist risks. But China is modernizing its military, and the theme of China as the great threat in Asia reemerged in Washington from the end of 2004 onward, notwithstanding Chinese efforts to maintain stability in the region and stress economics in its relations with other countries. A Pentagon report in July 2005 claiming China was a military threat to other nations in the region only managed to outrage the Chinese government, but it scarcely altered the reality. The administration needs potential enemies to justify its immense military expenditures, however, and China will play that role at least from time to time.

September 11 saved the Pentagon from great embarrassment, but it was confused and divided, and the military services were resisting major changes. The *Quadrennial Defense Review Report* was completely rewritten to respond to an entirely new situation the military establishment had scarcely contemplated. Congress subsequently appeared ready to approve almost whatever budget increases the calamity seemed to warrant, however, and there was no longer a concern with waste or deficits. Rumsfeld immediately shifted his statements from getting the maximum from a finite budget to appeals for much more funding. "We are perfectly capable of spending whatever we need to spend. The world economy depends on the United States [contributing] to peace and stability. That is what underpins the economic health of the world, including the United States."[4] The problem was that his assertions proved false.

Yesterday's budget-balancing conservatives were ready to endorse immense deficits. The size of the military was left untouched, but— money notwithstanding—the basic strategic problems the United States has inherited over a half-century are far greater than ever. It is impossible for it to operate effectively in all places, and its goals, priorities, and national interests do not match its virtually unlimited but vague military commitments. Financial costs are as unpredictable as the time required to win each conflict, and the US way of making war has proved far too expensive for the nation's great but ultimately finite resources.

The United States would now develop a "capability-based strategy" because in the "much more complex" world that now existed, all that seemed possible was to anticipate "the kinds of capabilities that could threaten us much better than we can predict exactly where that threat will come from or what entity or what country."[5] The report itself was sufficiently ambiguous to conceal service rivalries, but otherwise it was familiar. Forward stationing, airlift, sealift, research and development of new technology, and the like were essential to deny "asymmetric advantages to adversaries," but the report repeatedly stressed it could no longer predict the identities, location, or even the actors now threatening it. The very forms their hostility might take were now very much an open question.

These doubts have remained because they are permanent, and had actual and aspiring US leaders learned anything from defeats in Korea and Vietnam, they would not be making the same mistakes over and over again. Rumsfeld initially intended to end these strategic and costly conundrums and to make the military more rational and effective, beginning by eliminating some expensive but cherished advanced weapons projects, but he failed. "Transformation" was his word for this process. He took on his awesome task with supreme self-confidence in his eventual success, but he made enemies on every hand.

To project ahead, none of the problems Rumsfeld wanted to confront were resolved, and they will remain inherent in the bloated Pentagon budget. In the summer of 2005, when it was time to begin yet another four-year defense review, the military services were still as deeply divided as ever—the air force wanted to develop immensely costly space weapons, and the army was critical of the entire budget process—and the review remained as chaotic as ever. The army was scraping for manpower for Iraq among inadequately equipped and trained Reservists and National Guard and even asking the navy and air force to provide truck drivers and security personnel. The Pentagon could not fight anywhere and everywhere it chose to and admitted as much. The "war on terror," especially the Iraq War, had made Rumsfeld's plans just as irrelevant as those of his predecessors. Conventional institutions, along with conventional wisdom, were breaking down.

Old Enemies, Old Problems

Given the increasingly unpredictable context, Rumsfeld did not argue in detail for the need for an anti-ballistic missile (ABM) system, which is quite irrelevant, technically unworkable, and in any case has divided the military. But the Pentagon continued its development, and by late 2004, when it received $53 billion more to develop it over the next six years, it had already wasted $130 billion or more, a sum that some experts think is a small fraction of the ultimate cost of developing and maintaining it. An effort was made after September 11 to get the Russians to agree to changes in the 1972 Treaty Between the United States and the Union of Soviet Socialist Republics on the Limitation of Anti–Ballistic Missile Systems in return for alleged mutual reductions in strategic nuclear missiles; the Bush administration shifted its line from its implied willingness to unilaterally abrogate the treaty to getting Russia's assent to any changes. "I think it's enormously important that Russia look west," Rumsfeld commented in mid-November 2001.[6] So long as there was a war in Afghanistan, it was far more advantageous to the United States to have friendly relations with Russia, which momentarily gave Moscow substantially more leverage. As the war wound down, so too did the Bush administration's eagerness to get Russia's agreement on crucial questions of security. In mid-December 2001, the Russians having served their usefulness, the United States renounced the 1972 treaty. But to abolish it for an ABM system that does not work is the height of folly—all liabilities and no assets.

Despite protests from senior officers, who said there was no evidence it would work, in late 2004 the Pentagon decided to begin installing an extremely expensive ABM system that had never been proven in tests. It even began negotiating with the Poles and Czechs to establish major ABM bases on their soil—clearly meant for the Russians, who claimed that they were developing a missile that was invulnerable to the ABM. Russian-US relations reached their nadir by early 2005, and NATO's eastward expansion caused Russia to raise the prospect of breaking its treaty with the United States on intermediate-range missiles. In 2005 the United States still had as many as 480 nuclear weapons secreted in its military bases in Europe. President Bush was motivated more by principle than practicality when he returned instinctively to the profound unilateralism with which he began his presidency. Spending on the ABM will be $9 to 10 billion annually until 2009—a total of $63 billion from 2002 through 2009. Not only Russia but also US traditional allies are likely to deplore it, but the message is clear: the United States is the sole superpower and can define the rules that govern the world. In the end, the Bush administration has only renewed one of the worst legacies of the Cold War, the arms race.

In light of the 2001 Pentagon review's admission and the statements coming from its civilian leaders, it was not obvious why they believed that their traditional equipment and budgetary ambitions would solve the highly indefinable terrorist threat. The world was infinitely simpler for the Pentagon when it had the Soviet Union to preoccupy it. The Chinese signed up via the World Trade Organization to be a part of the global capitalist economic system and were highly unlikely to get into a war with the United States—one they were certain to lose even if they destroyed the United States.

The Pentagon's hastily rewritten 2001 review only compounded the nation's problems, and it avoided confronting the sheer variety and the complexity of the challenges now confronting the United States, much less why these problems existed in the first place. The location of challenges or even the identities of the specific enemies were explicitly left open. Osama bin Laden and Al-Qaida had to be brought to heel in the very near future, and terrorism was a far larger and more geographically diverse threat than originally thought, one that might take an indeterminate number of years to expunge. Indeed, as Rumsfeld put it, "in the decades ahead, we will face other threats that seem just as unimaginable to us today."[7] Terrorism replaced communism as the source of fear and loathing. Internal security would "become a permanent part of the way we live," Vice President Dick Cheney stated in October 2001.[8] War in Iraq solved only one dimension of this basic threat.

The War in Iraq

The US invasion of Iraq on March 19, 2003, was the beginning of major surprises and, essentially, defeats for Washington, a nightmare for the Iraqi people, and a series of calamities that has greatly accelerated the transformation of the international order. It confirmed once more the lesson of the past century: any war, including those fought with high-tech weapons, is a dirty, messy, and protracted affair that quickly goes askew.

It revealed again that accurate intelligence is ignored if it conflicts with preconceived policies, making "preemption" simply another excuse for dangerous, frivolous interventions likely to make the invader's expectations a chimera. The distinction between truth and falsity ceased to have meaning; what was important is that US leaders have justifications for their actions. Next, it shattered amicable relations between the United States and nations it once considered allies, transforming the internal politics of a great many of them to make alliances with the United States anathema and dangerous for politicians in power. It further alienated the Islamic world and won adherents to terrorist and radical causes. And perhaps worst of all for the future of US power and its high-tech way of making war, the United States was now in Iraq, mired hopelessly, as it had been in Vietnam about four decades earlier, confronting most of the same problems.

Many of the Bush administration's critical decisionmakers, including Cheney and Rumsfeld, had expressed the desire to remove Saddam Hussein from power well before September 11, but that, by itself, does not explain what was in the last analysis a war of choice. Most of these decisionmakers had uttered similar statements about the leaders of other nations—the "axis of evil" had long included North Korea, Iran, Cuba, and others. As Wolfowitz admitted in May 2003, when September 11 occurred, the question of attacking Iraq became a part of global US strategy, with only the timing to be decided. One must not make too much, or too little, of Israel's role or that of the Jewish neocons who saw US interests and those of Israel as identical and were now in high office. That there should be a US war in the Middle East to transform the politics of the vast region was a proposition that predated September 11, and there was surely a receptive mood for war against Hussein, but the same was true of other nations on other continents. Israel's highest priority, by far, was Iran, and although its intelligence "was a full partner to the picture presented by US and British intelligence regarding Iraq's non-conventional capabilities," to quote an Israeli military specialist, Israel hoped that the US invasion of Iraq would next lead them to Iran and Syria. "The war in Iraq is just the beginning," former prime minister Shimon Peres said in February 2003.[9]

Israel's influence over US policy since 2000 has been inordinate by virtue of the many Jewish neocons who were appointed to important positions by Bush, but basic US policy in the region had been formulated decades earlier. There are many non-Jewish figures who also influence US policies, and even Iran had a great deal to gain by removing Hussein from power. There was, ironically, a coincidence in short-term interests between Israel, the neocons, Iran, and others, but it simplifies matters greatly to attribute the Iraq War exclusively to any of them. More crucial was the aggressive mood that prevailed in Washington from January 2001 onward—what Rumsfeld termed the need to be "forward-leaning."[10]

Geopolitical Consequences of the Iraq War

In fact, although it was in Israel's interest to encourage the US adventure in Iraq, it did not want to see them stuck there. Instead, the geopolitics of the region—especially after the Iraqi elections in January 2005 brought the Shiites to power—shifted much further in favor of Iran and against both the United States and Israel. For many key Shiite clerics, Iran remains an inspiration. As for weapons of mass destruction (WMD), the UN inspectors could not find them after combing Iraq carefully for years, and the Central Intelligence Agency's (CIA's) experts were convinced that by 1995 Hussein had few, if any, left. The single most important US public justification for the Iraq war proved to be an utter falsehood.

This catastrophic lie will haunt the United States for years to come. Although it proved in Iraq that it could quickly defeat what was, at best, a second-rate army, it has no political credibility whatsoever. Official US reports in late 2004 merely confirmed what was known all along. The Bush administration dismissed arguments that even if Hussein had WMD, there was a decisive deterrent to his employing them, and that the power equilibrium that had kept the peace between the United States and Soviet Union for decades would also operate in the Middle East. Until early 2004, the neocons in the Pentagon suppressed the CIA's view that there was no link between Iraq and Al-Qaida, which was also the position of Israeli intelligence, and in late 2004 Rumsfeld admitted there was no proof of a connection. Many CIA analysts complained publicly that the administration was forcing them to lie on these issues.

That the Bush administration chose to ignore a great deal of accurate intelligence and rely on useful false arguments was part of a much older pattern, also engaged in by leaders of other nations, that one pays no attention to inconvenient facts if they contradict policies that have a rationale of their own. That the net effect of its doing so was to accelerate the destruction of traditional alliances was unintended. In January 2003 the National Intelligence Council warned the president that the worst-case scenarios in Iraq and throughout the region were entirely possible and that insurgency in Iraq and mounting terrorism elsewhere were real prospects to consider. Many senior officers and former advisers to Republican presidents also gave dire warnings, but September 11 represented a geopolitical opportunity in the region. Rumsfeld had argued throughout 2002 that a revamped and modernized Pentagon would be more lethal and need less manpower—there would be more bang for the buck, as the Eisenhower administration had argued in the 1950s—and the neocons dismissed Army Chief of Staff Erik K. Shinseki's February 25, 2003, estimate that "several hundred thousand soldiers" would be required. The war would be short and cheap too. "There is a lot of [oil] money to pay for this that doesn't have to be US taxpayer money," Wolfowitz assured Congress.[11]

"A liberated Iraq," Bush declared on February 26, 2003, "can show the power of freedom to transform that vital region by bringing hope and progress into the lives of millions. . . . Success in Iraq could also begin a new stage for Middle Eastern peace and set in motion progress towards a truly democratic Palestinian state."[12] His senior advisers believed the region would welcome the spread of Yankee values, as if the entire Muslim world were waiting for Texans to free and enlighten them and US wars brought democracy rather than death and more dictators. Statements such as these were an aspect of the administration's reflexive hyperbole—and naiveté. The president even conjured up the image of Iraqis throwing flowers at US troops. The assumption was that the Islamic masses were like Eastern Europeans before the fall of communism, waiting to be liberated. It was wrong.

It is impossible to dissect the extent to which everything that was said preceding the invasion of Iraq was sincerely believed or the cynical manipulation of the media—or a combination of both. Cheney and Rumsfeld were unquestionably wholly aware of the disparity between their repeated statements and the truth. September 11 offered the Bush administration the precious excuse to fulfill the grandiose goals that its most important members had always cherished. There is a tremendous amount of evidence that few senior US leaders believed Hussein had WMD, and they repeated conscious falsehoods over and over, but the very same people sincerely thought that the Middle East would be transformed by using the sword, a proposition that strikes intellectual adults as fantasy. The problem is that much of Washington accepts such illusions and assumes there is a transcendent danger that it cannot explain or identify coherently. But its nominal historical allies concluded that the United States has power and ambition but that it lacks the essential reasoning relevant in today's world—it had lost touch with reality and is therefore incredibly dangerous.

Alienating Friends, Wrecking Alliances

The destruction of existing alliances and the transformation of the politics of many European nations because of the Iraq War surprised the United States. The controversy over NATO's future was exacerbated by Secretary of Defense Rumsfeld's attacks on "Old Europe" and the disdain for Germany and France that he and his close adviser, Richard Perle, expressed. But the underlying problems over the alliance's future had been smoldering for years. The US justification for its attack on Iraq compelled France and Germany to become far more independent on foreign policy, far earlier, than they had intended or were prepared to do.

Together, the nations that opposed the US war in Iraq and the Middle East will influence the future profoundly. A reunited Germany is far too powerful to be treated as it was a half-century ago, and Germany has its own interests in the Middle East and Asia to protect. Germany and France's power is now economic as well as political and moral, and wholly inept US propaganda on WMD and the relationship of Iraq to Al-Qaida, as well as overwhelming antiwar public opinion outside the United States, reinforced it. If Russia cooperates with them, they will be much more powerful, and President Vladimir Putin's support for their position on the war makes that a real possibility.

The Eastern European nations of "new Europe" may say what Washington wishes on Iraq, but economically they are far more dependent on Germany and those allied with it. When the fifteen nations in the European Union met in February 17, 2003, their statement on Iraq was far closer to the German-French position than the US position, reflecting the antiwar nations' economic clout as well as the response of some otherwise prowar political leaders to the massive antiwar demonstrations that took place in Italy, Spain, Britain, and the rest of Europe in the months before and after the war began. The Iraq War put NATO's future role in grave doubt and made it much more likely there will be some sort of European military force independent of NATO and US control. The United States emerged from this crisis in NATO more belligerent and more isolated and detested than ever. Washington has decided that its allies must now accept its objectives and work solely on its terms.

The United States submitted the Iraq issue to the UN Security Council in early February 2003 only because of a vain effort by Secretary of State Colin Powell to stem the unilateralism of the dominant entourage around President Bush, but the entire crisis revealed the impotence of traditionalists in the State Department. The Americans based their case for military action on the alleged existence of Iraqi WMD, as well as Hussein's purported links with Al-Qaida terrorists. By doing so, the United States lost a great deal of prestige and credibility. No one, quite rightfully, believed what it said, further isolating it and reinforcing the conviction that the Bush administration was dangerous. Subsequent documents confirmed that the case for war was built on deliberate falsehoods: crucial decisions to go to war were made long before diplomacy was tried, US intelligence reported that Hussein did not possess the weapons he was publicly alleged to have, and the like. CIA leaders ignored information that showed that foregone policy conclusions were dangerous fantasy, and the administration paid no heed to State Department warnings that the lack of serious planning for postwar Iraq condemned the entire war to unpleasant, protracted surprises. It was if the entire Vietnam experience was being repeated all over again and the United States was creating another quagmire for itself.

But France saw the issue as primarily one of the rule of international law in guiding the international affairs of all nations and regarded US behavior as both arbitrary and unilateral. To this extent, the Iraq crisis impinged directly on NATO's future. The French and Germans refused to support what was an obvious US obsession both to eliminate a regime that it deplored and vindicate the efficacy of its advanced military technology, although the Security Council could not constrain its dangerous action.

Turkey's response was an even bigger surprise than Europe's, and it had serious immediate consequences for the United States. Turkey was obliged to define its own interests in the likely political outcome of a war with a neighboring country. The highly favorable vision the United States held of the war's political consequences, for which it had no proof whatsoever, stretched the credulity of its long-time allies and especially their people. It failed badly—on virtually every count.

Turkey's problem was simple: the US pressured it to allow US troops to invade Iraq from Turkey—in effect, to enter the war on its side. The United States asked NATO to aid Turkey in order to strengthen the Ankara government's resolve to ignore overwhelmingly antiwar domestic opinion. Washington was furious about Germany, France, and Belgium's refusal, under Article 4 of the NATO treaty, to protect Turkey from an Iraqi counterattack because that would prejudge the Security Council's decision on war and peace, but its alleged distemper was only a contrived reason for confronting fundamental issues that have simmered for many years. The dispute was far more about symbolism than substance, and the point was made: some NATO members refused to allow the organization to serve as a rubber stamp for US policy, whatever it may be.

In addition, the arms and assistance Turkey was to receive from NATO were superfluous. The Turks have always been far more concerned with Kurdish separatism in northern Iraq spilling over to Turkish soil, rekindling the civil war that Kurds—who comprise one-fifth of the Turkish population—have fought in Turkey since the 1990s, and the regional implications of the Kurdish enigma put Washington in a difficult position. The Kurds demanded a separate country that would completely recast the borders of four Middle Eastern nations. The United States, in various ways, has relied on Kurdish forces in northern Iraq as their functional military allies, helping them with arms and funds. The United States naively took Turkey for granted, as it has for many decades.

An important faction of the Turkish government deliberately protracted negotiations with the United States in the hope of preventing the war altogether. When that failed, Turkey's best—and most obvious—defense was to stay out of the war, which the vast majority of Turks wanted. After incessant haggling, it ended up doing so, and its relations with the United States have become increasingly strained, perhaps irreparably. Washington alienated a nation that has been a loyal ally since 1947. Turkey has since protested US attacks on northern cities where Turkmens live, thereby helping the Kurds further extend control over the region. Meanwhile, tens of thousands of Turkish troops are massed at the Iraqi border, and Ankara says they will march if the Kurds declare de facto independence or in some way threaten Turkish interests. Even if they do not leap into the Iraqi imbroglio, for the United States it is a nightmare that could become a reality.

Foreign affairs, as the attack on a Madrid train station dramatically showed in March 2004, are too volatile to permit uncritical endorsement of US policies. Parties in power can pay dearly, as in Spain, where the people were always overwhelmingly opposed to entering the war in Iraq and the ruling party snatched defeat from the jaws of victory. The triumphant party pledged to remove Spain's troops in Iraq and promptly did so. What happened in Spain was a harbinger of the future, further isolating the US government in its adventures.

More important are the innumerable victims among the citizens of the countries that joined the US coalition. The nations that have supported the Iraq war enthusiastically, particularly Britain, Italy, the Netherlands, and Australia, have made their populations especially vulnerable to terrorism. They now have the expensive responsibility of trying to protect them. Even the firmest US allies began to ask themselves if issuing blank checks to Washington was in their national interest or if it undermines the tenure of parties in power.

Global public opinion polls, as I note above, showed growing and overwhelming opposition to the US role in the world. The United States planned to restructure the Middle East to make it more congenial to itself as well as Israel, but the plan failed. Arab opinion—even among those once friendly to the United States—is overwhelmingly antiwar and passionately angry, a fact that will only increase terrorism's appeals and its dangers to Americans and their allies. The vast majority of Arabs believe that the outcome of the war on Iraq will be instability for the entire region. In Europe, right after the political debacle in Spain, the president of Poland, where a growing majority of the people has always been opposed to sending troops to Iraq or keeping them there, complained that Washington "misled" him on Iraq's weapons of mass destruction and hinted that Poland might withdraw its 2,400 troops from Iraq earlier than previously scheduled. In Italy, by May 2004, 71 percent of the people favored withdrawing the 3,000 Italian troops in Iraq no later than June 30, and leaders of the main opposition have already declared they will withdraw them if they win the spring 2006 elections—a promise they and other antiwar parties in Britain and Spain used in the mid-June 2004 European Parliament elections to significantly increase their power. In Great Britain, the Labour Party lost nearly 100 seats in parliament. The vote in the May 2005 election—35 percent of the total as opposed to 41 percent in 2001—was the lowest for a victorious party in modern history, and it was entirely due to prime minister Tony Blair's enthusiastic support for the Iraq war. Of the 32 nations that have sent troops to Iraq, about six have already withdrawn troops, and more have indicated they will do so or have reduced their numbers. Although some may keep troops there indefinitely, the issue now is whether nations like Poland, Britain, or Italy can afford to isolate themselves from the major European powers and their own public opinion to remain a part of the increasingly quixotic and unilateralist US-led "coalition of the willing." The political liabilities of staying close to Washington are obvious, the advantages nonexistent.

Life in Iraq

Daily life in Iraq after March 19, 2003, was increasingly violent. Like Afghanistan, Iraq has become another predictable—and predicted—US disaster. In the eighteen months after the US invasion, according to a team of experts at the Johns Hopkins University School of Public Health, the war caused about 100,000 "excess deaths," fifty-eight times higher than before the war. Civilian deaths due to combat were at least 25,000 in the two years after the US invasion began, 37 percent due to US fire, but that figure does not include deaths unreported in the news media. Another study reported that the malnutrition rate among children less than five years old has doubled since the invasion, reaching levels that exist in the poorer African countries. The median income fell by almost half from 2003 to 2004, and by 2005 over half of Iraq's population lived below the poverty line. The "lethality" Rumsfeld boasted about—airpower in particular—was mostly responsible, but violence of every sort also ensued.[13] Large cities, like Fallujah, have been destroyed. The Iraqi response to the war was not at all what the US leaders had expected; the resistance has grown over time.

US intelligence experts had warned the administration in January 2003 that unless it quickly restored essential services in Iraq and transferred control to popular leaders, an invasion would create a nationalist backlash—with the risk of insurgency. The Baathist regime's lack of popularity would not prevent chaos. But key administration officials initially calculated that the existing structure, from police to service ministries, would continue operating essentially as normal, and all that was necessary was to replace their Baathist leadership. They planned to withdraw the vast majority of the 150,000 US forces within three to four months. The Pentagon indeed reduced troops levels to 108,000 in February 2004, when they started rising again to approximately 138,000 and then 150,000. Even at the latter level, they were still far from sufficient. If the ratio of soldiers to the population had been the same as that used in Bosnia, 364,000 troops would have been needed. Hussein's army quickly capitulated, no WMD existed for it to use, and the Americans won a decisive military victory. There was scarcely any resistance to the "lethal" US invasion, but time was of the essence. Chaos ensued, and the pessimistic warnings they had received proved too cautious.

By any measurement one uses, the US occupation has failed, and with failure there came a mounting insurgency that increasingly taxed US forces, which comprised about 90 percent of the 175,000 total troops in Iraq. By June 2004, in thirteen of eighteen Iraqi provinces, which had a population of 20 million people, electricity was below the already low prewar levels. Widespread looting dismantled the complex electrical network. Electricity was a key element in reconstruction, but in the year after May 2003, as the insurgency sabotaged it, the electricity supply fell sharply throughout the country. In late 2004, Norwegian experts working with Iraqi authorities estimated that 85 percent of the households had no reliable supply of electricity, almost half lacked access to clean water, and nearly two-thirds were not connected to a sewage system. Median household income had fallen by almost 50 percent since the invasion. US and foreign contractors brought in to repair it were much slower than cheaper locals. Fraud and incompetence were a problem at every level of reconstruction—as much as four-fifths of the reconstruction funds were wasted, and some estimates are even higher.

The court system and police—law in general—broke down. Records were disorganized, but the Coalition Provisional Authority (CPA) ministries were severely understaffed, by as much as two-thirds in some cases, even though they were the biggest item in the existing budget. Of the $58 billion that had been pledged by June 2004—three-quarters of it US money—at most only $14 billion had actually been spent, much of it to replace stolen equipment. But some Bush administration officials put the expenditures at much less. Two years after the overthrow of Hussein, the Iraqi gas and thermal generators were still producing electricity at about one-third of their capacity. Even at the end of 2005, Iraq's oil production was well below the prewar peak, depriving it of great revenue. US firms were given prime contracts, and gross overcharges and serious delays and breakdowns compelled the State Department in April 2005 to reevaluate the entire program.

Reconstructing Iraq

For the first month, the Americans tried to reconstruct Iraq with the bureaucracy and resources that existed. But from May 2003 onward, when L. Paul Bremer took over and the first American in charge was removed, it was the policy to fire everyone—about 500,000 people—who had belonged to the ruling Baath Party and to privatize the approximately 200 state firms that were crucial to a functioning economy. The neocon ideologues had their chance to put their theories into practice, and they believed that eliminating the state-run economic sector would usher in prosperity. The theory essentially matched the typical International Monetary Fund (IMF) conditions, and the fund has a great role in managing Iraq's economic future. The immediate result was sharply rising unemployment, which fed the insurgency, and chaos.

Data on Iraqi unemployment, again according to Norwegian experts, estimated it was about 20 percent at the end of 2004. It reached 70 percent in some parts of Baghdad—where Hussein's 350,000-man army had returned after it was dissolved—and those with government jobs sometimes went without wages.

The successive political policies the Americans pursued—too many to be detailed—were all responses to the failure of the political strategy that had preceded it. Washington was not attaining the goals it had set for itself. But all strategies stressed, to varying degrees, the importance of exiles in the leadership of a future Iraqi government, and the Byzantine intrigues usually gave exiles inordinate control of power. Different US agencies had their own preferences, most of whom had taken US money, but looking for exiles who would act as proxies for US interests was the rule rather than the exception. These exiles fought hard, whatever their differences, to preserve their own jurisdictions and power.

Ahmad Chalabi had been the preferred choice of the neocons in the Pentagon, and his assiduous courtship of Israel and its lobby had much to do with it. Chalabi, however, had been utterly opportunistic in secretly eliciting support outside approved channels—especially Shiite and Iranian—and what he would do when in power was too debatable. He repackaged himself much too often to be trusted. The CIA favored Ayad Allawi, a former Baathist and secular Shiite who had been in exile and had long-standing ties with the agency. But Iraqi politics is very complicated and constantly changing, and pervasive opportunism makes it impossible to predict what aspiring leaders will do. They all hope to manipulate the existing political system to their advantage, and truly free elections are anathema to most of them. Allawi's success was due to his responsiveness to US desires insofar as they can be defined, and his advocacy of recruiting former Baathists for the government represents a reversal of the original US policy of purging them all. His party comprises mostly former Baathist officials, many of whom returned to their old posts and even the same methods—including massive corruption—

that existed under Hussein. The nominal transfer of authority to his government on June 28, 2004, which merely gave the CPA a new name, was
ceremonial and meaningless.

The United States based its initial political strategy on brokering
deals with regional ethnic interests and local urban councils, some of
which had come into existence spontaneously, self-selected without
votes, and some of which the Americans simply created. As administrative units, they failed to remedy the vacuum that existed nationally, and
they had paltry budgets. The initial US commitment to an unequivocal
purge of Baathist officials deprived it of their skills and experience,
driving many into the resistance. Allawi pragmatically shifted partway
on this issue. The Bush administration replaced its own administrators
and modified the technical conditions of its political goals several
times, but the exile politicians remained crucial in the CPA, and they
fought hard to keep power. At the same time, the Americans made certain that the CPA's economic strategy enshrined the principles of private, as opposed to state control, of the economy and that US firms got
the largest chunk of the lucrative reconstruction contracts. Politics based
on ethnicity, which has always been a reality, strengthened the latent
divisions in a country that was little more than an arbitrary British creation established after the destruction of the Ottoman Empire during
World War I. But the United States stressed making deals with the
important tribes, religions, and parties, many of whom actually run their
turf, at the same time assuring that its wishes were respected, including
its desire for permanent bases in the future. All the major ethnic groups
are deeply divided. Although the Shiites constitute about 60 percent of
the population, they too are split—many look to Shiite Iran for inspiration, which made a truly democratic election and representation risky
for the United States. Iraqi politicians who want much closer relations
with Iran, which in the summer of 2005 included Prime Minister Ibrahim
al-Jaafari, were well placed—which was reflected in the intimacy that
developed between the two nations. But even a crucial section of the
Kurds supports friendlier relations with Iran. Iran, for its part, favors
elections. But so long as Iran, a charter member of the "axis of evil,"
stands to gain so much strategic influence from the US war against Hussein's regime, the United States will keep troops in Iraq. At stake is
domination of the entire region.

The net effect of US efforts—despite its nominal commitment to
elections—is to encourage those forces that will divide the country, de
facto if not formally, making the former Yugoslavia the model for its
future. Regional and local leaders are becoming stronger, and the central
government is growing weaker. But the threat of secession has existed in

the Kurdish north for decades, and the Kurds claim the oil-rich region around the city of Kirkuk as their own—as well as Mosul, originally a non-Kurdish city, and other strategic areas in the north from which they will expand their largely autonomous, if not independent, orbit. Like the Shiites, they control many of the nominally Iraqi army and police forces in their area. They also assert that they have the right to sign contracts granting oil exploration leases, and they have exercised it. The three provinces around the southern city of Basra, which has the most oil in Iraq, have already met to discuss creating an "autonomous" district—a symptom of the fragmentation of the country that very well may lead to civil war. Turkey has watched these developments with mounting dismay, and the Turks correctly regard US reliance on the Kurds to control northern Iraq as a recipe for secession, even though the federal self-rule they enjoyed until July 2004 has been eliminated in return for their being given charge of the crucial defense and foreign affairs ministries. They still control the northern region and demand autonomy and veto power over central government decrees. The Kurdish problem will eventually explode again.

The worst case scenario is civil war in Iraq. The country could just break up peacefully, and the federalism embodied in the constitution ratified in October 2005 is a major step in that direction. Many Shiites want to follow Islamic laws and create a theocracy like that in Iran. Kurds are mainly secular and seek de facto autonomy, if not independence. Both want control over their region's oil revenue, and that is the nub of all the still unresolved debates over the constitution and the form of future governments. The Sunnis ruled Saddam Hussein's regime and are now no more than a small minority, though they are located in a crucial region. It is impossible to know what Iraq will become five or ten years hence—not for us, nor for those in Washington who went to war there so blithely.

"Insurgency" and Resistance

To many Iraqis, the large majority of whom were glad to see Saddam Hussein's regime gone, the question was increasingly a matter of when the Americans and foreign invaders would exit. A growing nationalism, nuanced by ethnic, religious, and tribal differences, accompanied the failure of the occupation to return the country to something like normal, and with this alienation violence increased greatly. To the extent hatred of the occupiers exists in every country, there has been a national consensus and degree of unity.

There was no resistance of importance in the months immediately after March 2003, and what there was posed few problems for US forces. In February 2004 there were 411 "significant insurgent attacks," as defined by the CPA, and 1,169 in May, and over 2,300 in September 2004—a thousand in Baghdad that last month, when no place in that city was immune from attack. But Pentagon numbers were considerably higher: from 700 in March 2004 to 2,700 in August. At least twenty-two cities were under insurgent control by October 2004. Not a single province had been spared an attack, and at the end of September Secretary of State Powell admitted the insurgency was getting worse. Violence has increased steadily since then, but much of it was directed at other Iraqis as the risk of civil war among the religious factions mounted. Some, indeed, belong to the same religion but are struggling with each other for power. The insurgents were mostly Iraqis, rather than foreigners attracted to Iraq to fight a jihad against Americans—though some existed—and their numbers were debated. Some sources gave numbers as high as 120,000, but 8,000 to especially 12,000—full-time—are the figures used by the US military. But this number increases to over 20,000 when sympathizers are included, and the insurgency is growing both in size and skill.[14]

The insurgents are a very motley bunch; at least thirty-five organizations identified themselves with the resistance after the US invasion. Nationalism is a common denominator for most of them, and although officers and soldiers of the former Iraqi army—sometimes against their will—have given them expertise they did not have at the inception, especially in Sunni regions, insurgents are recruited from very diverse elements, and the majority are anti-Baathist. Some are simply local tribal warriors, others are criminals posing as patriots, but many are part of diverse religious militia and are therefore potentially more threatening. Religious fundamentalists are growing increasingly important among the resistance. Some have joined the insurgency because Americans have killed members of their family and they seek revenge. US firepower has been incredibly destructive, but it has also galvanized people to resist who otherwise would not—and that it creates a self-fulfilling prophecy is one of its basic contradictions. There are many factions within the resistance, and all they share is their hatred of Americans. Nationalism unites otherwise divided constituencies. Jordanian-born Abu Musab Zarqawi plays a role as a facilitator with arms and money, but his importance, along with that of foreign fighters, is greatly exaggerated. The CIA says he does not coordinate with Al-Qaida but merely has common aims.

A major reason for insurgent success is the vast size of the country and the inability of the limited number of US forces to occupy it. There are towns that are infrequently, if ever, patrolled, and the tendency is for a significant number of US officers to make accommodations with local leaders and police to maintain order for them—many of these towns thereby become safe havens for insurgents. These deals solve an immediate US problem, but who actually controls an area is always in doubt—and insurgents and locals can exist a very long time in such an environment. Cities and important areas fall into insurgent hands by default, and gaining them back is often a major operation. US forces can easily win battles for cities, but they cannot hold them without tying down most of their soldiers—a fact that some senior officers concede. The option, which is to increase the number of US forces greatly to occupy and pacify the entire country, does not exist without reinstating the draft in the United States. Both manpower shortages and costs, not to mention the patience of the American people and the sinking morale of US troops in Iraq, make the war quixotic.

The ultimate US solution for preventing its troops from being mired for years in Iraq is an "exit strategy"—as Rumsfeld put it in October 2004, to "build up Iraqi forces, [and] we will be able to relieve the stress on our forces and see a reduction in coalition forces over some period of time."[15] This strategy was only reluctantly adopted well into 2004, when it became apparent that the insurgency was growing stronger and US forces were unable to defeat it alone. In mid-2004 there were nominally about 220,000 men in Iraqi armed forces, police, and civil defense units, but in fact there are far fewer. The police were to have 135,000 trained men but by mid-2005 had about half that number, nearly all of whom were useless. When fighting begins, many of them disappear. The Iraqi National Guard had a target of 61,900 recruits, but only 38,300 were trained. The police had 41 percent of their required weapons and 25 percent of the vehicles they needed. Independent experts think the Iraqi army will not be able to replace US forces for five years—some say a decade. No one, including the Pentagon, knows what the real strength of Iraqi forces is, but both in numbers and discipline, it is considerably less than they claim. Worse yet, it is unsure of the extent to which Shiite, Kurdish, tribal, and even criminal elements have joined these armed forces in order to exploit the freedom, money, and guns that the United States is eager to provide them. The Pentagon is contemplating establishing a number of permanent bases in Iraq, ostensibly to prevent civil war in the country, but their number and troop requirements have to wait until the insurgency is over. There is scant chance the United States will leave Iraq willingly. The administration now estimates it may be there in force many years from now.

The United States disbanded Hussein's 350,000-man army soon after arriving in Baghdad, which caused massive unemployment and drove some of them—especially officers—into the resistance. But there was disagreement in Washington over this strategy, and some of these soldiers were still given nominal salaries. The chief American in Baghdad soon after the invasion, L. Paul Bremer, made the decision to build a new army battalion by battalion in the hope it would fight other Iraqis as the United States wished. Yet apart from the fact that roughly only one-third of the personnel essential to train these forces existed in September 2004, no one trusted these new recruits. Roughly 5 percent of them, up to the highest levels, were insurgents who had infiltrated these forces to obtain arms and intelligence. A far larger proportion was simply taking salaries as a way of making a living, but many have tribal and other ties to the insurgents. They were often neutral, but in Fallujah in May 2004 the brigade the Americans formed gave 800 AK-47 assault rifles, twenty-seven pickup trucks, and fifty radios to the insurgents, and some joined them. In Samarra, 300 of 750 soldiers abandoned their battalion before an offensive began. By mid-2005 only three of the 107 military and paramilitary Iraqi battalions the US had created could plan, execute, and sustain independent counterinsurgency operations. But then that number fell to one by late 2005. On the whole, "Iraqization" is a failure.

The United States has never been able to rely on proxies to save it from grave failures. In that crucial regard, Vietnam and Iraq are alike. The United States pursued a very similar strategy by attempting to "Vietnamize" the war there, with the identical result: defeat.

The Failure of US Strategy

Over 2,000 US soldiers had been killed in the Iraq War by late 2005, most after Baghdad was occupied, and the number rose as the insurgency became more proficient.

The Iraq War, like virtually all wars fought by all nations before it, turned out to be a nightmare for the United States, destroying all predictions and expectations. It has compelled the Pentagon to wholly rethink Rumsfeld's strategy for "transformation" of US military power—which is predicated on very short wars that "shock and awe" its enemies. Putting aside its immense geopolitical and strategic consequences for the moment, everything went wrong from the beginning. The existence of weapons of mass destruction was the one justification for attacking Hussein "that," as Wolfowitz commented in May 2003, "everyone could agree on."[16] But there were none, and although most leading US officials knew this all along, others—including the president—very likely did not, and the principal vindication of the war, which alienated more of its former allies than any other, proved an embarrassing falsehood. But it was scarcely the only example of the uselessness of its intelligence. The Americans began the war by attacking fifty "high-value" targets that were supposed to contain the regime's leaders, and all were unsuccessful. From the inception, US intelligence was very expensive but poor, and in July 2004 the Pentagon admitted it did not know whether the insurgency in Iraq was coordinated. Meanwhile, the war in Iraq was a gift to Osama bin Laden and the terrorist cause. Secretary of State Powell admitted in September 2004 that "we have seen an increase of anti-Americanism in the Muslim world," a point that Saudi Arabians, who have experienced growing extremism, made even more strongly the following month.[17] The insurgency in Iraq was getting stronger; the Muslim world was being radicalized, and it is more anti-American than ever.

US officers in Iraq found the war utterly different than the conditions for which Rumsfeld's high-tech expensive equipment was suited. Technologies designed for Cold War conditions were irrelevant in low-tech environments. Indeed, in 1998, long before Rumsfeld had the opportunity to revamp the military, the size of each battalion was reduced by a company—or as much as one-third—in order to pay for high-tech weapons, and the army had substantially less manpower for the war than it later required. Field-training opportunities for young officers dropped by half from 1995 onward, and the number of captains leaving the army doubled over this period. The emphasis was on high-tech, not conventional war. But in Iraq soldiers had to go down narrow alleyways in slums full of children. If they used firepower, they risked high civilian casualties and further alienation of the people—which might induce insurgents to fight. The war became increasingly costly in US lives lost. Although Bush won reelection easily and initial polls on his handling of the situation in Iraq showed he was very popular at home, the fact was that the entire US force structure in Iraq was under mounting pressure and poorly trained. It could concentrate and win battles for specific cities, as it did often, but at the cost of abandoning earlier victories and predominance elsewhere. Iraq was simply too big to be conquered without greatly increased manpower. The Reserves and National Guard were called upon to provide personnel, and at the beginning of 2005 they made up at least half of the US forces in Iraq. But they were also stretched to the limits and could no longer provide the soldiers needed. The duration US soldiers were required to stay in Iraq was extended far beyond what was once deemed normal, causing morale to plummet even further. Recruitment in the National Guard fell nine-tenths as a consequence. As in Vietnam, war was producing a crisis in the US army.[18]

Since the Pentagon counted on a short war in Iraq and had no formal plan for it until seven months after it began, there was soon a severe shortage of spare parts and maintenance for sophisticated equipment. US forces used many of the helicopters at two to three times, and armored vehicles up to six times, their expected rate. The wear and tear on all this technology cost roughly $10 billion annually to repair. Then there were dangerous, expensive logistical problems in supplying an army spread out over a vast terrain. To complicate matters, as in the Vietnam War, there were too many generals and senior officers, each with their own fiefdoms and career ambitions, out to serve their six- to twelve-months duty without reports of failure, get home, and be promoted.[19]

The Iraq War, conforming to Rumsfeld's plans to increase the military's "lethality," is heavily reliant on capital-intensive technology but also much more on private contractors. These contractors employ at least 20,000 workers, who do everything from servicing sophisticated equipment to providing guards and drivers. To an unprecedented extent, the war has been privatized. Foreigners often receive very high wages for extremely dangerous work; Iraqis, the large bulk of their employees, are estimated to receive 27 percent of every dollar spent. Contractors make inordinately large profits for their efforts; enormous contracts are often made with no bidding to firms that have friends in Washington, like Halliburton, which has about $13 billion in contracts. Vice President Cheney was formerly its chairman. But like most wars in most nations, this one was also mediated by the existing power structure and those who possess influence and friends in high places rather than rational criteria; it was therefore far more expensive than it might have been. Yet even under the best of circumstances, an open-ended, protracted war whose conclusion cannot be measured in the usual conventional ways will be very costly—and Iraq *is* such a war. Unfortunately, most wars in the recent past, and increasingly those in the future, are politically and militarily far more complex, and arms have increasingly limited value in confronting these problems. Indeed, they may not merely be irrelevant but, as Vietnam showed, counterproductive. Destruction in a technologically efficient fashion may galvanize people to oppose what the United States is seeking to accomplish—and wars that are not won politically are lost, weaponry notwithstanding.

With a federal budget deficit of nearly a half-trillion dollars in fiscal 2004, the Bush administration unquestionably has been warned it cannot afford the global war on terrorism that the president threatens to take well beyond Afghanistan and Iraq. The Iraq War cost about $50 billion by July

2003, but the Pentagon's prognosis for it was initially optimistic, and it expected to withdraw most troops by the end of the year. In October 2004 the Bush administration, assuming a force level in Iraq of about 130,000, asked for a $70 billion supplemental for both its wars, but it implied that it might ask for more—and did. The two and one-half years in Iraq will cost at least $225 billion by the fall of 2005. The Iraq War, the heads of the four services told Congress in November 2004, was now costing at least $70 billion annually. Adjusted for inflation, it will by 2005 exceed the cost of World War I and will reach nearly half of what the Vietnam War cost over nine years. The Iraq War will be, by far, the most expensive in US history. In early 2005 the Congressional Budget Office calculated the ten-year costs of the wars in Iraq and Afghanistan at $1 trillion—and $1.4 trillion at the current level of operations, even assuming these wars are gradually phased down. Some informed estimates are even higher, especially if treatment for returning veterans is calculated. But the cost of the war has increased because of the much greater reliance on private contractors for essential services, widespread fraud and corruption among Iraqis and Americans in charge of reconstruction and oil revenues, and the haste and desperation that the chaos in Iraq now evokes from those in power.

By the middle of 2003 some US senior officers were apprehensive about the war, but as the insurgency grew and improved, so too did pessimism at the highest levels. In June 2004 General William E. Odom, former head of the National Security Agency, published a scathing attack on the premises of the war and its outcome, arguing that bin Laden and Iran were its winners so far. Hussein's Baath regime had been destroyed, but any successor was going to be anti-American, and civil war, including a Turkish invasion of the Kurdish region, was quite possible. The United States simply did not possess the land forces to reverse the descent into further chaos: "The United States should begin a strategic withdrawal from Iraq because it was never in the interests of the United States to invade that country in the first place." Odum compared Iraq to Vietnam for mindlessness, but stated that this situation "is far graver than Vietnam" because the strategic implications in the region were far more ominous. Transferring the war to an Iraqi force to win against enemies "we can't defeat stretches the imagination."[20]

A confidential National Intelligence Estimate in July 2004 was no less pessimistic, though a CIA official observed "we're telling them something they don't want to hear." The CIA, which had about 300 employees in Iraq at the end of 2004, has become increasingly bleak about the war with time, infuriating the White House. The CIA, in fact, sent the White House similar analyses before the war began and again in late 2003. It stated that Iraq's security force was unlikely to provide the Americans with a face-saving exit strategy and that the best-case scenario was a "tenuous stability" through 2005; the worst was that Iraq might succumb to a civil war. In September 2004, the Royal Institute of International Affairs in London predicted that Iraq might dissolve and civil war ensue, leaving the entire region highly unstable. In September 2005 the Saudi foreign minister reiterated this gloomy prognosis, warning that Iraq was hurtling toward disintegration and could drag the entire region into war. Iran has already begun to use its prestige and funds among its coreligionist Shiites in Iraq, and its power there can only increase.[21] Iraq and Iran signed a pact in July 2005 that covered everything from Iranian help in training troops, to building a billion dollars' worth of schools and hospitals, to constructing a pipeline between Basra and Abadan that will lead to a merger of their oil economies. The worst neocon nightmare is coming to pass, and Rumsfeld has already made it clear that US troop departures will be affected by the extent of Iranian influence.

There is no coherent strategy, one US officer observed: "We rush from one crisis to the next." "We are losing the war," another concluded.[22]

The Geopolitical Consequences of the Iraq War

There is no longer an Iraqi balance to Iranian predominance in the Persian Gulf, a fact that has untold geopolitical implications. Washington supported Hussein in his war with Iran throughout the 1980s, to repeat a crucial fact I noted earlier, providing him credits, intelligence, and vital military support, solely to contain Iran. Turkey is likely to intervene, one way or another, to control the Kurds in northern Iraq—what may occur there is wholly unpredictable. But although the United States intends to maintain a much larger military presence in the region for many years to come, using Iran as an excuse, it cannot oppose the Turks without shattering the illusion of its alliance with it—and NATO. War with Iraq has created a vast number of uncontrollable dangers throughout the region. Iran is more likely than ever to dominate the Gulf and attain its regional geopolitical ambitions. This is especially the case should the Shiites in Iraq—who form 60 percent of the population—take over the Iraqi government via elections or other means and open a new era of friendship between the two nations. Such a prospect especially worries Iraq's Sunni neighbors, Saudi Arabia and Jordan.

Iran's role is of overwhelming importance to the United States—and to Israel. It is militarily far more formidable than Iraq and will have nuclear weapons in due course—only the timing is disputed. Iran's principal concern is Israel and its nuclear weapons and delivery systems, and Iran has neither the intention nor the technology to reach beyond it. Even though Iran's possession of nuclear weapons will merely create an essentially stabilizing deterrent to Israel using its bombs, once Iran has nuclear weapons, then it is very likely Saudi Arabia and Turkey will want them too—and the Saudis are very close to Pakistan, whose nuclear weapons development they helped to finance. The obvious solution—which Iran has proposed for some time and is a precondition for its abandoning its race for nuclear weapons—is to create a Middle Eastern nuclear-free zone enforced by international inspection, an option Israel is most unlikely to accept. Israel has often stated it regards Iran as a much greater threat to it than Iraq, and it hoped that war against the latter was only a preliminary to transforming the Middle East, as Bush indeed promised.[23]

Will the United States "drain the swamp" in the region, as the neoconservatives advocate, even including Saudi Arabia among the regimes to be toppled? Washington has been committed to an aggressive foreign policy globally for decades, never more than at the present time, but it is divided on the issue of new regional adventures, and it lacks manpower for what would be a much larger war with Iran than with Iraq. What inhibits it most is Iraq's political chaos, which utterly surprised the White House despite expert warnings it was inevitable; the United States is obligated to end this disorder before it confronts more nations militarily, a process that may take many years. All speculation on when and if the Americans will get out of Iraq remains just that—speculation. The coterie around Bush is deeply divided on the issue of withdrawal, wracked with unrealistic ambitions that often border on the fantastic. It is a question that Americans are likely to live with for a far longer time than they imagined, as in Vietnam, and predictions are likely to be wrong. But the United States was astonished in Iraq by the immense costs of the US way of making war, and it does not have the needed manpower. Weapons are not, despite the illusions Rumsfeld shares with most of his predecessors, sufficient for victory.

Vietnam and Iraq: Has the US Learned Anything?

There are great cultural, political, and physical differences between Vietnam and Iraq that cannot be minimized, and the geopolitical situation is entirely different. But the United States has ignored the major lessons of the traumatic Vietnam experience and is today repeating many of the errors that produced defeat there.

In both places successive US administrations slighted the advice of its most knowledgeable intelligence experts. In Vietnam they told Washington's decisionmakers not to tread where France had failed and urged them to endorse the 1954 Geneva Accords provisos on reunification. They also warned against underestimating the communists' numbers, motivation, or independent nationalism.

In the 1960s the Pentagon had an uncritical faith in its overwhelming firepower, modern equipment, mobility, and mastery of the skies. It still does, and Defense Secretary Rumsfeld believes the military has the technology to "shock and awe" all adversaries. But the war in Vietnam, as in Iraq, was highly decentralized, and the number of troops required only increased even as the firepower became greater. When they reached a half-million Americans in Vietnam, the public turned against President Johnson and defeated his party.

Wars are ultimately won politically or not at all. Leaders in Washington thought this interpretation of events in Vietnam was bizarre and continued to ignore its experts whenever they frequently reminded them of the limits of military power. The importance of Vietnamese politics was slighted, escalations followed, and the credibility of US military power—the willingness to use it and win no matter how long it took—became their primary concern.

In both Vietnam and Iraq the American public was mobilized on the basis of cynical falsehoods that ultimately backfired, causing a "credibility gap." People eventually ceased to believe anything Washington told them. The Tonkin Gulf crisis of August 1964 was manufactured, as the CIA's leading analyst later admitted in his memoir, because "the administration was seeking a pretext for a major escalation."[24] Countless lies were told during the Vietnam War, and eventually many of the men who counted most were themselves unable to separate truth from fiction. Many US leaders really believed that if the communists won in Vietnam, the "dominoes" would fall and the Chinese and Soviets would dominate all Southeast Asia. The Iraq War was initially justified because Hussein was purported to have weapons of mass destruction and ties to Al-Qaida and because Iraq was a base for terrorism everywhere.

There are about 161,000 US troops in Iraq at the time of this writing, the greatest number since the war began. But, as in Vietnam, their morale is already low and sinking. The United States desperately needs many more soldiers in Iraq, and other nations will not provide them. In Vietnam, President Richard M. Nixon tried to "Vietnamize" the land war and transfer the burdens of soldiering to Nguyen Van Thieu's huge army to win the victory that US forces failed to attain. "Iraqization" of the military required to put down the resistance will not accomplish what has eluded the Americans, and in both Vietnam and Iraq the United States greatly underestimated the length of time it would have to remain and cultivated illusions about the strength of its friends or collaborators.

The idea that an Iraqi army will be loyal to US goals or be militarily effective is nonsense. As in Vietnam, where the Buddhists opposed the Catholic leaders the United States endorsed, Iraq is divided regionally and religiously, and Washington has the unenviable choice between a protracted insurgency that the insufficiency of US troops makes likely or civil war if it arms Iraqis. Elections so far have exacerbated these differences, not resolved them. Despite plenty of expert opinion to warn it, the Bush administration has scant perception of the complexity of the political problems it confronts in Iraq. Afghanistan looms as an immediate reminder of how military success depends ultimately on politics and how things go wrong.

Key members of the Bush administration are far less confident of what they are doing than they were early in 2003. But as in Vietnam, when Defense Secretary Robert McNamara eventually ceased to believe that victory was inevitable, it is too late to reverse course. Now the credibility of US military power is at stake, and Bush increasingly invoked it as a justification for persevering in Iraq.

Ultimately, domestic politics takes precedence over everything else in most nations—wars over the past century have usually ended with a profoundly alienated public. That was surely the case in the Vietnam War, and it is very likely to be repeated in Iraq also. By 1968 the polls were turning against the Democrats, and the Tet offensive in February caught President Lyndon Johnson by surprise because he and his generals refused to believe the CIA's estimates that there were really 600,000 rather than 300,000 people in the communist forces. Nixon won because he promised a war-weary public he would bring peace with honor. After ten years, Vietnam proved that even the American public has limited patience. Despite Bush's reelection in November 2004, that is still true.

US leaders never learned the lessons of the Vietnam War.

Abandoning a Conservative Economic Program

Events, not ideology, beliefs, or rational calculations, have determined how all administrations, whether Republican or Democrat, have managed US foreign policy and economic programs. The unintended, generally negative consequences of their actions have compelled them to adapt far more than they will ever confess.

The September 11 calamity appeared to rescue the Bush administration's attempt to reform the Pentagon and its budget from the same failure that has been the fate of its predecessors, and Rumsfeld did not have to admit that he could not overcome the services' opposition to its grandiose organizational schemes. But it was really less able than ever to articulate a strategic plan that was relevant to the political and military realities of the twenty-first century. It could postpone, perhaps permanently, designating China as its likely future enemy, a step that was fraught with incalculable danger. The president and the Pentagon now called a scruffy band of terrorists—desperate fanatics who exist in tiny numbers and in many places—their principal enemies for the indeterminate future. As problematic as the war in Afghanistan and Iraq may seem in terms of lives and cost, much less the time and political complexities that the destabilization of South Asia and the Middle East may very well involve, it would have been far more dangerous for the United States and the peace of the world had the Pentagon called China the major threat to US welfare and existence. Treating China so cavalierly is a major error in judgment, for the Chinese primarily want to do business, and in their own way and time its leaders are discarding what little is left of their Leninist-Maoist heritage.

The Bush administration's economic program was also a victim of the September 11 events and Iraq war, and what was to be a conservative agenda was discarded in favor of what is best termed a variety of military Keynesianism. The bipartisan consensus in Congress not only eliminates many of the normal political processes but compounds its problems because there is far less opposition—on both sides of the very narrow political spectrum—to the executive doing as it wishes with the economy. The president has never been so powerful in all domains as after September 11, not merely in the draconian restrictions on civil liberties he proposed but, above all, the economy. There is a general mandate for its confusion and loss of priorities, one that is inherent in what in the last analysis is consensus politics and the fact that the two parties share far more than they wish to admit. Indeed, these shifts have happened so easily that it makes clear that Bush never had any sincere economic convictions to begin with and that his conservative stance was merely designed to get him nominated as the Republican presidential candidate in 2000.

The economy began entering a recession in March 2001, and the high-technology sector was in especially serious trouble. Tax rebates had no impact, commercial real estate was in the doldrums, jobs were cut back, and unemployment mounted. The question of what the administration would do, given its initial fiscally conservative pledges, was very much in doubt. September 11 decided that.

Huge losses in the stock market, airlines, and the like meant the federal government had to come to their rescue with subsidies, and immense deficits became the rule from that time onward. The Pentagon's budget was increased by 13 percent, and its share of the economy grew from 3.0 percent in 2000 to 3.6 percent of gross domestic product (GDP) in 2003; the United States in 2004 accounted for 47 percent of world outlays on defense spending. The post–Cold War peace dividend died. Even more money was allocated to the war on terrorism, and at the beginning of 2002 the military services were told they should prepare for the crisis to endure at least six more years. The Pentagon was committed in 2004 to buying well over a trillion dollars of futurist weapons, allowing it to fight anywhere in the world in the only way it knew how—with high firepower and expensive technology of dubious effectiveness.

The president in spring 2001 had promised a budget surplus of $236 billion for fiscal 2001 and a cumulative surplus of $5.6 trillion over the following decade. Bush immediately enacted a $1.35 trillion tax cut over the decade based on these estimates, mainly benefiting upper-income earners. He now faced far lower revenues and greater expenses, proving that all long-range projections are highly speculative. Indeed, the White House asked Congress to raise the debt ceiling limit another $2.23 trillion, and it was $8.18 trillion at the end of 2004. In 2004 the actual gross federal debt was already $7.3 trillion, on which it paid annual net interest of $176 billion. The immense shortfall was a result of the tax cuts, the costs of September 11 and the Iraq War, and greatly increased defense spending, as well as the recession that was well advanced by then. No effort has been made to balance the budget, and deficits in federal spending have been growing, reaching 3.6 percent of the GDP in 2004. The actual deficits created over the next decade depend on many unpredictable variables, not the least of which will be the cost of repairing the immense damage that hurricanes inflicted on the gulf states in late 2005. Future deficits are now only educated guesses, but in 2004 the deficit was at the very least $450 billion and was far higher than the previous record of $290 billion in 1992. If Bush's tax cuts last a decade, as he has pledged, then US debts will grow at least $2.3 trillion by 2015—but some estimates are almost twice that sum.

The US current account deficit has also grown significantly since Bush took office, from 4.4 percent of the GDP when he came to power to over 6 percent, mainly to finance government borrowing. That is well over two-thirds of the current account surplus of China, Germany, Japan, and all the surplus nations put together, and it makes the United States increasingly dependent on foreigners willing to loan it money. Some economists regard it as precarious folly. The value of the US dollar against the euro and yen began falling in 2002, and by the end of 2004 it had dropped almost one-third against the euro. The members of the Organization of Petroleum Exporting Countries have begun to shift their holdings from the dollar to the euro. The consequences of such trends could be exceedingly serious.

All the pillars of the conservative faith have crumbled, and overwhelming bipartisan approval of bailouts, public spending in the name of defense or fiscal stimulus, and projected deficits confirmed that conservatives were no more true to their articles of ideological faith than liberals. Most conservatives want favors for their powerful constituents, and some of their proposals for tax cuts go well beyond what even the president has advocated. Despite the conservative pretensions, virtually everyone in Washington has become a Keynesian, at least in the sense of favoring deficits. They still retain their deeply rooted belief that the United States is a model to the world, not seeing that attitude as the least bit inconsistent or hypocritical, and that free markets are the only efficient way to organize economies—a doctrine that academic economics has transformed into absolute truths and the IMF has attempted to implement in many dozens of nations. According to Rumsfeld, the United States is special: "If one looked down from Mars on earth you would find that only a handful of countries are really capable of providing for their people, and where people provide for themselves . . . where the political and economic structures are such that the maximum benefit for the people is achieved."[25]

Getting ideology and practice to conform to each other is the historical contradiction of the US economy. It began with an increasingly elaborate regulatory structure initiated at the end of the nineteenth century and continues today in antidumping duties on imports, tax advantages to upper-income earners, and immense subsidies to upper-income groups (for example, the wealthiest top tenth of farmers received two-thirds of the $72 billion in agricultural subsidies from 1996 to 2000).

But public opinion was with the president, and he won reelection in 2004 despite the war in Iraq, Enron, and other scandals, in large part because the Democrats offered no alternatives and failed to capitalize on Bush's consistent decline in the polls. And although Bush is genuinely popular, his ad hoc and essentially opportunistic economic measures showed clearly how events rather than rational priorities or ideology play the decisive role in guiding US leaders. There was no consistency in President Bush's actions or ideas, but he is a consummately ambitious and highly successful politician, and reelection was what counted most before November 2004. As in the case of the Vietnam War, public opinion changes slowly, but eventually it becomes more critical. Polling results differ somewhat, but by mid-2005 they all pointed in the same direction: the American people increasingly disapproved of the war. In June 2005, for example, a Washington Post–ABC survey found 52 percent of the public believed the war in Iraq had not improved the long-term security of the United States, and the same figure disapproved of Bush's job as president. Other polls were even more negative, recording an increasing public opposition to a martial foreign policy. Hurricanes Katrina and Rita in August and September 2005 traumatized public opinion, deepened its opposition to the Iraq War's costly drain on essential domestic spending, and further lowered Bush's overall approval rating to 40 percent—the lowest ever. Later polls were even lower, and support for war in Iraq fell from 74 percent in June 2003 to 44 percent in October 2005, with more people for a speedy troop withdrawal than for US troops remaining there. Bush's domestic economic policies have only aggravated the public's alienation, and there will be immense political consequences in the future.

The United States Faces Reality

Like all warring nations before it, reality for the United States is totally different than its theories and expectations. The future of the world, whether there is war or peace, now depends on what happens in Washington; how the United States deals with its mounting frustrations and dilemmas will decide the future of much of the entire world.

Reality has always been an antidote for dreamers since time immemorial, but dreamers with illusions have repeatedly harmed the world because realism follows rather than precedes armed conflicts and disastrous failures. But never before was there such destructive weaponry in so many hands. War and peace is more important to humankind's future than ever, and to a very great extent that issue is increasingly dependent on what the United States does or does not do.

Doctrinally, there is no constraint on US action; indeed, the Bush administration only finely honed the reasons for taking initiatives that were articulated before 2001 and took them to their logical conclusion: it believes passionately in action. But war in Iraq again confirmed what Korea and certainly Vietnam had revealed much earlier: militarily and politically, the US way of making war is no better than those of the Germans, French, English, or Russians. War simply does not resolve problems between nations, whatever they may be, and those that attempt it invariably end up far worse than when they began, and unforeseen complications create crises it may never resolve. Wars have profoundly and increasingly scarred the human condition for centuries.

The war the United States chose to fight in Iraq after March 2003 only reiterates these truisms, but the war there, like most before it, went badly from the inception. It is also incredibly costly, and there are limits to US budget deficits, including the willingness of foreigners to hold dollars. During 2003, the forthcoming presidential election in November 2004 inhibited adventures further afield than Iraq, but so too did overextension of the US military. Iraq was supposed to be a short war, but it became protracted and expensive in both manpower and money. Alliances were crumbling, and the most powerful nations, save the United Kingdom, rejected the war from its inception; plans for reforming the US military were in abeyance; and the goals and doctrines the Bush administration had when it took office and retained after September 11 were in tatters. Something went wrong for the United States, as it has for virtually every ambitious warring nation before it: there are countless surprises.

In theory, Bush's notion of preemption still exists, even if it was more a description of the conduct of US foreign policy since at least the beginning of the twentieth century than an original strategy. There were other aspects to his more lofty utterances, such as democratizing most of the Middle East, if not all of it, stamping out terrorism, taking unilateral US action when necessary, and the like, all underpinned by the illusion that the country's ambitious goals were honorable and US power was unlimited. But the legitimacy of preemption depended at home and abroad on getting facts right and accepting the best evidence possible on the nature of reality. Iraq's utter lack of WMD showed the United States in the worst possible light. Its credibility was zero. The world was astounded by the notion—floated in late 2004—that action was justified if a nation merely thought of or intended to get such weapons in the future. The capriciousness of such thinking showed how unpredictable, threatening, and dangerous the United States had become. It is a rogue nation—out of control. The net effect of US bellicosity for members of the "axis of evil," including those who feared future inclusion in it, was to convince them that safety was to be found in building a nuclear deterrent. And compared to the period before 1990, it is far easier and cheaper to obtain them.

Intelligence has never been the basis of any great nation's foreign policy, and accurate information was ignored if it failed to reinforce what political and military leaders wished to hear. The United States is scarcely alone in this regard. There are situations in which information may impose constraints on options, but they are overwhelmingly tactical rather than strategic choices. There are also times when accurate information is utterly ignored even tactically, involving timing or clarity in the minds of decisionmakers, and this relatively rare condition probably exists among a great many in Washington at the present moment. Then important people prefer to deceive themselves, and they surround themselves with sycophants who confirm the wisdom of their profound illusions and ignorance. Analytically, we do not often know which people are deliberately issuing falsehoods—there are surely some who do this as a matter of routine—and which people are deluding themselves, much less which are doing both. Motives are difficult to fathom. But history is replete with individuals who leave us bewildered as to what they truly believe.

A larger structural and ideological environment constrains the use of intelligence, and foreign policies generally foredoom efforts to base actions on informed insights. Even when knowledge is far greater than ignorance, there are decisive boundaries to its role. Wars have afflicted the world again and again, for centuries, precisely because blindness and stupidity combine with spurious ideas and the irresponsibility that power allows. Americans have never been alone in this myopia, and the Bush administration is not much different than those that preceded it. CIA directors are often political appointees with their own agendas. The press reports what it is told and is usually reverential of leaks coming from the White House, but ultimately the problem is far less information than policy. Unfortunately, the world is far more dangerous than it was fifty years ago, and destructive weapons are more universally distributed than at any time in history. The consequences of doing the wrong thing make truth that much more precious.

Intelligence, in the sense of accurate information about specific topics, can become inaccurate because of policy predilections but also because there is too much of it and one is therefore free to believe what one wishes. The bad, good, or irrelevant are all mixed together. In fact, US intelligence agencies have some very bright people working for them, and they often know a great deal about their topics. The United States spent at least $200 billion on signal intelligence from supersecret satellites after creating the National Reconnaissance Office (NRO) in 1961. The NRO picked up everything and overwhelmed the intelligence systems, allowing senior analysts to support their politically correct evaluations with all kinds of data—which in Iraq's case of WMD, to cite but one of many examples, turned out to be completely inaccurate and at total odds with an immense amount of publicly available information. Allies abandoned the United States, its credibility has fallen immeasurably, and the doctrine of preemption is simply another reason for aggression rather than what Bush claimed he intended it to be—forestalling real threats.

The real danger confronting any nation, especially the United States, is the belief that it is strong when it is not and faith in the power of weapons and technology when they are in fact wholly irrelevant—or even defective. That was surely the moral of the Vietnam War, which the United States fought more than a decade, investing tremendous resources and manpower in it, and lost completely. That lesson is being relearned in Iraq at the time of this writing.

US weapons are incredibly expensive, and their cost is increasing. The F-15, including its maintenance system, costs about $100 million. US headquarters in Qatar and Kuwait had forty-two times the bandwidth available during the first Gulf War, allowing them—in theory—to maintain contact with all front-line units and equipment in Iraq. Some of the expensive contract employees in Iraq service this equipment. Innovations such as these—"force transformation"—allowed Rumsfeld to think that future wars could be fought more "lethally" with far smaller forces, and even the Joint Chiefs of Staff had already proclaimed in June 2000 that information-based military technology would lead to "full spectrum dominance" and make the United States invincible in any context by 2020. But this kind of war is exceedingly complicated, and its software, computer codes, and much else must work perfectly in tandem. Although such military technology will not be finally completed until 2014, a great deal is installed now and is being used in the Iraq War. Its very existence was one of the reasons the Bush administration believed the war would be over very quickly. In fact, however, most of the system broke down immediately. US headquarters in Qatar and Kuwait received so much airborne sensor data that it overwhelmed them, forcing them to stop the machines. Convoys could not go too fast or too far, making them better targets. Such simple things as adequate water were ignored beforehand, and much of it had to be trucked in from Kuwait. Links did not function well, computers crashed for ten to twelve hours at a time; vehicles outran their radio connections, and the like. The chain of command broke down often, and information technology did not operate in the front lines, where it counted most. "We had terrible situational awareness" was the universal judgment of the commanders.[26] Given the immense federal deficit, spending on useless technology was doubly counterproductive.

All wars depend on soldiers, and they are the unpredictable variable. It was surely the case during World War I, when morale plummeted, and soldiers even started the revolution in Russia. During the Vietnam War the soldiers who were supposed to fight there nearly destroyed the military with everything from drug addiction to killing their officers. There were 1.4 million active duty troops in 2003 and 1.2 million Reservists and National Guards. These part-time soldiers are committed to a weekend every month and two weeks in the summer training, often to supplement their income. Most are married and have regular, usually lower income, jobs. They have poor unit cohesion, they are not good soldiers, and their equipment is inferior. A few incidents of their refusal to obey orders or go to Iraq have been publicized, but they are the tip of the iceberg. The army sends them to Iraq for twelve months or longer, which is twice the length of time in combat zones that it introduced after the Vietnam War. The army freely admits that is too long but says it has no option. At least half of the US forces in Iraq are from the Reserves and National Guard—and the percentage is rising. "The war in Iraq is wrecking the Army and the Marine Corps," wrote a former navy officer in July 2004.[27]

Recruitment for the Reserves and National Guard has fallen, and the all-volunteer army can no longer meet the extraordinary demands imposed on it. Although it is politically unpopular, the draft is being reconsidered. In August 2004 a Pentagon advisory panel argued that the existing US military force "will not sustain our current and projected global stabilization commitments," and one alternative is to "scale back" the number and objectives of these missions.[28] That is not likely to happen.

US military power has ceased to be credible in Iraq, and it is again on its way to defeat. Its pretensions and technology have proved hollow. Its key alliance, NATO, is crumbling, and Washington has scant time or resources to deal with the challenges it faces elsewhere. Meanwhile, a crucial part of South America is veering leftward, toward far greater independence, and that will end a century of US hegemony in that vital area. South America may become far more united, far more economically developed, and independent in crucial ways that may for the first time challenge and neutralize US domination of the vast, rich region. The Bush administration's inclination before September 11 to make China, already one of the world's great economic powers, its adversary has been temporarily sidetracked by the crisis in the Islamic world. The United States has improved its relations with India and Southeast Asian states and installed bases in Central Asia, but some in Washington still want to confront China before its rapid economic growth and military buildup, which now includes missiles and nuclear weapons, makes it far too powerful for the United States to even dream of confronting it.

Ambition Versus a Big World

The world is escaping US control. Power of every sort—economic and military above all—is becoming far more diffuse, and whether it is effectively multipolar now or will become so in the near future is debatable, but the direction the world is taking is not. The postwar world of transatlanticism and NATO cannot be resurrected, and the leaders of France and Germany are on record as being in favor of a new international system. Although its contours are vague, because in virtually all domains the United States has pursued a unilateral course, it has guaranteed that the world will now be rebuilt without its participation. In no area is this dispersion of power more crucial than nuclear weapons.

Eight nations, as of this writing, possess nuclear weapons. At least thirty nations could retool their peaceful nuclear programs and make nuclear weapons fairly quickly, according to the UN. In the near future, the proliferation problem comes less from the states that already have nuclear weapons than the far greater number that have the capacity to make or acquire them. Pakistan, one of the eight, has sold weapons information and equipment to at least twenty nations. The head of Pakistan's nuclear bomb project, Abdul Qadeer Khan, remains a national hero who was pardoned by Musharraf for selling virtually everything anyone needs, from centrifuges to blueprints, to make weapons. It is a mystery who or how many customers he had. Pakistan, which got help from China when it began its research in the early 1980s, has been far too important to the United States in Afghanistan since 1980 to warrant more than relatively polite reprimands. But apart from Pakistan, which purchased much of what it needed in other countries, there are also other networks, composed of entrepreneurs, criminals, scientists, and government agents, ready to make the development or acquisition of nuclear bombs easier.[29]

In a world where the United States threatens preemption against countries that harbor terrorists or allegedly possess WMD, every incentive exists for those nations in the "axis of evil" to develop nuclear weapons as quickly as possible as a deterrent. The United States never signed the Comprehensive Test Ban Treaty, it is developing a whole spectrum of new nuclear weapons, it wants to weaponize space, and it opposes the verification provisions other states think essential to an effective international treaty on enriching key nuclear weapons materials. It also opposes a verification regime for the Biological Weapons Convention and additional monitoring and inspection measures for the May 2002 Strategic Offensive Reductions Treaty with Russia, which was unenforceable and immediately ignored by both sides. But Washington's threats greatly encourage potential victims to build nuclear weapons.

It is only a question of time until Iran and North Korea obtain nuclear weapons, and North Korea may have them already (both now have missiles). Ambiguity, as the Israelis have shown, keeps possible attackers guessing and is itself a powerful deterrent. South Korea has mastered the basic technology, Brazil will not allow inspectors look at its nuclear power installations, and Iran is quite aware that Brazil is permitted to ignore the rules. Once Iran's possession of nuclear bombs is beyond doubt, Saudi Arabia and Turkey are likely to obtain their own to deter Iran's domination of the region. Japan has the technical knowledge and funds to quickly build a bomb, and an arms race in East Asia may occur. In due course, many more nations will possess nuclear weapons. They may admit it but are more likely to use ambiguity as a deterrent—and develop nuclear weapons. As for "dirty bombs" based on freely accessible radioactive waste used with ordinary explosives, which cause far less damage but creates panic, they can easily be constructed by small groups and set off anywhere. Sooner or later, such groups may also acquire real nuclear bombs.

Options exist, the ideal being a ban on nuclear weapons with enforceable inspection, which can be done regionally. The Iranians favor such a solution as part of an overall Middle Eastern peace accord. Like the North Koreans, Iran would also demand guarantees against US attack. The Israelis claim to agree to regional nuclear disarmament but want an acceptable peace agreement implemented first rather than linked discussions—which is tantamount to refusing nuclear disarmament. But to accomplish anything would require radically different premises than those the Bush administration now embraces, and the solution to the proliferation problem in every region must deal with the political aspects of security, or it will fail.

All these are exceedingly dangerous trends, but this nightmare is our reality. We live in an age of perpetual wars. The world is far more perilous than it was fifty or one hundred years ago.

6

Conclusion:
The Age of Perpetual Conflict

ALL WARS IN THE TWENTIETH CENTURY BOTH SURPRISED AND disillusioned world leaders, whatever their nationality. Given the political, social, and human elements involved in every conflict and the near certainty that these mercurial ingredients will interact to produce unanticipated consequences, leaders who calculate the outcome of wars as essentially predictable military events are invariably doomed to disappointment. The theory and the reality of warfare conflict immensely, for the results of wars can never be known in advance.

Blind men and women have been the motor of modern history and the source of endless misery and destruction. Aspiring leaders of great powers can neither understand nor admit before embarking upon adventures that their strategies are extremely dangerous; statecraft by its very nature always calculates the ability of a nation's military and economic resources to overcome whatever challenges it confronts. To reject such traditional reasoning, question the value of conventional wisdom, and react to international crises realistically on the basis of past failures would make them unsuited to command. The result is that politicians succeed in terms of their personal careers, states make monumental errors, and people suffer. Greed, ambition, and ignorance, in a word, erode the integrative functions of ruling systems and those who guide them. The great nations of Europe and Japan put their illusions into practice repeatedly before 1945.

At the beginning of the twenty-first century, only the United States has the will to maintain a global foreign policy and to intervene everywhere it believes necessary. Today and in the near future, the United States will make the decisions that will lead to war or peace, and the fate of much of the world is largely in its hands. It possesses the arms and a spectrum of military strategies all predicated on a triumphant activist role for itself. It believes that its economy can afford interventionism and that the American public will support whatever actions necessary to set the affairs of some country or region on the political path it deems essential. This grandiose ambition is bipartisan, and details notwithstanding, both parties have always shared a consensus on it.

The obsession with power and the conviction that armies can produce the political outcome a nation's leaders desire is by no means an exclusively American illusion. It is a notion that goes back many centuries and has produced the main wars of modern times. The rule of force has been with humankind a very long time, and the assumptions behind it have plagued its history for centuries. But unlike the leaders of most European nations or Japan, US leaders have not gained insight from the calamities that have so seared modern history. Folly is scarcely a US monopoly, but resistance to learning when grave errors have been committed is almost proportionate to the resources available to repeat them. The Germans learned their lesson after two defeats, the Japanese after World War II, and both nations found wars too exhausting and politically dangerous. The United States still believes that if firepower fails to master a situation, the solution is to use it more precisely and much more of it. In this regard it is exceptional—past failures have not made it any wiser.

Wars are at least as likely today as any time over the past century. Of great importance is the end of Soviet hegemony in Eastern Europe and Moscow's restraining influence elsewhere. But the proliferation of nuclear technology and other means of mass destruction have also made large parts of the world far more dangerous. Deadly local wars with conventional weapons in Africa, the Balkans, Middle East, and elsewhere have multiplied since the 1960s. Europe, especially Germany, and Japan, are far stronger and more independent than at any time since 1945, and China's rapidly expanding economy has given it a vastly more important role in Asia. Ideologically, communism's demise means that the simplified bipolarism that Washington used to explain the world ceased after 1990 to have any value. With it, the alliances created nominally to resist communism have either been abolished or are a shadow of their original selves; they have no reason for existence. The crisis in the North Atlantic Treaty Organization (NATO), essentially, reflects this diffusion of all forms of power and the diminution of US hegemony. Economically, the capitalist nations have resumed their rivalries, and they have become more intense with the growth of their economies and the decline in the dollar—which by 2004 was as weak as it has been in over fifty years. These states have a great deal in common ideologically, but concretely they are increasingly rivals. The virtual monopoly of nuclear weapons that existed about a quarter-century ago has ended with proliferation.

Whether it is called a "multipolar" world, to use French president Jacques Chirac's expression in November 2004, in which Europe, China, India, and even eventually South America follow their own interests, or something else, the direction is clear. There may or may not be "a fundamental restructuring of the global order," as the chairman of the Central Intelligence Agency's (CIA's) National Intelligence Council presciently reflected in April 2003, but the conclusion was unavoidable "that we are facing a more fluid and complicated set of alignments than anything we have seen since the formation of the Atlantic alliance in 1949." Terrorism and the global economy have defied overwhelming US military power: "Our smart bombs aren't that smart."[1]

Wars, whether civil or between states, remain the principal (but scarcely the only) challenge confronting humanity in the twenty-first century. Ecological disasters relentlessly affecting all dimensions of the environment are also insidious because of the unwillingness of the crucial nations—above all the United States—to adopt measures essential for reversing their damage. The challenges facing humanity have never been so complex and threatening, and the end of the Cold War, although one precondition of progress, is scarcely reason for complacency or optimism. The problems the world confronts far transcend the communist-capitalist tensions, many of which were mainly symptoms of the far greater intellectual, political, and economic problems that plagued the world before 1917—and still exist.

Whatever the original intention, US interventions can lead to open-ended commitments in both duration and effort. They may last a short time, and usually do, but unforeseen events can cause the United States to spend far more resources than it originally anticipated, causing it in the name of its credibility, or some other doctrine, to get into disastrous situations that in the end defeat the United States. Vietnam is the leading example of this tendency, but Iraq, however different in degree, is the same in kind. Should the United States confront even some of the forty or more nations that now have terrorist networks, then it will in one manner or another intervene everywhere, but especially in Africa and the Middle East. The consequences of such commitments will be unpredictable.

The United States has more determined and probably more numerous enemies today than at any time, and many of those who hate it are ready and able to inflict destruction on its shores. Its interventions often triumphed in the purely military sense, which is all the Pentagon worries about, but in all too many cases they have been political failures and eventually led to greater US military and political involvement. Its virtually instinctive activist mentality has caused it to get into situations where it often had no interests, much less durable solutions to a nation's problems, repeatedly creating disasters and enduring enmities. The United States has power without wisdom and cannot, despite its repeated experiences, recognize the limits of its ultrasophisticated military technology. The result has been folly and hatred, which is a recipe for disasters. September 11 confirmed that, and war has come to its shores.

That the United States end its self-appointed global mission of regulating all problems, wherever, whenever, or however it wishes to do so, is an essential precondition of stemming, much less reversing, the accumulated deterioration of world affairs and wars. We should not ignore the countless ethical and other reasons it has no more right or capacity to do so than any state over the past century, whatever justifications they evoked. The problems, as the history of the past century shows, are much greater than the US role in the world; but at the present time its actions are decisive, and whether there is war or peace will be decided far more often in Washington than any other place. Ultimately, there will not be peace in the world unless all nations relinquish war as an instrument of policy, not only because of ethical or moral reasoning but because wars have become deadlier and more destructive of social institutions. A precondition of peace is for nations not to attempt to impose their visions on others, adjudicate their differences, and never to assume that their need for the economic or strategic resources of another country warrants interference of any sort in its internal affairs.

But September 11 proved that after a half-century of interventions the United States has managed to provoke increasing hatred. It has failed abysmally to bring peace and security to the world. Its role as a rogue superpower and its promiscuous, cynical interventionism has been spectacularly unsuccessful, even on its own terms. It is squandering vast economic resources, and it has now endangered the physical security of Americans at home. To end the damage the United States causes abroad is also to fulfill the responsibilities that US politicians have to their own people. But there is not the slightest sign at this point that voters will call them to account, and neither the American population nor its political leaders are likely to agree to such far-reaching changes in foreign policy. The issues are far too grave to wait for US attitudes and its political process to be transformed. The world will be safer to the extent that US alliances are dissolved and it is isolated, and that is happening for many reasons, ranging from the unilateralism, hubris, and preemptory style of the Bush administration to the fact that since the demise of communism, the world's political alignments have changed dramatically.

Communism and fascism were both outcomes of the fatal errors in the international order and affairs of states that World War I spawned. In part, the Soviet system's disintegration was the result of the fact it was the aberrant consequence of a destructive and abnormal war, but at least as important was its leaders' loss of confidence in socialism. And suicidal Muslims are, to a great extent, the outcome of a half-century of US interference in the Middle East and Islamic world, which radicalized so many young men and women ready to die for faith. Just as the wars of 1914–1918 and 1939–1945 created Bolsheviks, the repeated grave errors of the United States, however different the context or times, have produced their own abnormal, negative reactions. The twenty-first century has begun very badly because the United States continues with its aggressive policies. They are far more dangerous than those of the twentieth century. The destructive potential of weaponry has increased exponentially, and many more people and nations have access to it. What would once have been considered relatively minor foreign policy problems now have potentially far greater consequences. It all augurs very badly. The world has reached the most dangerous point in recent, or perhaps all of, history. There are threats of war and instability unlike anything that prevailed when a Soviet-led bloc existed.

Even if the United States abstains from interference and tailors its actions to fit this troubled reality, there will be serious problems throughout much of the world. Internecine civil conflicts will continue, as well as wars between nations armed with an increasing variety of much more destructive weapons available from outside powers, of which the United States remains, by far, the most important source. Many of these conflicts have independent roots, and both principles and experiences justify the United States staying out of them and leaving the world alone. Both the American people and those involved directly will be far better off without foreign interference, whatever nation attempts it.

US leaders are not creating peace or security at home or stability abroad. The reverse is the case: its interventions have been counterproductive, and its foreign policy is a disaster. Americans and those people who are the objects of successive administrations' efforts would be far better off if the United States did nothing, closed its bases overseas and withdrew its fleets everywhere, and allowed the rest of world to find its own way. Communism is dead, and Europe and Japan are powerful and both can and will take care of their own interests. The United States must adapt to these facts. But if it continues as it has over the past half-century, attempting to satisfy its vainglorious but irrational ambition to run the world, then there will be even deeper crises and it will inflict wars and turmoil on many nations as well as on its own people. And it will fail yet again, for all states that have gone to war over the past centuries have not achieved the objectives for which they sacrificed so much blood, passion, and resources. They have only produced endless misery and upheavals of every kind.

Notes

"Introduction"

1. Budget figures in this chapter are taken from *Economic Report of the President,* 2005, Table B-80.

Chapter 1: "Warfare at an Impasse: The Road to Vietnam"

1. Kolko 1988, p. 50. See also Kolko and Kolko 1972, pp. 671, 705–707.
2. Kolko and Kolko 1972, pp. 671–672; Bitzinger 1989; Gaddis 1982, pp. 139–145.
3. Kolko and Kolko 1972, pp. 706–707; Kolko 1988, pp. 48–52; Gaddis 1982, pp. 130–131, 144–145; Shafer 1988, chap. 5.
4. Aldrich 2004. See also Aldrich 2001, pp. 618–619.
5. Kolko 1988, pp. 55–57.
6. Ibid., pp. 56–57.
7. Blechman and Kaplan 1978, pp. 30–52; Shafer 1988, chap. 2, p. 279; Betts 1977, pp. 202–203, chap. 10; Betts 1978, pp. 62ff.; Kolko 1988, pp. 49–57; Booth and Sundrum 1985, p. 26; Janvry 1989, p. 416; Bairoch 1979, pp. 671ff.
8. Halper and Clarke 2004, pp. 140–144; Kolko 1988, pp. 74–77, 274.
9. The reader wishing a more comprehensive account of the Vietnam War may consult my *The Anatomy of a War: Vietnam, the United States, and the Modern Historical Experience* (New York: New Press, 1994).
10. Kolko 1985, pp. 15, 39–41, 60–67, 93–99, 130; Trullinger 1980, pp. 91ff.; Bergerud 1991, pp. 55ff., 76, 335.
11. Kolko 1985, pp. 143–144, 180–181, 194–195; Mrozek 1988, chap. 2; Momyer 1978, pp. 80–95; US Senate 1985, p. 316; Smith 1989, pp. 182ff.; McChristian 1974; Halberstam 1972; Deitchman 1976, pp. 113, 134; Betts 1977, pp, 189–191; Wilensky 1967; and especially Allen 2001.

179

12. Krepinevich 1986, p. xi. See also Kolko 1985, pp. 126–127; Mrozek 1988, pp. 164–165, 178–179, especially 184.
13. Kolko 1985, pp. 189–192, 357; Palmer 1984, pp. 58, 62; Krepinevich 1986, p. 127.
14. Taylor 1974, p. 14.
15. Kolko 1985, p. 197. See also pp. 284ff.; Halberstam 1972, pp. 733–740, 782–783; Taylor 1974, p. 25; Palmer 1978; Heiser 1974, pp. 22–23, 48, 60–61.
16. Heiser 1974, p. 23. See also Palmer 1984, pp. 70–71, 168–169.
17. Mueller 1973, pp. 54–57, 124–125, 130, 138–139; Kolko 1985, p. 172; US Senate 1985, pp. 580–592.
18. Kolko 1985, pp. 359–364.
19. Halberstam 1972, p. 667. See also Kolko 1985, pp. 200–201.
20. Palmer 1984, pp. 167–168.
21. Kolko 1985, pp. 144–145, 200–202; Mrozek 1988, 132–145.
22. Kolko 1985, pp. 202–207.
23. Trullinger 1980, pp. 143–144, 182–203; Deitchman 1976, pp. 386–403; Bergerud 1991, pp. 295–296; Mrozek 1988, pp. 178–179, 184.
24. Kolko 1985, pp. 234–236, 253–260, 523ff.

Chapter 2: "Prelude to Permanent Crises: The Background"

1. Philippines 1990, pp. 22, 26, 29; Booth and Sundrum 1985, pp. 138–142; Janvry 1989, pp. 396ff.; Bairoch 1979, p. 677; Williams 1986, p. 198; Brockett 1988, p. 55.
2. Inter-American Development Bank 1990, p. 121.
3. Kolko 1994, p. 440.
4. Roberts 1978, pp. 7, 94, 174; Binnendijk 1987, pp. 118–119; *Financial Times* (London), Sept. 9, 1991, Oct. 1, 1992, and Nov. 24, 1992; *Far Eastern Economic Review,* July 26, 1990, p. 48; UNCTAD 2003, pp. 19–22.
5. *Finance and Development* (IMF), Dec. 1990, p. 18; Sept. 1992, pp. 3, 9–12; *IMF Survey,* Sept. 10, 1990, pp. 258–259; Inter-American Development Bank 1990, pp. 3, 127, 129; Inter-American Development Bank 1992, p. 103.
6. Cardoso and Helwig 1992, pp. 22–26; Inter-American Development Bank 1991, p. 99; Jain 1975.
7. All data from the US Energy Information Administration, various fact sheets.
8. Acheson 1969, p. 562.
9. Kolko 1988, pp. 70–72.
10. Macmillan 1969, p. 635.
11. *Department of State Bulletin,* January 28, 1957, p. 128.
12. Stockwell 1978, p. 43.
13. For excellent accounts of all aspects of this war, see Hiro 1991; and Hiro 2001, pp. 27–34.
14. *Los Angeles Times,* Feb. 26, 1992.

15. Gates 1996, pp. 144–145; Brzezinski interview reprinted in *Counterpunch,* Oct. 8, 2001.

16. Matthias 2001, p. 323.

17. Caspar Weinberger, "The Uses of Military Power," Nov. 28, 1984, Department of Defense press release.

18. Levine 1987, p. viii.

19. Gates 1996, p. 145.

20. Ibid., p. 433.

21. Matthias 2001, p. 314. See also pp. 4, 166, 294.

22. Beschloss and Talbott 1993, pp. 106, 346. See also pp. 170, 176, 443.

23. US Joint Chiefs 1991, pp. 1–2; Richard Haass, US Information Service, London, Sept. 24, 1991.

24. Beschloss and Talbott 1993, p. 192. See also pp. 187, 191.

Chapter 3: "The World Comes Apart: The 1990s"

1. *New York Times,* Sept. 20, 1990.

2. Bamford 2004, p. 103.

3. *New York Times,* Aug. 31, 1990. See also Carney 2002, pp. 224–226.

4. See Cooley 2002 for an excellent overview of US policy on Islam.

5. White House press briefing, June 25, 1999.

6. US Department of Defense 2000, pp. 3, 5.

7. Richard Cohen, Department of Defense press release, Dec. 5, 2000.

8. Anonymous 2004, pp. 170–171.

9. US Department of Defense, "1996 Annual Defense Report," May 19, 1997, pp. 1, 4–5, 12–13.

10. Gompert and Isaacson 1999, p. xx.

11. Cohen, Department of Defense press release, July 5, 2000. For the more general intelligence estimate, see Hutchings 2003.

12. Lieutenant General Patrick M. Hughes, statement to US Senate, Select Committee on Intelligence, Jan. 28, 1998, p. 3.

13. Stiglitz 2003, pp. 21, 28.

14. World Health Organization, *Global Health: Today's Challenges,* February 24, 2004, chap. 1; International Labour Organization (ILO), "Global Employment Trends," January 2004, pp. 1–5; ILO, February 24, 2004, report, pp. 35–45; *Los Angeles Times*, August 27, 2004; *Financial Times,* December 19, 2003.

15. CIA 2000, p. 39.

Chapter 4: "The Twenty-First Century: The United States and War on the World"

1. Paul Wolfowitz, Department of Defense press releases, Aug. 16, 2001; June 14, 2001.

2. US Department of Defense, *Quadrennial Defense Review Report,* Sept. 30, 2001, pp. 1–2.

3. Woodward 2004, p. 19. See also Halper and Clarke 2004, p. 110.

4. US Department of Defense, "The United States Security Strategy for the East Asia–Pacific Region," Nov. 23, 1998, pp. 4, 11; US Department of Defense, "Nuclear Posture Review," January 8, 2002.

5. *International Herald Tribune,* Jan. 8, 2001. See also Woodward 2004, p. 12.

6. Donald Rumsfeld, Department of Defenses press releases, July 24, 2001, and July 30, 2001; Wolfowitz, quoted in *Washington Times,* Aug. 29, 2001. See also Spinney 1997.

7. US Department of Defense, "The United States Security Strategy for the East Asia–Pacific Region," Nov. 23, 1998, pp. 4, 11. See also Cheng 2004.

8. *Financial Times,* Sept. 21, 2004.

9. Speech by President George W. Bush to Congress, White House press release, Sept. 20, 2001; *Washington Post,* Oct. 21, 2001; White House press briefing, Sept. 18, 2001.

10. Rumsfeld, Department of Defense press release, Oct. 24, 2001.

11. White House press release, Nov. 6, 2001.

12. *Washington Post,* Nov. 7, 2001, and Nov. 28, 2001.

13. *Washington Post,* Sept. 27, 2001.

14. Anonymous 2004, p. x; *Washington Post,* Aug. 14, 2004. See also *Los Angeles Times,* Oct. 31, 2004.

15. *USA Today,* Oct. 23, 2003.

16. Corum 2004.

17. *Washington Post,* Sept. 20, 2001; Rumsfeld, Department of Defense press release, Nov. 14, 2001; *Guardian* (London), Nov. 10, 2001; White House press release, Nov. 6, 2001.

18. *International Herald Tribune,* Oct. 18, 2001.

19. *Los Angeles Times,* Sept. 12, 2004. For politics, see Anonymous 2004, pp. 54–56; *Los Angeles Times,* June 20, 2004; for drugs, see *Los Angeles Times,* Sept. 1, 2004, and Oct. 4, 2004; *Financial Times,* Oct. 5, 2004; *New York Times,* Nov. 19, 2004.

20. *Financial Times,* Oct. 12, 2001.

21. *International Herald Tribune,* Nov. 22, 2001, and Nov. 26, 2001.

22. *Boston Globe*, Oct. 22, 2001; *Financial Times,* Nov. 5, 2001. See also Anonymous 2004, pp. 54–55.

23. *Washington Post,* July 14, 2001; Wolfowitz, Department of Defense press release, Aug. 16, 2001.

24. US Department of State, Bureau of Democracy, Human Rights, and Labor, "Supporting Human Rights and Democracy: The U.S. Record, 2002–2003." Washington, DC, June 24, 2003.

25. *Los Angeles Times,* Aug. 13, 2004. See also *Los Angeles Times,* Feb. 25, 2004, July 18, 2004, and Dec. 6, 2004; Reuters, Feb. 25, 2004; *Washington Post,* July 16, 2004; Blank 2004.

26. *Los Angeles Times,* March 26, 2004.

27. Rumsfeld, Department of Defense press releases, Sept. 25, 2001, and Sept. 27, 2001.

28. Ibid.

29. Halper and Clarke 2004, pp. 237–239; Pew Research Center, "Views of a Changing World 2003," June 3, 2003; Pew Research Center, "U.S. Image Up Slightly, but Still Negative," June 23, 2005; *Financial Times,* Sept. 2, 2004, and Sept. 9, 2004; *New York Times,* Sept. 4, 2004.

Chapter 5: "Things Go Wrong: The United States Confronts a Complex World"

1. *Washington Post,* Oct. 21, 2001; Rumsfeld, Department of Defense press release, Oct. 24, 2001.

2. *Washington Post,* July 14, 2001; Wolfowitz, Department of Defense press release, Aug. 16, 2001.

3. Wolfowitz, Department of Defense press release, Sept. 14, 2001; Defense Department, *Quadrennial Defense Review Report,* Sept. 30, 2001, p. 4.

4. Rumsfeld, Department of Defense press release, Oct. 12, 2001.

5. Rumsfeld, Department of Defense press release, Sept. 30. 2001; *Quadrennial Defense Review Report,* p. iv. For the later period, see Elaine Grossman's reports in *Inside the Pentagon,* June 2 and 16, 2005; Ippolito 2005; *New York Times,* May 3, 2005, and July 5, 2005.

6. Rumsfeld, Department of Defense press release, Nov. 14, 2001.

7. *International Herald Tribune,* Nov. 2, 2001.

8. *Washington Post,* Oct. 21, 2001.

9. Wolfowitz, Department of Defense press release, May 9, 2003, p. 4; Brom 2003, pp. 1, 4; *Ha'aretz,* March 21, 2003, and Sept. 25, 2003.

10. Woodward 2004, p. 19.

11. *Washington Post,* Feb. 26, 2003; *Power and Interest News Report,* Nov. 1, 2004. See also Woodward 2004, pp. 249, 288, 295, 442.

12. *Washington Post,* Aug. 1, 2003; *Los Angeles Times*, Sept. 27, 2004; ABC radio text, Oct. 29, 2004; *Financial Times,* Nov. 20, 2004.

13. *New York Times,* Sept. 8, 2004, and July 20, 2005; *Los Angeles Times,* June 16, 2005.

14. Knight Ridder dispatch, June 29, 2004; *New York Times,* Sept. 29, 2004, Oct. 22, 2004, Nov. 18, 2004, July 24, 2005, and Aug. 25, 2005; *Washington Post,* Oct. 31, 2004, and April 24, 2005; *Los Angeles Times,* Aug. 31, 2004, Sept. 28, 2004, and Nov. 9, 2004; *Guardian,* Aug. 22, 2005.

15. Yahoo news, Reuters, Oct. 10, 2004. See also *Los Angeles Times,* July 6, 2004; Anthony Cordesman, quoted in *Financial Times,* Sept. 20, 2004, and Oct. 18, 2004; *New York Times,* Oct. 22, 2004, and Nov. 23, 2004.

16. Wolfowitz, Department of Defense press release, June 3, 2003, p. 9. See also *Los Angeles Times,* March 11, 2005.

17. Department of State press release, Sept. 26, 2004. Also *New York Times,* June 13, 2004, and Oct, 14, 2004; Anonymous 2004; *Los Angeles Times,* July 6, 2004, and Nov. 7, 2004.

18. See the insightful articles by Elaine Grossman, *Inside the Pentagon,* Sept. 23, 2004, Sept. 30, 2004, and Nov. 4, 2004.

19. Grossman, *Inside the Pentagon*, Nov. 4, 2004, pp. 2, 4; *Los Angeles Times*, Oct. 19, 2004; *Washington Post*, Oct. 18, 2004, and March 19, 2005; *New York Times*, Jan. 7, 2005.

20. William E. Odum, *National Interest* (Summer 2004), p. 33; *Guardian*, Sept. 16, 2004; see also *Los Angeles Times*, July 11, 2003, Oct. 20, 2004, and Nov. 18, 2004; *Washington Post*, July 13, 2003, and Oct. 26, 2004.

21. *Washington Post*, Sept 29, 2004, and Oct. 7, 2004; *Los Angeles Times*, Sept 2, 2004. See also *New York Times*, July 3, 2004, Sept 16, 2004, Dec. 7, 2004, and July 31, 2005; *Los Angeles Times*, Sept 16, 2004, and Oct. 25, 2004.

22. Grossman, *Inside the Pentagon*, Sept. 30, 2004.

23. *Financial Times*, Sept. 13, 2004; *Ha'aretz*, March 29, 2003.

24. Allen 2001, p. 183. See also Kolko 1994 for a detailed account of the Vietnam War.

25. Rumsfeld, Defense Department press release, Oct. 12, 2001.

26. David Talbot, "How Technology Failed in Iraq," *Technology Review* (Nov. 2004; MIT), p. 2. See also US Joint Chiefs of Staff, *Joint Vision 2020*, June 2000.

27. John Byron, "The U.S. Military Is in Bad Shape," *Naval Institute Proceedings*, July 2004.

28. Grossman, *Inside the Pentagon*, Sept. 23, 2004. See also *New York Times*, Sept. 24, 2004.

29. For nuclear proliferation in general, see the *Guardian*, Sept. 20, 2004; *Ha'aretz*, July 8, 2004; *Financial Times*, Feb. 17, 2004, April 7, 2004, and Nov. 30, 2004; Seymour Hersh in the *New Yorker*, March 9, 2004; *Los Angeles Times*, Feb. 22, 2004, and May 24, 2004; *New York Times*, Jan. 4, 2004; *Washington Post*, Feb. 6, 2004, Feb. 8, 2004, and Feb. 21, 2004.

Chapter 6: "Conclusion: The Age of Perpetual Conflict"

1. Hutchings 2003, pp. 1–2, 4. See also *New York Times*, Nov. 18, 2004.

Bibliography

Acheson, Dean. 1969. *Present at the Creation: My Years in the State Department.* New York: W. W. Norton.

Aldrich, Richard J. 2001. *The Hidden Hand: Britain, America, and Cold War Secret Intelligence.* London: John Murray.

———— [National Security Archive]. 2004. "The Creation of SOIP-62: More Evidence on the Origins of Overkill," July 13.

Allen, George W. 2001. *None So Blind: A Personal Account of Intelligence Failure in Vietnam.* Chicago: Ivan R. Dee.

Anonymous [Mike Scheuer]. 2004. *Imperial Hubris: Why the West Is Losing the War on Terror.* Washington, DC: Brassey's.

Bairoch, Paul. 1979. "Le Volume des productions et du produit national dans le Tiers monde." *Revue Tiers Monde* 20 (October–December), pp. 669–691.

Bamford, James. 2004. *A Pretext for War: 9/11, Iraq, and the Abuse of America's Intelligence Agencies.* New York: Doubleday.

Bergerud, Eric M. 1991. *The Dynamics of Defeat: The Vietnam War in Hau Nghia Province.* Boulder: Westview.

Beschloss, Michael, and Strobe Talbott. 1993. *At the Highest Levels: The Inside Story of the End of the Cold War.* Boston: Little, Brown.

Betts, Richard K. 1977. *Soldiers, Statesmen, and Cold War Crises.* Cambridge: Harvard University Press.

————. 1978. "Analysis, War, and Decision: Why Intelligence Failures Are Inevitable." *World Politics* 31 (October), pp. 61–89.

Binnendijk, Hans, ed. 1987. *Authoritarian Regimes in Transition.* Washington, DC: Foreign Service Institute.

Bitzinger, Richard A. 1989. *Assessing the Conventional Balance in Europe, 1945–1975.* Santa Monica: RAND Corporation N-2859.

Blank, Dr. Stephen J. "Toward a New US Strategy in Asia." US Army Strategic Studies Institute, Feb. 24, 2004.

Blechman, Barry M., and Stephen S. Kaplan. 1978. *Force Without War: US Armed Forces as a Political Instrument.* Washington, DC: Brookings Institution.

Booth, Anne, and R. M. Sundrum. 1985. *Labour Absorption in Agriculture: Theoretical Analysis and Empirical Investigations*. New York: Oxford University Press.

Brockett, Charles D. 1988. *Land, Power, and Poverty: Agrarian Transformation and Political Conflict in Central America*. Boulder: Westview.

Brom, Shlomo. "The War in Iraq: An Intelligence Failure?" *Strategic Assessment* 6 (Nov. 2003; Jaffee Center for Strategic Studies, Tel Aviv).

Cardoso, Elena, and Ann Helwig. 1992. "Below the Line: Poverty in Latin America." *World Development* 20 (January), pp. 19–37.

Carney, John T., and Benjamin F. Schemmer. 2002. *No Room for Error: The Covert Operations of America's Special Tactics Units from Iran to Afghanistan*. New York: Ballantine.

Cheng, Joseph Y. S. "Challenges to China's Russian Policy in the Early Twenty-First Century." *Journal of Contemporary Asia* 34 (2004), pp. 480–498.

CIA (Central Intelligence Agency). 2000. "Global Trends 2015." December.

Cooley, John K. 2002. *Unholy Wars: Afghanistan, America, and International Terrorism*. London: Pluto.

Corum, Lieutenant Colonel James S. "Fighting Insurgents—No Shortcuts to Success." U.S. Army Strategic Studies Institute, May 2004.

Deitchman, Seymour J. 1976. *The Best-Laid Schemes: A Tale of Social Research and Bureaucracy*. Cambridge: MIT Press.

Ford, Harold P. 1998. *CIA and the Vietnam Policymakers: Three Episodes, 1962–1968*. Washington, DC: CIA Center for the Study of Intelligence.

Gaddis, John Lewis. 1982. *Strategies of Containment: A Critical Appraisal of Postwar American National Security Policy*. New York: Oxford University Press.

Gates, Robert M. 1996. *From the Shadows: The Ultimate Insider's Story of Five Presidents and How They Won the Cold War*. New York: Simon and Schuster.

Gompert, David, and Jeffrey Isaacson. 1999. "Planning a Ballistic Missile Defense System of Systems." RAND Issue Papers. Santa Monica, CA: Rand Corporation.

Halberstam, David. 1972. *The Best and the Brightest*. New York: Viking Press.

Halper, Stefan, and Jonathan Clarke. 2004. *America Alone: The Neo-conservatives and the Global Order*. Cambridge: Cambridge University Press.

Heiser, Joseph M., Jr. 1974. *Logistic Support*. Vietnam Studies series. Washington, DC: US Department of the Army.

Hiro, Dilip. 1991. *The Longest War: The Iran-Iraq Military Conflict*. New York: Routledge.

———. 2001. *Neighbors, Not Friends: Iraq and Iran after the Gulf Wars*. London: Routledge.

Hutchings, Robert L. 2003. Speech by the CIA National Intelligence Council chairman, April 8, 2003. Distributed by the CIA.

Inter-American Development Bank (IADB). 1990. *Annual Report, 1989*. Washington, DC: IADB.

———. 1992. *Annual Report, 1991*. Washington, DC: IADB.

Ippolito, Dennis S. "Budget Policy, Deficits, and Defense: A Fiscal Framework for Defense Planning." US Army Strategic Studies Institute, June 2005.

Jain, Shail. 1975. *Size Distribution of Income: A Compilation of Data*. Washington, DC: World Bank.

Janvry, Alain de, et al. 1989. "Land and Labour in Latin American Agriculture from the 1950s to the 1980s." *Journal of Peasant Studies 16* (April), pp. 390–423.

Kolko, Gabriel. 1988. *Confronting the Third World: United States Foreign Policy, 1945–1980*. New York: Pantheon.

———. 1994. *Anatomy of a War: Vietnam, the United States, and the Modern Historical Experience*. New York: Pantheon.

———. 1994. *Century of War: Politics, Conflicts, and Society Since 1914*. New York: New Press.

Kolko, Gabriel, and Joyce Kolko. 1972. *The Limits of Power: The World and United States Foreign Policy, 1945–1954*. New York: Harper and Row.

Krepinevich, Andrew F., Jr. 1986. *The Army and Vietnam*. Baltimore: Johns Hopkins University Press.

Levine, Robert A. 1987. *The Arms Debate and the Third World*. Santa Monica: RAND Corporation N-3523.

Macmillan, Harold. 1969. *Tides of Fortune, 1945–1955*. London: Macmillan.

Matthias, Willard C. 2001. *America's Strategic Blunders: Intelligence Analysis and National Security Policy, 1936–1991*. University Park: Pennsylvania State University Press.

McChristian, Joseph A. 1974. *The Role of Military Intelligence, 1965–1967* Vietnam Studies series. Washington, DC: US Department of the Army.

Momyer, William W. 1978. *Airpower in Three Wars*. Washington, DC: Air Force History and Museums Program.

Mrozek, Donald J. 1988. *Air Power and the Ground War in Vietnam: Ideas and Actions*. Maxwell Air Force Base, AL.

Mueller, John E. 1973. *War, Presidents, and Public Opinion*. New York: John Wiley.

Palmer, Bruce, Jr. 1984. *The 25-Year War: America's Military Role in Vietnam*. Lexington: University of Kentucky Press.

Palmer, Gregory. 1978. *The McNamara Strategy and the Vietnam War: Program Budgeting in the Pentagon, 1960–1968*. Westport, CT: Greenwood Press.

Philippines Department of Agriculture, Bureau of Agricultural Statistics. 1990. *Agricultural Development Trends in the 80's: Philippines vs. Other Selected Countries*. Manila: Philippines Department of Agriculture.

Roberts, Bryan. 1978. *Cities of Peasants: The Political Economy of Urbanization in the Third World*. Beverly Hills, CA: Sage.

Shafer, D. Michael. 1988. *Deadly Paradigms: The Failure of US Counterinsurgency Policy*. Princeton: Princeton University Press.

Smith, Russell Jack. 1989. *The Unknown CIA: My Three Decades in the Agency*. Washington, DC: International Defense Publishers.

Spinney, Franklin E. "Porkbarrels and Budgeteers: What Went Wrong with the Quadrennial Defense Review." *Strategic Review* 25 (September 1997).

Stiglitz, Joseph E. 2003. *The Roaring Nineties: A New History of the World's Most Prosperous Decade*. New York: W. W. Norton.

Stockwell, John. 1978. *In Search of Enemies: A CIA Story*. New York, W. W. Norton.

Taylor, Leonard B. 1974. *Financial Management of the Vietnam Conflict, 1962–1972*. Vietnam Studies series. Washington, DC: US Department of the Army.

Trullinger, James Walker, Jr. 1980. *Village at War: An Account of Revolution in Vietnam*. New York: Addison-Wesley.

United Nations Conference on Trade and Development (UNCTAD). 2003. *Economic Development in Africa: Trade Performance and Commodity Dependence*.

US Army. 1999. "Posture Statement," May.

US Department of Defense. 1998. "The United States Security Strategy for the East Asia-Pacific Region," November 23.

———. 2000. "Report to Congress, Kosovo Operation Allied Force After-Action Report," January 31.

———. 2001. *Quadrennial Defense Review Report,* September 30.

US Joint Chiefs of Staff. 1991. *1991 Joint Military Net Assessment*. Washington, DC: March.

US Senate, Committee on Armed Services. 1985. *Report: Defense Organization: The Need for Change*. 99th Congress, 1st session. Washington, DC.

Westad, O. S. 1996–1997. "Concerning the Situation in 'A': New Russian Evidence on Soviet Intervention in Afghanistan." *Cold War International History Project Bulletin,* nos. 8–9, (Winter), pp. 128–184.

Wilensky, Harold D. 1967. *Organizational Intelligence: Knowledge and Policy in Government and Industry*. New York: Basic Books.

Williams, Robert G. 1986. *Export Agriculture and the Crisis in Central America*. Chapel Hill: University of North Carolina Press.

Woodward, Bob. 2004. *Plan of Attack*. New York: Simon and Schuster.

Index

Acheson, Dean, 41
Afghanistan, 51–56; Al-Qaida training camps in, 55, 104; Central Intelligence Agency in, 54; civilian casualties in, 55; communism in, 52; complexity of politics in, 109, 110; costs of wars in, 54; elections in, 110, 111, 113; Islamic fundamentalism and, 55; military aid to, 54; as narco-state, 114; Northern Alliance in, 109, 110, 111, 112, 121; Pashtuns in, 51, 55, 109, 113; reconstruction in, 114; relations with Pakistan, 52; Soviet Union in, 51, 54, 55; Taliban in, 55, 56, 82, 107, 110, 111, 113, 114, 115; tribal/ethnic divisions in, 51, 110; US intervention in, 51–56, 108–114; US political failure in, 92, 108–114; war in, 108–114; warlords in, 51, 110, 113, 114
Africa: agricultural exports from, 35; arms expenditures, 36; economic growth in, 85; terms of trade and, 36; unemployment in, 86; US intervention in, 10
Agriculture: in Asia, 11; in Central America, 34; exploitation of, 35; for export, 35; land issues and, 34, 35; in Latin America, 11; in Third World, 11
AIDS, 85
Albania, 68, 70
Allawi, Ayad, 149, 150
Alliance for Progress, 35

Alliances: as cause of wars, 129; destruction of, 120–128, 133, 142, 143–147; fear of communism and, 58; future of, 77–78; with Israel, 46; military, 7; regional, 7; risks of, 58; with Saudi Arabia, 46; US dilemmas with, 67–70; US perceptions of as constraints, 69
Al-Qaida, 55, 83, 103, 104, 107, 116, 118, 139; numbers trained by, 106
Anglo-Iranian Oil Company, 42
Angola: liberation movements in, 47; US intervention in, 12, 53
Argentina: real wages in, 37; US intervention in, 12
Arms market: human rights and, 81, 82; US share of, 81, 82
Arms race, 18, 45, 121; fear requirement in, 4; public mobilization during, 5
Army Concept, 19
Army of the Republic of Vietnam (ARVN), 30, 31
Asia: agricultural exports from, 35; agricultural production in, 11; land issues in, 34
Atlanticism, 130, 131
Australia: public opinion on Iraq War, 146
Axis of evil, 47, 99, 108, 127

Balkans: civil war in, 33; destabilization of balance of power in, 33, 34;

About the Book

IN THIS COMPREHENSIVE, SUCCINCT—AND PROVOCATIVE—OVERVIEW of the past five decades of US foreign policy, Gabriel Kolko gives special emphasis to the period since 2000.

Kolko argues that, as dangerous as the Cold War era was, we face far more instability and unpredictability now; the international environment is qualitatively more precarious than ever. Ranging from the Vietnam War to the war in Iraq, he critically appraises US responses to a world of complex new challenges. The result is a book with a unique voice.

Sure to capture the attention of readers concerned with the troubled world we live in, *The Age of War* will also stimulate classroom discussion, serving as a powerful pedagogical tool.

Gabriel Kolko is distinguished research professor emeritus at York University in Toronto. He is the author of more than a dozen widely acclaimed books, including *Century of War: Politics, Conflicts, and Society Since 1914* and *Anatomy of a War: Vietnam, the United States, and the Modern Historical Experience*.